THE COMPLETE IDIOT'S GUIDE® TO

Meals in 30 Minutes or Less

by Tod Dimmick

ALPHA
A member of Penguin Group (USA) Inc.

To Jen. Thank you.

ALPHA BOOKS

Published by the Penguin Group

Penguin Group (USA) Inc., 375 Hudson Street, New York, New York 10014, USA

Penguin Group (Canada), 90 Eglinton Avenue East, Suite 700, Toronto, Ontario M4P 2Y3, Canada (a division of Pearson Penguin Canada Inc.)

Penguin Books Ltd., 80 Strand, London WC2R 0RL, England

Penguin Ireland, 25 St. Stephen's Green, Dublin 2, Ireland (a division of Penguin Books Ltd.)

Penguin Group (Australia), 250 Camberwell Road, Camberwell, Victoria 3124, Australia (a division of Pearson Australia Group Pty. Ltd.)

Penguin Books India Pvt. Ltd., 11 Community Centre, Panchsheel Park, New Delhi—110 017, India

Penguin Group (NZ), 67 Apollo Drive, Rosedale, North Shore, Auckland 1311, New Zealand (a division of Pearson New Zealand Ltd.)

Penguin Books (South Africa) (Pty.) Ltd., 24 Sturdee Avenue, Rosebank, Johannesburg 2196, South Africa

Penguin Books Ltd., Registered Offices: 80 Strand, London WC2R 0RL, England

First edition originally published as *The Complete Idiot's Guide to 5-Minute Appetizers*, *The Complete Idiot's Guide to 20-Minute Meals*, and *The Complete Idiot's Guide to Quick and Easy Low-Carb Meals*

International Standard Book Number: 978-1-61564-146-8
Library of Congress Catalog Card Number: 2011910191

14   13   12   8   7   6   5   4   3   2   1

Interpretation of the printing code: The rightmost number of the first series of numbers is the year of the book's printing; the rightmost number of the second series of numbers is the number of the book's printing. For example, a printing code of 12-1 shows that the first printing occurred in 2012.

Printed in the United States of America

Note: This publication contains the opinions and ideas of its author. It is intended to provide helpful and informative material on the subject matter covered. It is sold with the understanding that the author and publisher are not engaged in rendering professional services in the book. If the reader requires personal assistance or advice, a competent professional should be consulted.

The author and publisher specifically disclaim any responsibility for any liability, loss, or risk, personal or otherwise, which is incurred as a consequence, directly or indirectly, of the use and application of any of the contents of this book.

Most Alpha books are available at special quantity discounts for bulk purchases for sales promotions, premiums, fund-raising, or educational use. Special books, or book excerpts, can also be created to fit specific needs.

For details, write: Special Markets, Alpha Books, 375 Hudson Street, New York, NY 10014.

Publisher: *Marie Butler-Knight*

Associate Publisher: *Mike Sanders*

Executive Managing Editor: *Billy Fields*

Senior Acquisitions Editor: *Brook Farling*

Senior Development Editor: *Christy Wagner*

Senior Production Editor: *Kayla Dugger*

Cover Designer: *Kurt Owens*

Book Designers: *William Thomas, Rebecca Batchelor*

Indexer: *Tonya Heard*

Layout: *Ayanna Lacey*

Senior Proofreader: *Laura Caddell*

Contents

9   Lunchbox-Worthy Sandwiches and Wraps 99

Part 4: Satisfying Snacks and Appetizers......................... 111

10   Quick Bites 113

Introduction

You lead a busy life. Between work, school, kids, sports, hobbies, pets, and whatever else you and your family have going on, you don't have a lot of time left over to spend in the kitchen. But you still want to feed your family delicious, nutritious food that didn't come from a drive-thru window. And there's just something special about the whole family sitting down to a weeknight dinner together.

As a father of a young family that's always on the move, I know where you're coming from. That's why I designed this cookbook to help you get good food on the table (or in the lunchbox), fast. The 500+ recipes in this book, which range from breakfast to dessert and everything in between, take about 30 minutes or less to prepare, cook, and get on the table.

Your time is valuable. Their tummies are grumbling. Let's go!

How This Book Is Organized

This book is divided into seven parts:

Part 1, Quick Meals, Delicious Meals, helps get you started on the right foot by telling you what you need to get in and out of the kitchen quickly, from pantry staples, to spices and herbs, to the right pots and pans and utensils.

In **Part 2, Starting Your Day Off Right,** gives you breakfasts that get you going and keep you going until lunchtime. I've included recipes for leisurely weekend morning breakfasts as well as make-and-go recipes for rushed workday mornings.

Part 3, Let's Do Lunch, is—you guessed it—all about lunch. From salads, to soups, to sandwiches, I hope you'll find many recipes you'll love to fill your lunchbox with.

Turn to **Part 4, Satisfying Snacks and Appetizers,** when you need a quick snack or want to wow your party guests with amazing appetizers.

Part 5, Delightful Dinners, helps you get dinner on the table without taking all evening. Seafood, beef, poultry, vegetarian, pasta, pizza, and even kid-approved meals are all included.

What would dinner be without sensational side dishes? **Part 6, Stars on the Side,** gives you many ideas for rounding out the dinner menu.

My editor isn't shy to tell me **Part 7, And for Dessert ...,** is her (and her sweet tooth's) favorite part. With dozens of sweet and decadent desserts, it might be your favorite, too!

Extras

Throughout the book, you'll notice little extra nuggets of information housed in sidebars. Here's what they all mean:

> **DEFINITION**
>
> Look to these sidebars for cooking-related words you might not be familiar with.

> **MINUTE MORSEL**
>
> Check these sidebars for information that helps cooking make sense—and even more fun!

> **ON THE CLOCK**
>
> In these sidebars you'll find tips on how to make something simpler, quicker, faster, and easier.

> **TIME WASTER**
>
> Be sure to heed these alerts about common misunderstandings, mistakes, or potential hazards.

You'll also notice some icons among the recipes.

This icon marks recipes that contain healthy, low-carb ingredients, and/or reduced sugar. If you're watching your weight, turn to these recipes to help you stay on track.

10 This icon indicates recipes that should take you about 10 minutes to prepare.

20 Recipes with this icon should take you 20 minutes.

30 This icon flags recipes that take a little longer—around 30 minutes.

Of course, everyone cooks and works in the kitchen at a different pace, so if it takes you less time or it takes you a little longer, still enjoy the process—and especially the results!

Acknowledgments

Many thanks to my editors at Alpha Books, Senior Development Editor Christy Wagner, Senior Production Editor Kayla Dugger, and Senior Acquisitions Editor Brook Farling, for identifying the opportunity of this book and for their endless patience and eye for detail as we compiled the magnum opus.

I am grateful to my friends, all passionate cooks, who helped with recipe testing.

Trademarks

All terms mentioned in this book that are known to be or are suspected of being trademarks or service marks have been appropriately capitalized. Alpha Books and Penguin Group (USA) Inc. cannot attest to the accuracy of this information. Use of a term in this book should not be regarded as affecting the validity of any trademark or service mark.

Quick Meals, Delicious Meals

Getting a delicious, nutritious meal on the table in 30 minutes or less isn't impossible, but it does require a little advance planning. In Part 1, I share everything you need to know to set yourself up for 30-minute-meal success.

For starters, I explain the benefits of quick cooking and give you tips on how to think like a quick cook. I also list the basic supplies and ingredients you should keep on hand in your pantry, refrigerator, and freezer, so you're always ready to whip up something tasty. I talk about herbs and spices, too—those magic seasonings that add flavor and interest to a meal.

And with the right tools, getting in and out of the kitchen is quick and painless, so to help with that, I share some of the essential pots, pans, tools, and equipment that make cooking easier and help speed you on your way.

Faster and Better

In This Chapter

- The importance of good meals
- Focusing on quality and taste
- It's all about adjusting your perspective
- Setting realistic mealtime goals … and achieving them

When you wake up late on a busy weekday morning, making a few extra minutes to fix yourself breakfast and pack a healthy lunch seems like an impossible task. After a tiring day, sometimes the last thing you want to do when you get home is spend a ton of time in the kitchen fixing dinner. This book helps you make the most of your time in the kitchen so you can get in there, create a delicious and nutritious meal, and get out of there quickly.

In these pages, I give you step-by-step guidance in getting started, from stocking your pantry to creative meal ideas. First, we're going to, together, assemble all the tools you need to get in motion, including the knowledge of how things go together, so that just *knowing* a pork tenderloin is waiting in the fridge is inspiration to create something.

That sense of inspiration leads to a second goal: to change your outlook on cooking. To change meal preparation from a grudging chore to an opportunity to create is a critical perception, because it helps us *want* to cook. With that outlook, preparing a meal becomes a soothing segue from the day at the office to an evening with the family … made special by something you've put together for them. What a difference!

Today's Mealtime Reality

Once upon a time, Mom spent the afternoon preparing the family meal. At least that's how the story goes. Time was no issue, because after all, what could be more important than preparing dinner? These days, no matter how many adults are in the household, they're probably all working. Working long hours. Because of this, the time available to make a meal is shrinking toward zero.

To cope with this time crunch, busy people turn to fast food, instant meals, or the Same Old Thing. It's a sad state because these alternatives are often more expensive, and certainly less healthy, than a home-cooked meal. Even worse, fast food tends to dull the taste buds and turn your attitude toward food from one of anticipation and pleasure to a necessity, a fuel stop.

How did we get here? It's simple, really. We're all busy, and all of us have the same minutes in a day. Because learning is time-consuming, many of us fall into routines that, although they might conserve time, shield us from anything new. Take it from a guy who served his wife chili for 7 days in a row early in his marriage: variety makes everyone happier.

MINUTE MORSEL

It always takes longer to do something the first time, from driving, to your job, to cooking. That's called a learning curve. This book is designed to make that curve as short as possible.

Fast, tasty, healthy meals are not only possible, they're easy … with a bit of knowledge and preparation. The purpose of this book is to enable a practical and fun approach to 30-minute cuisine.

An Oasis in a Busy Week

The 30 minutes you spend preparing a meal can be so much more than simply "cooking." A slightly different perspective creates new energy and enthusiasm, and a requirement suddenly becomes fun. A meal serves several purposes, after all. Of course, food is fuel—we all have to eat. But mealtime, at least until this frenzied day and age, has always been the one part of a busy day when people come together as family and friends.

But how is a good meal possible in only 30 minutes? Through efficient use of time and a little bit of advance planning. By having all your ingredients on hand, the meal is simple to prepare, and the cooking methods are quick and reliable. The result: a meal that brings people together and tastes like it took much longer than 30 minutes to prepare!

It's our choice whether we view the time we spend on food as a chore or a pleasure, something to endure, or something to anticipate. I suspect most of us are ready for a little more pleasure. Many people receive a great deal of joy and satisfaction from creating something for the table.

Setting Reasonable Expectations

To keep sane, it's important that 30-minute cuisine avoids involving a mad dash. As a parent, I am well aware that frenzy is often the name of the game, but at mealtime, you can use many tricks to keep the schedule, and your heart rate, under control. My experience is that a successful meal is made possible through planning, preparation, and *reasonable expectations*. Accordingly, on these pages you will find that …

- We're not going to attempt multiple-step menus, because just reading the recipe could take 30 minutes.

- We'll keep things simple in terms of preparation and cleanup.

- We'll avoid recipes with large numbers of ingredients, in the interest of saving time.

- We'll also avoid expensive or hard-to-find ingredients.

- We'll focus on our objective, quick preparation, so we can enjoy our meal.

Even with these parameters in mind, we have a world to explore. Picture asparagus sautéed in butter with tarragon. Linguini tossed with garlic, olive oil, scallops, and lemon. Warm rhubarb sauce over vanilla ice cream. All these are quick and simple to make, yet serve them and—after the silence of appreciative eating—you're likely to hear comments like "Delicious!" "Elegant!" or even "Gourmet!"

Quality Control

For our purposes, the quality of the food we eat can be considered in two ways: the ingredients in a meal, and the nutritional value.

One of the great satisfactions of preparing a meal is control over what goes in each dish. This might sound simple, but think about fast food a minute. When you prepare a meal, you know what goes in it. I know I sleep just a bit better knowing what I feed to people I care about.

Quality also affects taste, and taste affects how we enjoy a meal. We would all rather have fresh warm bread than stale, a crunchy carrot over a limp old one, and as for old chicken, well, you get my point. Fresh is good, and fresh is under your control when you're in charge of a meal.

MINUTE MORSEL

If you're a gardener, or if you visit your local farmers' market, you know the quintessential pleasure of summer is a fresh, ripe tomato, just picked from the vine. The flavor is incredible and just can't be duplicated by an unripe fruit that's traveled by truck or plane from the other side of the planet.

Less Is More

At some high-end restaurants, patrons expect to be pampered. They seek out unusual hors d'oeuvres, exotic salads, entrées from Bulgaria, desserts from France. They're paying for the careful blending of spices and herbs, for subtle seasonings and dishes that took three people an hour to prepare. A gourmet meal at such a place will cost a pretty penny, and if it's prepared well, it might even be worth it. Will we be able to replicate such a meal with our limited time and budget? Not likely.

Increasingly, however, new types of gourmet restaurants are appearing on the scene. They insist on quality and freshness—in fact, it's their reason for existence. Although the occasional exotic ingredient works its way into the menu (after all, it wouldn't be "high end" without some rather unusual elements), the focus is on incredibly fresh, often local, ingredients prepared in somewhat unusual ways. Think squash ravioli with fried sage, or asparagus with ginger. Visitors seek creativity and quality, not necessarily expensive ingredients. Ingredients readily available at a good farm stand, prepared in a slightly different way, can be amazing.

Such restaurants operate on the belief that with the freshest possible ingredients, your meal cannot go wrong. And while you might not have access to the same producers these restaurants do, I bet you do know a great farm store, a farmers' market, or a place where the peas are fresh and crisp and sweet, where the tomatoes are a meal by themselves. These flavors are sublime, and they beg to be served with a minimum of preparation and distracting seasonings so their own flavors can shine through.

Fresh can be easy, quick, and delicious. Fresh requires less work, and gives more flavor. Less is more.

Endless Possibilities

Even 30 minutes holds a lot of potential. I go into a great deal of detail later, but let me give you one example. My mother-in-law said she would love to see some ideas of what to do with a chicken breast. What a terrific suggestion.

A chicken breast to a cook is like a blank canvas to an artist. The possibilities are endless. It can be broiled, grilled, sautéed, pan-seared, poached, or even steamed. Each treatment, *absent any seasoning at all*, still results in a different taste. Then engage in some creative seasoning—perhaps one or more of salt, pepper, oregano, thyme, cumin, paprika, cayenne, nutmeg, even cinnamon—and a completely different experience emerges.

How about a marinade? Or perhaps a wine sauce, a cream sauce, a *reduced* broth, bursting with concentrated chicken flavor? Or cubes of chicken as an element in a pasta or rice dish, in a stir-fry, as part of a tomato sauce or a stew?

DEFINITION

To **reduce** is to heat a liquid such as a broth or sauce to remove some of the water content, resulting in more concentrated flavor and color.

It wouldn't be much of a stretch to say I could fill this cookbook with nothing but chicken breast recipes. (I've included some, but I've also included *so* much more.) Still, consider the number of meals you could make simply from this one ingredient, almost all of them fitting within the so-called "limits" of 30-minute meals. The same variety is possible with other meats (beef, pork, turkey), many vegetables (visualized marinated grilled zucchini), fruits, nuts, and more. The possibilities are indeed endless, so in this book we're in the fortunate position of limiting our suggestions to only the very best!

Part of successful 30-minute cuisine is in the approach. Treat it as fun, as an opportunity—and really believe it!—and suddenly the whole thing is something to anticipate rather than dread.

The Least You Need to Know

- Fast, tasty, healthy meals are not only possible, they're easy, thanks to a bit of knowledge and preparation.
- A meal is the one part of a busy day when family and friends come together to share a meal as well as their day.
- With the freshest possible ingredients, your meal cannot go wrong.
- Even in 30 minutes, there's an awful lot of potential.

Stocking Your Pantry

In This Chapter

- Essential ingredients to stock up on
- Fun foods handy to have
- Helpful herbs and seasonings
- Easy substitutions

When you have a stocked pantry, you have so many more options when it comes time to prepare meals. Opening that pantry door and seeing all those ingredients just waiting for you to combine them in a delicious dish makes meal planning so much easier.

In this chapter, I've included suggestions for the ingredients you need to get a good running start for preparing meals in 30 minutes or less. I love fresh ingredients—vegetables and fruits are a wonderful source of natural, quick flavors—but I've also recommended many canned or jarred ingredients. These preserved ingredients have a long shelf life and won't take up room in the fridge you could use for fresh ingredients instead. I've also included a short list of seasonings I find particularly useful, many of which you might already have.

So let's look at the basics—ingredients for the pantry, the fridge, and the spice rack.

The Perfect Pantry

A well-stocked pantry is a huge timesaver for the busy cook, as well as a potential source of inspiration. It's an area of the kitchen where you can conveniently reach all the basic ingredients necessary to prepare 30-minute cuisine. This inventory in this section isn't intended to dictate every food item in your house; rather, it provides a suggested building-block list of what you'll need for the recipes in this book.

I've divided this section into several categories, including baking (flours and meals), condiments and sauces, oils and vinegars, pastas and pasta sauces, rice and other starches, soups, meats and seafood, spices and herbs (more on this later in the chapter), sweeteners, and vegetables and grains. You could also include breakfast cereals, crackers, drinks (bottled or powdered), fruits, sweet snacks, and savory snacks. These items should be available at any supermarket or online.

MINUTE MORSEL

Preparing your pantry might feel like you're creating grocery store aisles in your house, but the resulting organization enables efficiency and speed when it comes to cooking crunch time.

Wherever possible, I suggest ingredients that are whole grain, low fat, and generally nutritious. I've found that food prepared with these ingredients just plain tastes better, not to mention lends peace of mind from eating healthy.

Baking

Flour and other dry staples are the lifeblood of any bread maker. Be sure to stock white flour, whole-wheat flour, breadcrumbs, cornmeal, oatmeal, cooking spray, baking powder, and baking soda. For fun, you could also include specialty flours (buckwheat, rye, etc.), whole-grain blends, and pancake and waffle mixes.

You might also want to keep on hand chocolate chips, baker's chocolate, vanilla extract, confectioners' sugar, cornstarch, cake mixes, and pudding mixes.

Buttermilk powder, chopped almonds, and chopped walnuts are also handy to have.

Condiments and Sauces

Condiments add flavor and texture to a dish. Often, like spices, a little goes a long way. Kosher salt, salad dressing or mix (I like to keep chunky blue cheese and Italian dressing on hand), capers, salsa, olives (especially my favorite, kalamata!), and ketchup are all good to stock up on.

Bruschetta topping mixture (tomatoes, garlic, peppers, and other ingredients), Dijon-style mustard, honey, horseradish, minced garlic, olive tapenade, and peanut butter also can play a role in your cooking.

ON THE CLOCK

For the sublime, rich flavor of peanuts to shine through in dips and sauces, choose all-natural peanut butter. You have to stir the peanut oil back in to the mix the first time you open the jar, but the overwhelming upside is flavor and the knowledge that you're bypassing a big dose of preservatives.

Oils, Marinades, and Vinegars

Kitchen liquids assist in the actual cooking process as well as add flavor. Here are the essentials: extra-virgin olive oil, canola oil, red wine vinegar, Worcestershire sauce, soy sauce, teriyaki sauce, and hot pepper sauce such as Tabasco.

Balsamic vinegar, walnut oil, peanut oil, and "hot" oil (oil infused with hot pepper) are also fun to work with.

Pasta

When it comes to pasta, consider whole-wheat pasta if you can find it; it has a unique, rich, nutty taste. Try different manufacturers of pasta, too, because ingredients and taste vary. Otherwise, your favorite shape will do fine.

Have spaghetti, linguini, shells, and angel hair in the pantry. And for the kids, pick up some rotelle, gemelli, holiday shapes, and macaroni (for macaroni and cheese!).

Rice and Other Starches

A critical element in recipes from across the globe, rice is a pantry must-have. Stock up on white long-grain rice (which cooks quickly) and nutritious brown and wild rice mixes (which take a little longer to cook).

Soups

The basic broths are useful for many recipes: low-salt chicken broth, beef broth, and vegetable broth. Cream of mushroom, cream of celery, and cream of chicken soups are the heart of many recipes for leftover poultry.

Meats and Seafood

Keep an open mind about seemingly commonplace items like deli-counter or canned chicken, ham, or tuna. These items can be used to create unusual and delicious appetizers, and because they're ready to use, they can be the basis of recipes that would otherwise take far too long. I won't tell anyone you got it from a can.

Anchovies, bacon and/or bacon bits, canned clams (chopped), canned crabmeat, capers, prosciutto, *sardines*, shrimp (cocktail size), and smoked salmon are other top picks.

DEFINITION

Anchovies and **sardines** are tiny, flavorful preserved fish that typically come in cans. The strong flavor from these tiny salted fish is a must in many recipes.

Herbs, Spices, and Seasoning Mixes

With the following seasonings in your pantry, you'll be equipped to prepare so many delicious dishes: allspice, basil, bay leaf, caraway seed, cardamom, chili powder, cinnamon, cloves, coriander, dill, ginger, marjoram, nutmeg, oregano, paprika, peppercorns, red pepper, rosemary, sage, tarragon, and thyme.

For lots more on these, turn to the "Helping Herbs" section later in this chapter.

Sweeteners

Items to sweeten things up a bit include brown sugar (light brown is fine), honey, molasses, and refined sugar. A number of low-calorie or no-calorie sweeteners, such as stevia extract, are now available.

Vegetables and Grains

Staples such as cannellini beans, corn, kidney beans, chickpeas, refried beans, split peas, canned tomatoes, tomato sauce, tomato paste (small, 4-ounce cans), sauerkraut, and water chestnuts form the foundation of many a terrific dish.

Almonds, hearts of palm, marinated artichoke hearts, mushrooms (marinated or not), pearl barley, roasted red peppers, sun-dried tomatoes, lentils, and walnuts are also good to stock up on.

In the Fridge

The fridge is a place of magic for the 30-minute cook. It's the holding tank for accessories and main ingredients kept fresh and ready to be used at a moment's notice.

Some items you'll find in my fridge include cottage cheese, plain yogurt, sour cream, cheddar cheese, mozzarella cheese, meats, vegetables, and fruits. Lurking up top you'll find Dijon mustard, olives, salsa, mayonnaise, lemon juice, barbecue sauce, butter, dill pickles, and yeast.

As with the pantry, this inventory is not intended to dictate every food item. I'll leave the particular kind of breakfast juice up to you.

Fresh Vegetables

Depending on what's in season and tastes the best, I like to have several of the following vegetables and fruits. One of my favorite pastimes is to peer into the produce drawer, see what I've got, and use that as the inspiration to create something. Fresh vegetables work magic in your meals. They bring flavor, texture, and visual appeal with little or no prep time.

Here are my favorites, but please add your own to the list: *Belgian endive*, carrots (both large carrots for recipes and "baby" carrots to serve), celery, chives (also available dried in the herbs and spices section of your grocery store), cucumbers, mushrooms (sliced or whole white button and portobello), scallions, spinach (fresh for wrapping appetizers and frozen as an ingredient in dips and spreads), sweet onions (such as Vidalia), tomatoes (grape and cherry), and zucchini squash.

DEFINITION

Belgian endive resembles a small, white, elongated, tightly packed head of romaine lettuce. The thick, crunchy leaves can be broken off and used as a terrific dipper for dips and spreads.

Fantastic Fruits

Fruits also bring freshness, flavor, and visual appeal. Some, such as avocados and coconut, bring an exotic richness while others (apples, dates, etc.) add sweetness.

Here's what I like to keep on hand: apples, avocados, coconut (shredded), dates, figs (dried), grapefruit, grapes, lemons (for fresh lemon juice, a critical component in many recipes), limes, melons (cantaloupe and honeydew), pears (Bartlett), and pine-apple (canned pieces are the easiest).

> **MINUTE MORSEL**
>
> In botanical terms, a fruit is the seed-bearing section of a plant, which includes not only apples and other obvious "fruits," but also tomatoes and other veg-etables with seeds. Because we're cooks, not botanists, I've listed tomatoes (and other seeded edibles) according to the way we use them, with the vegetables. A tomato pie, though, is actually delicious.

Bring on the Flavor!

Food is all about flavor. From the simple delight of a chicken grilled in its own juices to the rich layers of the same meat sautéed with a mélange of mushrooms and wine, flavor is what brings us in and gives us pleasure. The source of flavor might be the main ingredient itself (think of a rich fish), or the main ingredient might serve as a willing platform for a combination of added flavors brought on by herbs and spices.

Helping Herbs

The characteristic of an herb is often a fragrant or pungent smell, with a parallel effect on the food. Some herbs are used also for their color, such as saffron, which lends a deep yellow hue. Here are some of the characteristics of each recommended pantry herb:

Basil   A flavorful, almost sweet, resinous herb delicious with tomatoes and in all kinds of Italian or Mediterranean-style dishes.

Caraway   A spicy, distinctive seed used for bread, pork, cheese, and cabbage dishes. It helps reduce stomach upset, which is why it is often paired with, for example, sauerkraut.

Chili powder   Actually a mixture, but so commonly used I'm treating it as an herb, chili powder is usually made with hot peppers, cumin, and oregano. It provides the base "blast" for a flavorful chili, but that's only the beginning.

Chives   An easy onion flavor to add interest to any dish. Well, maybe not apple pie.

Coriander   A rich, warm, spicy herb used in all types of recipes, from African to South American, from entrées to desserts.

Dill   A slightly sour, unique flavor perfect for eggs, cheese dishes, and of course vegetables (pickles).

Marjoram   A sweet herb, similar to oregano (actually a cousin), also used in Greek, Spanish, and Italian dishes.

Oregano   A fragrant, slightly astringent herb used in Greek, Spanish, and Italian dishes.

Parsley   A fresh-tasting green leaf, adding color and interest to just about any savory dish.

Red pepper   Hot yet rich, crushed red pepper, used in moderation, brings flavor and interest to many savory dishes.

Rosemary   A pungent, sweet herb used with chicken, pork, fish, and especially lamb. A little of it goes a long way.

Sage   The lemon rind, fruity scent, and "sunny" flavor is a terrific addition to many dishes. My favorite: scrambled eggs.

Tarragon   A sour-sweet, rich-smelling herb perfect with seafood, vegetables (asparagus especially), chicken, and pork.

Thyme   Minty, zesty leaves are used in a wide range of recipes.

Each herb is distinctive, and many are complementary to each other. As with any combination, however, be it people, chemicals in the lab, or herbs, some combinations work better than others.

The Spice(s) of Life

Creative cooks have used spices for thousands of years. Generally the seeds, seed pods, shells, or even woody parts (cinnamon bark) of plants, spices are characterized by intense flavors and aromas. If herbs bring a fresh "green" flavor, spices bring an intense "brown" one.

Spices play an important role in regional cuisine as well (think cardamom with the Middle East and cinnamon with the Far East), where they tend to be strongly represented in warmer climates where spices do not spoil or, occasionally, where their strong flavors mask otherwise bad food.

Here are some spice characteristics:

Allspice Named for its flavor echoes of several spices (cinnamon, cloves, nutmeg), allspice is used in many desserts and in rich marinades and stews.

Cardamom An intense, nutty-smelling spice used in baking and coffee.

Cinnamon Rich yet spicy, cinnamon is commonly used in baking (apple pie!), but can also be used for delicious and interesting entrées.

Cloves The smell of cloves makes many people think of holiday ham; our culture has thrown the two of them together. The sweet, strong, almost wintergreen flavor is used in baking and with meats such as ham.

Ginger Flavors of citrus and a floral smell make this a terrific addition to many savory and sweet dishes.

Nutmeg A sweet, fragrant, musky spice used primarily in baking.

Paprika A rich, warm, earthy spice that also lends a rich brown-red color to many dishes.

Peppercorns Biting and pungent, freshly ground pepper is a must for many dishes, adding an extra level of flavor and taste.

This list of spices is a general guideline for what works. With a bit of experience, you'll start to recognize matches made in heaven.

ON THE CLOCK

For cooks, herbs are generally the leaves of flavorful plants characterized by fresh, pungent aromas and flavors, such as parsley, sage, rosemary, and thyme. Quick benefits from a combination of herbs and spices can be achieved with seasoning blends from a specialty spice company. With names like Southwest Seasoning, Beef Rub, and Cajun Chicken and Fish Spice, their suggested usage is clear, and you're one step closer to being done.

Spices send ripples throughout your dish; a little bit can go a long way. As with herbs, there are matches that work well, and there are matches to avoid. For a hot chili fan, for example, fiery pungent cumin is indispensable, but in that big savory batch, there's probably not more than a tablespoon of the powerful spice.

Substitutions

A substitute teacher is brought to class when the regular teacher can't be there. Just like with school, in the kitchen there are terrific substitutes … and one or two to avoid. Fortunately, however, substitutions are rather intuitive: successful substitutions stem from exchanging like with like. Let's look at a few guidelines.

Main Ingredients

As an example, pork, a mild white meat, might go well in a dish calling for chicken. If every other ingredient is kept constant, the resulting dish will taste quite similar.

On the other hand, inserting a completely different variable is likely to result in a different dish entirely … substituting bluefish for chicken, for example.

Seasonings

Substitutions can also be made between herbs and some spices with similar flavor and texture. That's where some basic knowledge is important.

Among the herbs, those that contribute a distinctive but not overpowering flavor—sage, oregano, basil, rosemary, for example—can be experimented with freely. Others such as cilantro, which lend a strong, possibly overpowering flavor, should be substituted with caution. It's probably fine to use basil in place of cilantro in a recipe, but not the other way around.

TIME WASTER

Cilantro lends a strong flavor, and should only be substituted for other herbs with caution, lest it overpower your helpless entrée.

Fats and Oils

Fats and oils are necessary elements in many methods of cooking, such as sautéing or frying, and in many baking recipes. While I'm a big fan of the flavor of butter, I'm not a fan of cholesterol and saturated fat. As a result, when preparing a recipe that calls for butter, I often use canola or olive oil. Yes, both of these oils are largely fat; however, vegetable fats tend to be unsaturated and lower in cholesterol. They taste great, and your doctor will be happier with you, too.

The implicit message, when you know that sage and oregano go well with both chicken and pork, is you're going to be safe substituting pork in a recipe originally calling for chicken. You'll find freedom and pleasure in exploring different combinations, and you'll make better use of what you happen to have on hand in the pantry or the fridge. Just go easy on the bluefish.

The Least You Need to Know

- A well-stocked pantry is a huge timesaver for the 30-minute cook, as well as a potential source of inspiration.
- Food prepared with healthy ingredients tastes better, not to mention the peace of mind from eating healthy.
- Food is about flavor; it's what brings us in and gives us pleasure. Quality ingredients, herbs, and spices are the magic that bring the flavor to the table.
- Don't be afraid to substitute, but remember that successful substitutions stem from exchanging like with like.

Essential Equipment

In This Chapter

- Pots, pans, and then some
- Kitchen tools and knives
- Use technology to get you there, fast
- Your helping hand: the freezer

If you've spent any amount of time leafing through a kitchenware catalog or browsing in a home store, you might be overwhelmed by the many kinds and types of kitchen equipment available. The challenge is limiting your purchases to what you really need. Not only do you need to consider how much money you might end up spending, but also where you'll store everything once you have it (let alone find it when you need it).

The truth is, a few carefully chosen items can do everything you need with a minimum investment of time and money. This chapter reviews the few, simple, invaluable implements and equipment you should have for preparing meals in 30 minutes or less.

Cookware Items

Important cookware items needed for 30-minute cuisine include a large skillet with a lid and spatter screen, a small skillet, a large (4-quart) saucepan with a lid, a medium (2-quart) saucepan with a lid, a large (2- or 3-gallon) cooking pot, a vegetable steamer, a pizza stone, a large casserole or baking dish with a lid, a medium casserole dish, a baking pan, and a muffin pan.

A fish poacher and a wok (if you have a gas cook top) are also fun to have—and enable quick cooking!

To help you prepare for 30-minute cuisine, not to mention having your kitchen well equipped for most tasks, let's review the basics.

On the Stovetop

For stovetop cooking, the following are good to have:

Skillet A skillet is the workhorse of the 30-minute kitchen. Remember, I suggest getting two. The larger one can handle an entire meal, from breakfast to dinner. It's an important part—maybe *the* most important part—of your quick-cooking arsenal.

A good skillet must have the heft to stand up to hard, repeated use, but even more importantly, it must be able to distribute heat evenly. A poor-quality skillet heats unevenly and burns food, whereas a sturdy, well-made frying pan gradually rises to the appropriate temperature and stays there.

There's no doubt high-end cookware manufacturers have mastered the art of heft, but there's no monopoly. A solid, cast-iron frying pan (like Grandma used to cook with) can be just what the doctor ordered. I have two cast-iron skillets for specific uses. One I use with breakfast foods such as pancakes. The other I use for savory dinner items, including such generally nonbreakfast items as garlic, onions, and hot peppers. Cast iron will sometimes hold flavors, regardless of cleaning effort, and the hint of garlic in griddlecakes is not a great thing.

The small skillet serves as a member of the flavor brigade, typically working in concert with other kitchen tools. I use the small skillet, for example, to sauté onions to a golden softness before using them as a topping on whole-wheat pizza, or to brown ingredients to be subsequently added to a stew or chili. Again *mass* is the magic word because even heating is critical to successful frying and sautéing.

A large spatter screen is a terrific idea for skillet cooking because there will be times when you want to cook without a lid but would prefer not to remember your meal through spatters on the ceiling.

ON THE CLOCK

I've used high-end skillets and inexpensive bargain store skillets, and to me, the secret of success can be summed up in one word: *mass*.

Saucepans   Saucepans are also an essential aid in the kitchen. Although I've suggested 2- and 4-quart sizes, an infinite range is available. As the name implies, saucepans are perfect for preparing sauces, from basic pasta sauce to wine reductions to cream sauces. They hold soups, steam vegetables (with a steam insert or steam top), and perform myriad other functions. Consistent with all cookware, the watchwords are *quality* and *durability*. You want saucepans that will stand up to daily aggressive use.

Large cooking pot   A large pot is kitchen magic for many cooks—I make good use of my 16-quart behemoth. The pot over the fire, a romantic image of the "good old days" comes to mind, where the pot was never really empty but gradually evolved as different ingredients were added to the stew. Today we empty the pot, of course, but that makes it no less useful. Boiled food, such as corn on the cob and lobsters, just aren't possible without a good-size pot.

For the person who plans ahead to save time, a large pot is a critical vehicle for savory stews, chili, and soups. A big batch can be assembled and cooked and then eaten over the course of the week or frozen for a busy rainy day.

Vegetable steamer   This handy piece of equipment takes two main forms: as an insert for a large saucepan, and as a special pot with tiny holes in its bottom designed to fit on another pot with boiling water. The insert is generally less expensive. It resembles a metal poppy flower that expands to touch the sides of the pot, with small legs to hold the food to be steamed above boiling water. Either way, steaming is a very quick cooking method that preserves flavor and texture and has a secure spot in the 30-minute cuisine kitchen.

Wok   A wok is a wonderful tool for quick cooking. Unfortunately, it's only suitable for use on a gas cook top, unless you purchase an electric version, which may not have the important capability of rapid heating characteristic of a wok over a gas flame. Large enough to hold an entire meal, different enough to inspire interest, a wok brings fun to a meal.

Fish poacher   For a seafood lover, a fish poacher is a great item in the 30-minute kitchen. A poacher is a long, rectangular pot with a separate metal basket designed to hold a fish inside the pot, either above boiling water for steaming or in simmering liquid for poaching. They come in varying sizes up to 24 inches, although an 18-inch version covers all but the largest meals. The method is quick and easy, resulting in a delicious, flaky fish that disappears in minutes from the dinner table.

In the Oven

Now let's take a look at some of the workhorses in the oven.

Pizza stone   This is the secret for the knowledgeable pizza chef. Preheated with the oven (I cook pizza at 450°F), the stone cooks a crust to a delicious, crispy, pizza-parlor texture. It also holds heat well, so a pizza removed from the oven on the stone will stay hot for as much as half an hour at the table. A pizza stone is also terrific for baking other kinds of breads that benefit from that crisp hearth texture, such as focaccia.

Casserole dishes   Primarily used in baking, casserole dishes hold liquids and solids together and keep moisture around ingredients that might otherwise dry out. Most recipes that call for a casserole dish require longer than 30 minutes, so the rationale for inclusion in this list is that a large casserole can be used for a dish that will dispense a delicious meal several times. Several recipes in this book call for using a casserole dish.

Baking pans   Baking pans round out the 30-minute kitchen. They also are versatile and can be used for tasks ranging from baking potatoes to chicken, from cookies to croutons. Cake pans are, of course, used for cakes, whether from scratch or from a mix. Related tools, such as cookie sheets, are also a nice addition; however, in a pinch, the cake pan will do the job. The use of a muffin pan is primarily limited to muffins, although I've found a few creative uses for savory muffin-shape entrées.

Kitchen Tools

Now that you've got that big skillet, you need something to stir the scallions, measure the marjoram, and flip the flapjacks. Important tools for 30-minute cuisine include the following:

Wooden spoons   Three, of varying lengths, are enough to start with.

Spatulas   Both a good-quality, sharp-edge spatula and a coated, nonstick spatula are useful for flipping pancakes and turning burgers.

Rubber spatulas   These are the magic wands of cookery. For those of you who can't stand waste, this handy tool enables you to save every last bit of sauce from the pan and frosting from the bowl. If you have a nonstick skillet, a coated, nonstick spatula (or a wooden one) will prevent damage to the surface.

Pasta spoon   One of these long-handled spoons with teeth for gripping pasta is very useful for life with spaghetti and other pastas.

Measuring cups for dry and wet ingredients   I recommend you have two sets of nested measuring cups for dry ingredients (flour, oatmeal, nuts, and so on). Sets of measuring cups usually include ¼ cup, ⅓ cup, ½ cup, and 1 cup. You also should have at least two glass measuring cups for liquid ingredients. These cups come in 1- and 2-cup sizes; I find the 2 cup to be the most practical and versatile. Glass measuring cups are graded along the side to indicate all amounts less than the 2-cup capacity and are used for all liquids, from water and milk to oils and sweeteners.

ON THE CLOCK

I've heard busy cooks lament that they can never get enough measuring cups and spoons. When you need that ⅓ cup measure, and it's in the dishwasher, the argument for an extra is pretty compelling. The cost isn't great, and the time savings is valuable. The same "have an extra on hand" rationale applies to measuring spoons; the busy cook always needs an extra teaspoon.

Measuring spoons   Measuring spoon sets typically include ⅛ teaspoon, ¼ teaspoon, ½ teaspoon, 1 teaspoon, ½ tablespoon, and 1 tablespoon.

Colander and large kitchen sieve   Pasta often saves a meal, and, unless you've got strong arms and a steady hand to pour off boiling water from the pot, a colander is necessary to make pasta happen. The colander's junior cousin, the sieve, can also be used for rinsing vegetables, fruits, and meats, and straining liquids to remove unwanted larger particles.

Wire whisk   For sauces, eggs, dry mixtures, and liquid, a whisk is a simple and effective mixing tool.

Garlic press   Here's another item where you get what you pay for, so look for a solid press, where the pivoting press head won't break. (I've destroyed several.)

Box grater (the kind with different size holes on each side)   This is very useful for creating small to tiny pieces of an ingredient, from vegetable shavings to grated Parmesan cheese.

Lime squeezer   This is an unusual yet practical tool for the 30-minute cook. It takes a half a lime (and fits some lemons) and presses out all the juice. In marinades and sauces, lime juice is a tasty, memorably fresh ingredient. A lime squeezer is also indispensable for making the perfect margarita.

Salad spinner   A simple gadget perfect for anyone who loves fresh greens and salads, a salad spinner enables you to thoroughly rinse or soak your greens to clean them and renew their crispness and then rapidly spin off the excess water.

Kitchen shears/scissors   These display their usefulness in unexpected places. They're valuable for cutting herbs, vegetables, flowers, and even pizza (to avoid harming a pizza stone).

Peeler   A peeler is helpful for peeling many fruits and vegetables of their inedible or unappetizing skin.

Melon scoop   A melon scoop provides a quick and easy way to prepare a dessert or salad.

Can opener   This device is critical for anyone who uses canned ingredients. There are manual and electric can openers, but I recommend purchasing an electric one. They're typically not expensive ($10 to $15).

Timer   If not built into your oven or microwave, get yourself a reliable timer to clock your creations.

Corkscrew   For the wine lover, this is as important as a skillet for the cook. Better get two.

Don't Forget the Knives!

Knives are a critical investment for the kitchen and one place where I heartily recommend a splurge. I've used cheap knives as well as more expensive versions, and from experience, I can say that you get what you pay for. That said, you don't need to invest $500 in a complete set that may contain items you'll rarely use.

These knives, whether in a block or in the drawer, are worth the investment:

Chef's knife   A sturdy knife with a straight (nonserrated) blade can be used for everything from chopping vegetables to slicing meat. This versatile knife comes in a variety of sizes, from 6 to 12 inches.

Paring knife   This short (usually 3- or 4-inch blade), straight-edge knife is used for delicate cutting, peeling, coring, and paring.

Bread knife   This long (8- to 10-inch) serrated knife is designed to easily cut through bread without crushing it.

Knife sharpener   You'll find two general types of sharpeners—manual and electric. Both work well, although electric sharpeners, while more expensive, are quicker.

ON THE CLOCK

I've included a knife sharpener in this list because a knife is only as useful as its cutting edge.

A knife block is a great idea if you invest in quality knives, not only for safety but also to help preserve the knife edge and keeping a knife from scraping against other cutlery. There are many choices, from the familiar stand-on-the-counter version to flat blocks (magnetized) that hold about six knives and fit in a drawer or can be hung on a wall.

Hold It: Kitchen Containers

This broad category covers storage as well as serving containers and is intended to round out the checklist of nonelectric items for your 30-minute kitchen. I'm not including crockery (plates, cups, serving platters, and so on), which I'm assuming you already have. In my kitchen, I make ongoing use of several containers that make quick, convenient cooking and serving easy.

Few things are more graceful or satisfying than a simple wooden bowl. It can be used for serving salad or fruit, for chopping nuts, or for any number of other tasks.

Mixing bowls are similar multitaskers, from mixing cakes and other batters to serving grapes.

Finally, inexpensive plastic containers can be used for everything from single ingredients (egg whites) to entire dishes (chili) and can go from the fridge to the microwave. Most home stores sell a collection of these containers, which should include several sizes: 1 cup, 2 cup, 4 cup, and 6 to 8 cup.

Machinery to Make Life Easier

I'm assuming you have a fridge, a microwave, an oven, and a stove. If you don't, there are ways around the challenge, but they'll involve more gadgets. Follow manufacturers' instructions carefully for using any electric appliance, particularly if its use calls for operation when you're not at home to prevent any risk of accident or fire (for example, a slow cooker).

Helpful machines for 30-minute cuisine include the following:

Rice cooker   A rice cooker is a simple, pot-shape device useful for its simplicity and speed. You can cook rice on the stove, of course, but it requires a bit more attention to avoid burning. A rice cooker only asks that you add rice and water and then forget about it. Most even have an auto shut-off function that switches to "warm" when the rice is done.

Mixer   There's a lot of choice in the type of mixer you use, from the reliable, inexpensive hand beater to the art deco KitchenAid that does the work for you. For preparing batters, cakes, and so on, you'll need to decide how much work you want to do and how much you want to spend.

Blender   A sturdy blender makes short work of ingredients that need to be liquefied and blended, from soups to fruit drinks.

Food mill   A food mill can assist you with everything from shredding cheese for pizza to shredding the onions to go on top to puréeing the sauce.

Slow cooker   A *slow* cooker? In the 30-minute kitchen? Yes. While it might seem counterintuitive, a slow cooker takes up to 8 hours to slowly cook a meal. Again the magic is in the time required on your part: a few minutes in the morning means dinner is ready when you get home.

Toaster   The ideal breakfast machine, a toaster turns last night's bread into the perfect vehicle for butter and jelly.

MINUTE MORSEL

I'd have trouble making the case that a popcorn maker is practical and necessary, but boy is it useful to have around when the kids need a quick snack!

The Freezer Is Your Friend

Years ago, I "borrowed" a large chest freezer from my parents, and it has proven to be indispensable for two reasons: storage and advance preparation. Part of the hassle of quick cooking is ensuring that the necessary main ingredients are all on hand when you need them. The freezer steps up, storing quantities of base ingredients in the cold until you need them.

In my freezer, I have supplies of separately frozen chicken breasts, pork chops, hamburgers, and other items that, after a quick microwave defrosting, have me off and running. Then when I've prepared a large dish, I go back to the freezer with serving-size containers of lasagna, or chili, or stuffed peppers, ready to be thawed out and used at a moment's notice.

I also use the freezer to store tomato sauce made fresh from the garden. It's not only quickly accessible but also extends the use of garden produce year round.

Oh, and I still haven't gotten around to returning the freezer to my parents.

The Least You Need to Know

- Stovetop cookware must have the heft to stand up to hard repeated use, but more importantly, it must be able to distribute heat evenly.
- A solid cast-iron frying pan and a large saucepan are two essential items for the 30-minute kitchen.
- A kitchen equipped with carefully chosen tools and knives (enough for what you need to do, but not so much to overwhelm) enables quick, efficient preparation of tasty meals.
- The right machinery can make your life easier.
- A collection of storage containers means that every timesaving ingredient that can be used later has a home in your fridge or freezer.

Starting Your Day Off Right

They say breakfast is the most important meal of the day, and I tend to agree. But when there's so much to do on already-rushed weekday mornings, sometimes a nutritious breakfast is pushed down the to-do list. That doesn't have to be the case!

With the good-start breakfasts in Part 2, you'll *want* to make time for breakfast. From quick pancakes, to french toast, to waffles, you'll schedule extra time for morning breakfasts.

I've also included some quick and easy to-go recipes for when you don't have time for a leisurely breakfast. These grab-and-go recipes will have you out the door in no time flat.

If you're in the mood for eggs, I've got a whole chapter to satisfy. From omelets to scrambles and so much more, there's an egg-cellent egg dish with your name on it.

Breakfast Time

In This Chapter

- Breakfast: the most important meal of the day
- Surefire breakfast recipes
- Delicious pancakes, french toast, and more

Breakfast brings both opportunity and, let's be honest, time pressure. We've all heard the notion that "breakfast is the most important meal of the day," yet too many people skip breakfast because it's an extra step on rushed mornings. With a few minutes of preparation, however, you can have light and fluffy pancakes, sweet french toast, and delicious muffins on the table in no time.

The homemade breakfast recipes in this chapter are healthy and surprisingly quick, and you'll feel good knowing you've sent off your family with a good breakfast in them.

Buttermilk Pancakes

 20

Serves:
8

4 TB. canola oil

1 cup eight-grain or whole-wheat
  flour

2 cups white flour

$\frac{1}{2}$ cup buttermilk powder

$\frac{1}{2}$ tsp. salt

$1\frac{1}{2}$ tsp. sugar

$1\frac{1}{2}$ tsp. baking soda

2 eggs

2 cups milk

1. Preheat a large skillet or griddle over medium heat, and add 1 tablespoon canola oil.

2. Preheat the oven to warm, and place your serving plates inside.

3. In a large bowl, mix eight-grain flour, white flour, buttermilk powder, salt, sugar, and baking soda. Add eggs, milk, and remaining 3 tablespoons canola oil, and mix until lumpy (not too smooth).

4. Using a $\frac{1}{4}$ cup measure to spoon batter, pour 4 pancakes, each about 3 inches in diameter. After about 2 minutes, when bubbles appear in batter, pop, and stay open, flip over pancakes. Cook for 90 more seconds, and slide finished cakes into the oven to keep warm. Repeat with remaining batter. Serve with margarine or butter and warm maple syrup.

 ON THE CLOCK

Don't forget about the convenience of having a "second breakfast" of pancakes in the fridge. The original pancakes might have taken about 20 minutes to make, but the second serving, clocking in at 4 minutes in the microwave, more than makes up the difference.

Whole-Wheat Pancakes

 20

Serves:
8

3 cups whole-wheat flour

½ tsp. salt

1½ tsp. baking soda

2 large eggs

2 cups milk

½ cup nonfat small curd cottage cheese

2 TB. canola oil

1. In a large bowl, mix whole-wheat flour, salt, and baking soda.

2. In a separate bowl, whisk together eggs, milk, and cottage cheese.

3. Stir egg mixture into flour, and mix until batter is still a little lumpy.

4. In a large skillet over medium heat, heat canola oil. Using a ¼ cup measure to spoon batter, pour 4 pancakes, each about 3 inches in diameter. After about 2 minutes, when bubbles appear in batter, pop, and stay open, flip over pancakes. Cook for 1 more minute. Repeat with remaining batter. Serve with fresh fruit or "light" syrup.

 ON THE CLOCK

Cottage cheese is a secret weapon when it comes to pancakes. It adds a rich, creamy texture without adding much in the way of carbs.

Cottage Griddlecakes

Hearty and creamy in the same griddlecake!

20	**Serves:** 8

4 TB. canola oil

1 cup white flour

1 cup whole-wheat flour

$\frac{1}{3}$ cup cornmeal

$\frac{1}{3}$ cup buttermilk powder

1 tsp. baking soda

$\frac{1}{2}$ tsp. salt

3 TB. sugar

2 eggs

1$\frac{2}{3}$ cups water

$\frac{2}{3}$ cup cottage cheese

1. Preheat a large skillet or griddle over medium heat and add 1 tablespoon canola oil.

2. In a large bowl, mix white flour, whole-wheat flour, cornmeal, buttermilk powder, baking soda, salt, and sugar.

3. In a separate bowl, whisk together eggs, remaining 3 tablespoons canola oil, and water.

4. Add liquid to flour mixture, mix until lumpy, and stir in cottage cheese.

5. Using a $\frac{1}{4}$ cup measure to spoon batter, pour 4 pancakes, each about 3 inches in diameter. After about 2 minutes, when bubbles appear in batter, pop, and stay open, flip over pancakes. Cook for 90 more seconds, and slide finished cakes into the oven to keep warm. Repeat with remaining batter. Serve with margarine or butter and warm maple syrup.

Healthy Buttermilk Waffles

A touch of cornmeal adds crunch and bite to these hearty waffles.

20	**Serves:**
	6 to 8

2 cups white flour

$\frac{1}{3}$ cup whole-wheat flour

$\frac{1}{3}$ cup cornmeal

1 tsp. baking soda

$\frac{1}{4}$ tsp. salt

3 eggs

$\frac{1}{3}$ cup vegetable oil

1 cup plus 2 TB. buttermilk

1. Preheat a waffle iron.

2. In a large bowl, mix white flour, whole-wheat flour, cornmeal, baking soda, and salt.

3. In a separate large bowl, whisk together eggs, vegetable oil, and buttermilk.

4. Pour liquid slowly into dry mixture, stirring until lumpy.

5. Pour about $\frac{1}{3}$ cup batter into the center of the waffle iron (use more batter on the next one if this isn't enough). Cook according to manufacturer directions for about 3 or 4 minutes or until waffle is crisp and light brown.

Quick and Healthy French Toast

A slight twist on the old standby, this good-for-you french toast is the perfect way to finish off a loaf of bread.

20	**Serves:**
	4

2 TB. canola oil

3 eggs

1 cup milk

$\frac{1}{2}$ tsp. salt

3 TB. sugar

8 slices white or whole-wheat
   bread

3 TB. wheat germ

1. Spread canola oil in a large skillet preheated over medium heat.

2. In a large bowl, whisk together eggs, milk, salt, and sugar. Set the bowl next to the heated skillet.

3. Dip 1 slice bread in egg-milk mixture, allowing it to be covered but not completely soaked. Quickly move bread to the skillet. Sprinkle each slice with a little wheat germ on the "up" side before flipping. Cook for 2 or 3 minutes, flip over french toast, and cook for 2 or 3 more minutes or until nicely tanned. Serve with butter and warm maple syrup.

Light French Toast with Fresh Strawberries

20	**Serves:** 4

2 TB. canola oil

3 large eggs

½ cup milk

8 slices 100 percent whole-wheat or low-carb bread

3 TB. wheat germ

1 pt. fresh strawberries, rinsed, tops removed, and cut into ¼-in. pieces

1. In a large skillet over medium heat, heat canola oil.

2. Crack eggs into a large bowl, add milk, and whisk. Set the bowl next to the heated skillet.

3. Dip 1 slice bread in egg-milk mixture, allowing it to be covered but not completely soaked. Quickly move bread to the skillet. Sprinkle each slice with a little wheat germ on the "up" side before flipping. Cook for 2 minutes, flip over french toast, and cook for 2 more minutes or until nicely tanned. Serve topped with a spoonful of strawberries.

Variation: Instead of strawberries, you can use "light" syrup, a sprinkling of sweetener, or simply butter.

George Ames's Blueberry Muffins

This large batch will last for two meals. Enjoy once on the weekend—30 minutes—and then get the second meal instantly during the week!

30	**Serves:** 6 to 8

4 cups white or whole-wheat flour	6 TB. sugar
6 tsp. baking powder	2 eggs
2 tsp. salt	2 cups milk
2 cups blueberries	¾ cup melted shortening

1. Preheat the oven to 425°F.

2. In a large bowl, mix white flour, baking powder, and salt.

3. In a separate bowl, mix blueberries and sugar.

4. In a large glass measuring cup, whisk eggs until they start to get foamy. Add milk and melted shortening. Pour liquid mixture into the bowl with dry ingredients, mixing and stirring until combined but still lumpy. (Don't mix until smooth; that actually will inhibit cooking.)

5. Mix in blueberries.

6. Spoon mixture into greased muffin pans, and bake for 24 to 28 minutes or until done. Delicious!

MINUTE MORSEL

Don't expect the overly sweet modern-day bakery-style muffins here. These authentic treats are designed to showcase the berries, not the sweet tooth. They're biscuitlike in flavor, with a tart spike from the blueberries. If your sweet tooth demands it, add more sugar.

Good-Start Breakfasts

In This Chapter

- Savory skillet stir-ups
- Outside-the-box quick breakfasts
- Light breakfast favorites
- Fantastic fruity starts

This chapter focuses on ultra-quick, light and healthy breakfasts, including some off-the-shelf solutions. First up, meats, vegetables, and whole grains offer nutritious building blocks for quick, hot breakfasts. With one of these dishes under your belt, you'll have energy to face the day.

And then there's yogurt. Years ago, my wife and I spent 2 weeks in Greece. Every country has its own interpretation of breakfast food, and where we were, breakfast meant yogurt. It was made from the milk of the livestock that roamed the hills around the town, and I swore I could taste the dried herbs of the countryside in the creamy mix. Yogurt was sold plain, so we bought things to mix in, including local honey, raisins, and fresh fruit. The yogurt was out-of-this-world delicious, and we began to wonder why. We finally figured out (the labels were in Greek) that the large, prominent "10" on the label must refer to fat content: 10 percent fat. Yikes. Still, we learned from this that plain yogurt can be used to create a beautiful thing, even at home where we could reduce the fat.

No discussion of breakfast is complete without bowing to the fruit bowl, the source of many lightning-fast, tasty, and healthy breakfasts. My approach to fruit for breakfast is to minimize preparation and time and take full advantage of fresh flavors. With this in mind, I share a few of my favorites in this chapter.

Broiled Bacon and Tomato Rafts

 Serves:
2

6 slices ready-cooked lean
Canadian back bacon

6 fresh tomato slices, each about
¼-in. thick

8 fresh basil leaves or 1½ tsp. dried
basil

¼ cup shredded mozzarella cheese

Salt

Black pepper

1. Preheat the broiler to medium.

2. Arrange bacon slices on a baking tray. Top each with 1 tomato slice and 1 basil
   leaf (or a pinch dried basil). Distribute mozzarella cheese among tomatoes, and
   broil on the next-to-highest rack for 4 minutes or until cheese is melted.

3. Distribute to serving plates, season with salt and pepper, and serve.

 ON THE CLOCK

Canadian back bacon comes fully cooked in thick, low-fat slices that serve as
sturdy supports for this flavor-intensive dish. If you have trouble finding it, ham is
a tasty alternative.

Skillet Chicken Sausage and Veggies

Serves:
2

2 TB. canola or olive oil

1 large green bell pepper, ribs and
seeds removed, and diced into
½-in. pieces

½ lb. cooked chicken sausage links,
sliced into ½-in. pieces

1 cup diced tomatoes in juice
(canned or fresh)

Dash hot pepper sauce

3 TB. shredded Parmesan cheese

Salt

Black pepper

1. In a small skillet over medium heat, heat canola oil. Add green bell pepper, and cook, stirring, for 3 minutes or until tender-crisp.

2. Add sausage, and cook, stirring, for 2 minutes or until sausage begins to brown.

3. Add tomatoes and hot pepper sauce, and heat, stirring, for 3 minutes.

4. Distribute to serving plates, and season with Parmesan cheese, salt, and pepper.

ON THE CLOCK

The meat section of your grocery store is likely to have a selection of fully cooked sausages, including options made with chicken (and various other ingredients). Just verify that the package says "fully cooked"; otherwise you'll have to add a few more minutes to cook them.

Light Blueberry Cinnamon Oatmeal

 20   **Serves:**
                              2

2 cups oatmeal

½ tsp. salt

Pinch ground cinnamon

½ cup ripe blueberries, rinsed

1. Cook oatmeal according to the package instructions, and season with salt.

2. Stir in cinnamon, distribute to serving bowls, and top with (or fold in) blueberries. I also like a splash of skim milk on my oatmeal.

Variation: If you like a bit more sweetness, a packet of sweetener will do the job. Instead of blueberries, diced apple with cinnamon is a classic combination. Chopped peaches, strawberries, cherries, and raspberries are all terrific as well.

MINUTE MORSEL

Oatmeal gets great press for being an extremely healthy food. When it comes to carbohydrates, many health experts believe that whole-grain, steel-cut oats, prepared with minimal processing, are the best choice. Skip packages of oatmeal with ingredients other than "oats," and choose oatmeal comprised of whole rolled oats or, even better, steel-cut oats. To me, this oatmeal also has the best taste.

Light Toasted Almond Wheat Cereal

 20

Serves:
2

2 cups wheat cereal

⅓ cup sliced toasted almonds
   (or raw)

¼ cup skim milk

1. Prepare cereal according to the package instructions.

2. Mix in almonds, distribute to serving bowls, and top with skim milk.

 ON THE CLOCK

To toast almonds, spread them on a baking sheet and slide them under the broiler on the top shelf. Toast for 1 minute, stir them around, and toast for 1 or 2 more minutes, watching closely to prevent burning.

 Raspberry Crunch Yogurt

 10

Serves:
1

1 (8-oz.) tub light raspberry yogurt

¼ cup raspberries, fresh or frozen
   (and thawed)

2 TB. wheat germ

1. In a small bowl, mix yogurt, raspberries, and wheat germ.

2. Serve immediately.

ON THE CLOCK

To avoid added sugar, I prefer plain yogurt and then mix in fruit to add sweetness.

Blueberry-Vanilla Breakfast Yogurt

10   **Serves:**
                     1

1 (8-oz.) tub nonfat plain yogurt
¼ cup blueberries, fresh or frozen
   (and thawed)

¼ tsp. vanilla extract
1 pkg. sweetener (optional)

1. In a small bowl, mix yogurt, blueberries, vanilla extract, and sweetener
   (if using).

2. Serve immediately.

Variation: Other unsweetened berries, such as raspberries, blackberries, or strawberries, also work well.

MINUTE MORSEL

Fresh fruits, such as blueberries, strawberries, and peaches, make terrific flavor contributions to any meal. Dried fruits are also delicious, but they also have more concentrated sugar than fresh fruit.

Breakfast Yogurt

 10   **Serves:**
4

1 (32-oz.) tub plain yogurt (nonfat, low-fat, or whole milk—your choice!)

¼ cup honey
¼ cup wheat germ
1 cup blueberries

1. In a medium bowl, mix yogurt, honey, wheat germ, and blueberries.

2. Portion into individual bowls, and serve.

 ON THE CLOCK

This might sound a bit strange as a recommendation for breakfast, but a small drizzle of Amaretto liqueur over a bowl of fresh fruit works flavor-enhancing magic. A very small amount.

Gingered Apple and Yogurt

 10   **Serves:**
2

1 fresh, crisp Fuji or Granny Smith apple, peeled, cored, and chopped into ¼-in. pieces
1 cup plain yogurt

1 tsp. fresh ginger root, peeled and grated
2 pkg. sweetener (optional)

1. In a medium bowl, mix apple, yogurt, ginger root, and sweetener (if using).

2. Serve immediately.

 ON THE CLOCK

Fresh ginger root is available in the vegetable section of many grocery stores. Its fresh, sweet flavor is unmistakable and very different from the powdered dry stuff. Buy a root, peel it, and keep it in a freezer bag in your freezer. When you need it, simply grate it frozen, and stick the rest back in the freezer for next time.

Orchard Fruit Mélange

 Serves:
6 to 8

About 1 lb. green or red seedless
grapes
2 apples, peeled, cored, and
chopped into grape-size pieces

2 ripe peaches, pitted and
chopped into grape-size pieces
½ pt. pitted cherries
½ pt. blueberries
Juice of ½ lemon

1. In a large bowl, combine grapes, apples, peaches, cherries, and blueberries.

2. Drizzle with lemon juice, toss gently, and serve.

Variation: For a **Tropical Fruit Mélange,** combine 2 bananas, peeled and sliced
into ¼-inch rounds, 1 (12-ounce) can pineapple chunks, ½ pint blueberries, and
½ muskmelon, carved into balls with a melon baler. Drizzle with lemon juice as
directed.

 ON THE CLOCK

If you use organic apples, rinse them and chop with the peels on for added
nutrition—and to save peeling time.

Frozen Berry Shake

 Serves:
2

1 cup plain yogurt

1 cup frozen mixed berries

⅓ cup water

2 pkg. sweetener (optional)

1. In a blender or a food processor, combine yogurt, mixed berries, water, and sweetener (if using), and pulse to a creamy consistency. Add a little more water if necessary to facilitate blending.

2. Serve on the veranda with a view of the grounds.

Variation: This shake is delicious made with frozen raspberries, blueberries, and strawberries. If you've got fresh fruit, use it! Your shake won't be as cold, but it will be just as irresistible.

ON THE CLOCK

This delicious shake can pass as breakfast, lunch, dessert, or snack, depending on the time of day (and the size of your masterpiece).

Excellent Eggs

In This Chapter

- Quick, delicious eggs
- Elegant omelets
- Scrambles with a twist
- Veggie, meat, and egg dishes

Eggs are the classic breakfast ingredient. They're packed with protein and nutrition, contain almost no carbs, and even the fat they contain is a balance of saturated and unsaturated. And did I mention ease of preparation and unmatched flavor? Once you experiment with a few egg recipes such as omelets and scrambles, you'll look for more ways to fit eggs into your day.

Omelets are fast—averaging 3 or 4 minutes to cook—and are easy to make with a little practice. Give yourself the chance to try them a few times. If you end up with scrambled eggs at first, don't worry. They'll still be delicious.

Sunny yellow scrambled eggs are one of the easiest, most flexible dishes you can make. Simple, healthy, and full of rich egg flavor, the scrambles in this chapter make me want to get up in the morning.

And don't limit yourself to eggs for breakfast. A hearty omelet also makes the perfect lunch or dinner.

Italian Herb Omelet

	Serves:
	1

1 TB. olive oil

2 large eggs

1 tsp. Italian seasoning

2 TB. shredded Parmesan cheese

Salt

Black pepper

1. In a small nonstick skillet over medium heat, heat olive oil.

2. Crack eggs into a bowl, add Italian seasoning, and whisk to combine. Carefully pour egg mixture into the skillet, and cook for 1 minute without stirring. Then, using a spatula that won't harm the skillet's nonstick surface, loosen eggs around the edges so omelet slides easily.

3. When eggs are almost cooked through, sprinkle Parmesan cheese over top and, using the spatula, fold omelet over on itself. Lift the skillet over the serving plate, and slide omelet out onto the plate. Serve, seasoning with salt and pepper.

 ON THE CLOCK

A good nonstick skillet is very helpful when it comes to cooking egg dishes, especially omelets. Without a nonstick skillet, you'll need to use a bit more oil. A nonstick spatula is also a good idea so you don't damage the skillet surface.

Chicken and Swiss Omelet

10	**Serves:**
	1

1 TB. olive oil

2 large eggs

Dash hot pepper sauce (optional)

¼ cup shredded Swiss cheese

½ (6-oz.) can water-packed chunk white chicken meat, drained and broken into small pieces

Salt

Black pepper

1. In a small nonstick skillet over medium heat, heat olive oil.

2. Crack eggs into a bowl, add hot pepper sauce (if using), and whisk to combine. Carefully pour egg mixture into the skillet, and cook for 1 minute without stirring. Then, using a spatula that won't harm the skillet's nonstick surface, loosen eggs around the edges so omelet slides easily.

3. When eggs are almost cooked through, spread Swiss cheese and chicken over eggs and, using the spatula, fold omelet over on itself. Lift the skillet over the serving plate, and slide omelet out onto the plate. Serve, seasoning with salt and pepper.

Variation: Chopped leftover chicken is a natural in place of canned. Or you can substitute your favorite shredded cheese.

Prosciutto Omelet

10	Serves: 1

1 TB. olive oil	3 TB. chopped *prosciutto*
2 large eggs	Salt
2 TB. shredded Parmesan cheese	Black pepper

1. In a small nonstick skillet over medium heat, heat olive oil.

2. Crack eggs into a bowl, and whisk. Carefully pour eggs into the skillet, and cook for 1 minute without stirring. Then, using a spatula that won't harm the skillet's nonstick surface, loosen eggs around the edges so omelet slides easily.

3. When eggs are almost cooked through, sprinkle on Parmesan cheese and chopped prosciutto and, using the spatula, fold omelet over on itself. Lift the skillet over the serving plate, and slide omelet out onto the plate. Serve, seasoning with salt and pepper.

> **DEFINITION**
>
> **Prosciutto,** a dry, salt-cured ham, is salty, rich, and evocative of Italy. It's popular in many simple dishes where its unique flavor is allowed to shine. Although prosciutto-style ham is now produced worldwide, the original, from Parma, has unique flavor thanks to the pigs' diet of whey and chestnuts.

Baby Shrimp Omelet

🕙 **10**	**Serves:** 1

1 TB. olive oil	2 TB. shredded Parmesan cheese
2 large eggs	Salt
Dash hot pepper sauce	Black pepper
1 (4-oz.) can tiny shrimp, drained	

1. In a small nonstick skillet over medium heat, heat olive oil.

2. Crack eggs into a bowl, add hot pepper sauce, and whisk to combine. Pour egg mixture into the skillet, and cook for 1 minute without stirring. Then, using a spatula that won't harm the skillet's nonstick surface, loosen eggs around the edges so omelet slides easily.

3. When eggs are almost cooked through, spread tiny shrimp and Parmesan cheese over eggs and, using the spatula, fold omelet over on itself. Lift the skillet over the serving plate, and slide omelet out onto the plate. Serve, seasoning with salt and pepper.

Variation: Crabmeat, available in cans the same size as shrimp, is a delicious substitution for shrimp. Be sure to pick over crab to remove any remaining shell fragments.

Scrambled Eggs

🕙 **10**	**Serves:** 2

2 TB. canola or olive oil	Salt
4 large eggs	Black pepper
¼ cup skim milk	

1. In a small skillet over medium-low heat, heat canola oil.

2. Crack eggs into a bowl, add skim milk, and whisk to combine.

3. Carefully pour egg mixture into the skillet, and cook, stirring slowly to bring uncooked eggs in contact with the skillet, for 3 or 4 minutes or to your desired consistency.

4. Distribute to serving plates, and season with salt and pepper.

Variation: Add $\frac{1}{3}$ cup shredded Swiss cheese (or your favorite) along with the milk.

TIME WASTER

Avoid high heat when cooking eggs. The secret to creamy, luxuriant scrambled eggs is leisurely cooking over medium or medium-low heat, stirring all the while. You'll add a minute to cooking time (to a huge 4 minutes), but the flavor and texture is worth it. As soon as your eggs reach the consistency you like, serve 'em up. The more eggs cook (or the higher the cooking temperature), the drier they get.

Scrambled Eggs with Sun-Dried Tomato and Sweet Onion

After you try this fast, rich egg dish, you'll know how to answer when someone asks you how you like your eggs.

 20   **Serves:**
2

2 TB. olive oil	Pinch dried thyme
$\frac{1}{2}$ cup finely chopped sweet onion such as Vidalia or Spanish Sweet	Pinch crushed red pepper flakes
	3 eggs
$\frac{1}{3}$ cup oil-packed sun-dried tomatoes, chopped into 1-in. pieces	$\frac{1}{3}$ cup skim milk
	Salt
	Black pepper

1. In a small skillet over medium heat, heat olive oil. Add sweet onion, sun-dried tomatoes, thyme, and crushed red pepper flakes, and sauté for 7 minutes.

2. Crack eggs into a bowl, add skim milk, and whisk to combine.

3. Reduce heat to low, and add egg-milk mixture to the skillet. Stir slowly for 3 minutes or until egg mixture is cooked but still soft and velvety.

4. Distribute to serving plates, and season with salt and pepper.

Southwest Scramble

10	**Serves:** 2

2 TB. canola or olive oil	⅓ cup no-sugar-added salsa (your favorite)
4 large eggs	Salt
¼ cup skim milk	Black pepper

1. In a small skillet over medium-low heat, heat canola oil.

2. Crack eggs into a bowl, add skim milk and salsa, and whisk to combine. Carefully pour egg mixture into the skillet, and cook, stirring slowly to bring uncooked eggs in contact with the skillet, for 4 minutes or to your desired consistency.

3. Distribute to serving plates, and season with salt and pepper.

ON THE CLOCK

Great omelet fillings are just as good in scrambled eggs. Almost all the usual suspects, including cheeses, meats, vegetables, and seasonings, are also perfect for light cooking with scrambled eggs.

Florentine Scramble

 10 | **Serves:**
2

2 TB. canola or olive oil	¼ cup skim milk
2 cups fresh baby spinach leaves, rinsed and stemmed, or ⅓ cup frozen spinach, thawed and squeezed dry	3 TB. shredded Parmesan cheese
	Salt
	Black pepper
4 large eggs	

1. In a small skillet over medium heat, heat canola oil. Add spinach, and cook, stirring, for 3 minutes or until spinach is cooked and, if using fresh, spinach has dramatically reduced in volume.

2. Crack eggs into a bowl, add skim milk, and whisk. Carefully pour egg mixture into the skillet with spinach, and cook, stirring slowly to bring uncooked eggs in contact with the skillet, for 4 minutes or to your desired consistency.

3. Distribute to serving plates, and season with Parmesan cheese, salt, and pepper.

Tex-Mex Microwave Scramble

10 | **Serves:**
1

1 large egg	2 TB. milk
3 TB. shredded Mexican-style cheese (or your favorite)	Salt
	Black pepper
3 TB. sugar-free salsa	

1. In a microwave-safe plastic container with a tight-fitting lid, combine egg, Mexican-style cheese, salsa, milk, salt, and pepper.

2. Crack the lid and cook on high for 1 minute. Stir, and cook for 1 more minute or until done.

Garden Herb Eggs

(10) | **Serves:**
4

3 TB. canola or olive oil

6 eggs

²/₃ cup milk

½ cup shredded cheddar (or other) cheese

2 TB. chopped fresh basil, or 2 tsp. dried basil

2 TB. chives, chopped

Salt

Black pepper

1. Preheat a large skillet over medium heat, and add canola oil.

2. In a large bowl, whisk eggs, milk, cheddar cheese, basil, and chives.

3. Carefully pour egg mixture into the skillet, and cook, stirring slowly to bring uncooked eggs in contact with the skillet, for 3 or 4 minutes or to your desired consistency.

4. Distribute to serving plates, and season with salt and pepper.

Colette's Bacon and Egg Buttie

Served to us by friends in Scotland, this easy British breakfast staple has successfully invaded our kitchen. It resembles a fast-food breakfast sandwich, but it's so very delicious.

(20) | **Serves:**
4 to 6

Butter

8 soft bread rolls or biscuits, split

½ lb. good-quality bacon, such as Canadian bacon, thickly sliced

8 eggs

Salt

Black pepper

1. Spread butter among rolls, and set aside.

2. In a large skillet over medium heat, cook bacon until crispy. Remove and distribute pieces among buttered rolls.

3. In the heated skillet, cook eggs in bacon fat to your preferred degree of doneness. (My favorite is over easy, with a barely runny yolk.)

4. Distribute cooked eggs to sandwich rolls on top of bacon, and season with salt and pepper.

ON THE CLOCK

In Scotland, you might find people seasoning this sandwich with "brown sauce," which is similar to steak or barbecue sauce. For something close, you might try barbecue or Worcestershire sauce, or even mustard, instead.

Crustless Spinach and Bacon Quiches

 20   **Serves:**
                  2

3 large eggs	3 slices crisp, cooked bacon, crumbled, or 1/4 cup bacon pieces
1/2 cup frozen spinach, thawed and squeezed dry	
1/4 cup skim milk	1/4 tsp. salt
3 TB. light sour cream	Pinch black pepper

1. Preheat the oven to 400°F. Grease 2 large muffin pan cups or 4 miniature cups.

2. In a large bowl, mix eggs, spinach, skim milk, sour cream, bacon, salt, and pepper with a fork. Distribute egg mixture among the greased muffin cups, and bake for 15 minutes or until eggs are firmly set. (When eggs are cooked, a fork or knife inserted into the middle will emerge uncoated.)

3. Gently pry those little beauties out onto a plate, and enjoy.

Variation: These breakfast delicacies are also delicious baked and served in oven-safe ramekins.

Skillet-Broiled Roasted Red Pepper Frittata

20	**Serves:** 2

1 TB. olive oil

1 tsp. chopped garlic

2 large eggs

1 TB. dried *minced onion*

1 cup water-packed roasted red peppers, drained, patted dry on paper towels, and cut into $\frac{1}{2}$-in. pieces

1 (8-oz.) pkg. shredded cheddar cheese

$\frac{1}{2}$ cup shredded Parmesan cheese

$\frac{1}{2}$ tsp. Italian seasoning

2 TB. chopped fresh chives

Salt

Black pepper

1. Preheat the broiler.

2. In a small, oven-safe skillet over medium-low heat, heat olive oil. Add garlic, and cook, stirring, for 1 minute.

3. In a medium bowl, mix eggs, minced onion, roasted red peppers, cheddar cheese, $\frac{1}{2}$ of Parmesan cheese, Italian seasoning, chives, salt, and pepper. Pour egg mixture into the skillet, and stir to incorporate garlic. Cook, without stirring, for 5 minutes or until frittata has solidified almost to the surface (test with a knife). Sprinkle remaining Parmesan cheese over top of frittata.

4. Transfer the skillet to the next-to-highest shelf under the broiler, and broil for 3 minutes or until frittata is set all the way through. Remove, cool for 5 minutes, and cut into slices.

Variation: Many vegetables and meats are delicious in place of (or in addition to) the roasted red pepper. Mushrooms, spinach, chopped ham, prosciutto, cooked chicken, and halved cherry tomatoes all come to mind.

DEFINITION

Minced onion, available in the spice section of your grocery store, brings an onion flavor without the chopping (and the crying). Be sure to give it time to soak up the moisture in a dish to allow the flavor to spread.

Portobello Eggs

20 **Serves:**
2

2 large (4-in.) bowl-shape portobello mushroom caps	2 large eggs
3 TB. olive oil	Salt
$\frac{1}{3}$ tsp. Italian seasoning	Black pepper

1. Preheat the broiler (if your broiler has multiple settings, select medium).

2. Remove mushroom stems, scrape out gills with a spoon, and wipe caps with a damp paper towel. Place caps on a baking tray, top side up, and brush with 1 tablespoon olive oil. Broil on the next-to-highest rack for 3 minutes.

3. Flip over caps, drizzle each with half of remaining olive oil, sprinkle with a pinch of Italian seasoning, and broil for 3 more minutes.

4. Slide sizzling mushrooms out of the oven, crack 1 egg in each cap, slide back under the broiler, and broil for 3 minutes or until egg is cooked to your liking.

5. Place each mushroom on a serving plate, season with salt and pepper, and serve with a knife and fork.

ON THE CLOCK

If the stem side of the portobello cap isn't sufficiently concave, the egg will slide off. So be sure to scoop out the gills so the egg will have a bowl in which to cook. If your mushroom caps are too rounded to sit well on the baking tray, use a sharp knife to cut a bit of the top off to give it a flat surface.

Scottish Eggs

10 | **Serves:**
2

2 TB. canola oil

2 slices 100 percent whole-wheat
   or low-carb bread

Butter or margarine

2 large eggs

4 oz. thinly sliced smoked salmon

Black pepper

1. In a medium skillet over medium heat, heat canola oil.

2. While skillet heats, toast and butter bread.

3. When a drop of water "dances" on hot oil, crack 1 egg into the skillet, and cook for about 1 minute or until egg white turns white about halfway to the surface. Carefully slide a spatula under egg, and flip it over.

4. Add $\frac{1}{2}$ of smoked salmon to the skillet, and cook for 1 more minute.

5. Place toast on a serving plate, slide salmon on top of toast, and place egg on salmon. Repeat with other egg, another piece of toast, and remaining salmon. Season with pepper.

MINUTE MORSEL

I met these Scottish Eggs in Scotland years ago, and I've loved them ever since. In the old country, they're served on what we'd call a white flour biscuit.

Freddie's Spanish Eggs

Serve this flavorful egg dish with crisp whole-wheat toast for breakfast, or serve with salad and hunks of baguette for dinner.

20	**Serves:** 4

6 eggs

½ cup skim milk

Salt

Black pepper

3 TB. olive oil

1 onion, chopped

1 clove garlic, minced

1 sweet red pepper, chopped into ½-in. pieces

2 fresh tomatoes, chopped into ½-in. pieces

2 tsp. balsamic vinegar

1. In a large bowl, whisk eggs, skim milk, and dash of salt and pepper, and set aside.

2. In a skillet over medium heat, heat 2 tablespoons olive oil. Add onion, garlic, and sweet red pepper, and sauté for 10 minutes.

3. Add tomatoes and balsamic vinegar, season with more salt and pepper, and cook for 8 more minutes.

4. Meanwhile, in a separate skillet over medium-low heat, heat remaining 1 teaspoon olive oil. Pour in egg mixture, and cook, stirring, for 5 minutes or until eggs are cooked to your desired consistency. (Remember, the more you cook eggs, the firmer they get.)

5. Divide eggs among 4 plates, and top each with ¼ tomato-pepper mixture. Season with more salt and pepper if necessary.

Over-Easy Egg Toast

20	**Serves:** 2

2 TB. canola oil

2 slices *100 percent whole-wheat or low-carb bread*

Butter or margarine

2 large eggs

Salt

Black pepper

1. In a large skillet over medium heat, heat canola oil.

2. While skillet heats, toast and butter bread. Using a sharp knife (or even a large glass or cookie cutter), cut a round piece, about 3 inches in diameter, in center of toast. Remove the round piece but keep it.

3. Place toast in the hot skillet, and crack 1 egg into each toast hole. Cook for 2 minutes per side or to your liking.

4. Slide toast and egg onto a plate, and replace round piece as a "lid" over egg. Season with salt and pepper.

DEFINITION

You'll see **100 percent whole-wheat bread** everywhere these days because it's not only more nutritious, but many people think it tastes better than white bread. But read the label carefully. The word *wheat* doesn't mean anything (almost all bread is made with wheat!). It needs to say *100 percent!*

Let's Do Lunch

You don't have to settle for a tasteless, nutritionally barren fast-food drive-thru meal at lunchtime. And those vending machine offerings might be convenient, but you know they're not all that healthy for you. After trying a few recipes in Part 3, you'll never crave those second choice foods again!

From surprisingly satisfying salads, to quick and easy soups and stews, to filling sandwiches and wraps, Part 3 gives you a menu full of options for your lunchbox.

As a bonus, many of the recipes in Part 3 are on the lighter side, calorie-, fat-, and especially sugar- and carb-wise. (That's true throughout the book, too.) So if you're watching your weight, you'll find plenty of delicious options in the following chapters. Never fall prey to the vending machine again!

Sensational Salads

In This Chapter

- The usual salad suspects—and then some
- Variations on greens
- Bean salads
- Hearty dinner salads

The beauty of a salad is its flexibility. From a simple combination of torn lettuce and dressing to mesclun with ripe and dried fruits, toasted nuts, balsamic vinegar, and fresh chevre, there's a salad for everyone.

Fresh salad ingredients bring their own terrific flavors, and it's hard to mess up something that's already good. Salad ingredients are, for the most part, unprocessed and, as a result, higher in vitamins, minerals, and fiber, and lower in chemicals and empty carbohydrates. And then there are the shell bean salads. With beans as an important component, these hearty, tasty salads are high in protein and fiber, not to mention flavor. Just the perk you need at lunchtime to help you get through the rest of the day!

In this chapter, I share some of my favorite salads that take minutes to make but can easily become addictive.

Chicken Chef Salad

10	**Serves:** 4

2 (6-oz.) cans chunk white chicken meat, drained

1/2 cup chopped walnuts, toasted or raw

1 (12-oz.) bag iceberg salad mix

1 crisp pear, cored and chopped into 1/4-in. pieces

1/2 cup shredded cheddar cheese (or light cheddar)

1/3 cup vinaigrette or Italian dressing, or to taste

1. In a large bowl, mix chicken and walnuts with a fork, breaking up any large chunks of meat.

2. Add iceberg salad mix, pear, cheddar cheese, and vinaigrette; toss to coat chicken; and serve.

ON THE CLOCK

When you need to wash greens, a salad spinner—a nifty hand-driven tool that whirls moisture out of salad—can be your best friend. It's much faster than allowing your greens to drip dry.

Iceberg Nests with Avocado, Bacon, and Tomato

20	**Serves:** 2

1/4 lb. sliced bacon

1 large head iceberg lettuce

2 medium, ripe avocados, peeled and cut into 1/2-in. slices

1 large fresh tomato, chopped into 1/4-in. pieces

1/4 cup toasted pine nuts

2 TB. lime juice

Salt

Black pepper

1. In a large skillet over medium heat, cook bacon until crisp and drain on a paper towel–lined plate.

2. Cut head of lettuce in half, and carefully separate into 2 bowl-shape "nests," reserving the center of head for another use.

3. Distribute avocado between lettuce nests, and top with tomato and pine nuts. Drizzle lime juice over top, and sprinkle with crumbled bacon.

4. Serve, seasoning each nest with salt and pepper.

Variation: Other sturdy lettuces, such as romaine, also work in place of iceberg. Real bacon pieces (from the spice section at your grocery store) are a quick substitute for cooking the bacon.

ON THE CLOCK

If you have fresh limes, use fresh lime juice on your salad. It's quick, and the flavor is much better than the bottled stuff.

Flower Bed Salad

 Serves:
4

1 medium head romaine lettuce, leaves broken into bite-size pieces

1 (7-oz.) pkg. baby spinach, stems removed

About 10 grape tomatoes, halved

1 handful arugula leaves, stems removed

2 TB. balsamic vinegar

2 TB. extra-virgin olive oil

Salt

Black pepper

8 to 10 fresh, young nasturtium flowers

1. In a large serving bowl, mix romaine, spinach, grape tomatoes, and arugula.

2. Drizzle balsamic vinegar and extra-virgin olive oil over top, sprinkle with salt and pepper, arrange nasturtium flowers on top, and present for multiple compliments.

MINUTE MORSEL

The nasturtium is only one of the delicious flowers found in many gardens. Another one of my favorites is the flower of the tiny signet marigold. (It really does taste like it smells.) Use only plants that haven't been sprayed with pesticides.

Apple and Toasted Pecan Salad

 Serves:
4

6 TB. walnut oil

2 TB. sherry vinegar or wine vinegar

1 tsp. Dijon-style mustard

1 TB. sherry

1 pkg. sweetener

¼ tsp. black pepper

1 (6-oz.) pkg. "spring mix" greens

1 crisp Granny Smith apple, sliced thinly

½ cup crumbled Gorgonzola or other blue cheese

½ cup toasted pecans

1. In a small bowl, mix walnut oil, sherry vinegar, Dijon-style mustard, sherry, sweetener, and pepper.

2. Arrange spring mix in a serving bowl, pour dressing over top, and toss to coat. Decoratively top salad with apple slices, sprinkle with Gorgonzola, top with toasted pecans, and serve.

Real Greek Salad

10   **Serves:**
6

2 large fresh, firm tomatoes, chopped into 1-in. pieces, or 1 pt. grape tomatoes, halved

2 large sweet green peppers, ribs and seeds removed, and chopped into 1-in. pieces

1 large English-style cucumber (or 2 small cucumbers), striped, sliced in half lengthwise, and cut into $\frac{1}{2}$-in. pieces

$\frac{1}{2}$ large sweet onion, cut into $\frac{1}{2}$-in. pieces

$\frac{1}{2}$ cup (about 10 large leaves) fresh basil, chopped

3 TB. extra-virgin olive oil

2 TB. red wine vinegar

$\frac{1}{2}$ (8-oz.) pkg. feta cheese, sliced into $\frac{1}{4}$×3-in. pieces

$\frac{1}{2}$ cup kalamata olives

Salt

Black pepper

1. In a large bowl, combine tomatoes, sweet green peppers, cucumber, sweet onion, and basil. Drizzle extra-virgin olive oil and red wine vinegar over top, and toss to coat. Arrange feta wedges across the top, and sprinkle with kalamata olives.

2. Serve, being careful that a slice of feta cheese and some olives make it into each serving, and season with salt and pepper.

ON THE CLOCK

Salads like this are the place to splurge on high-quality extra-virgin olive oil. I've heard good olive oil described as "liquid sunshine." Who wouldn't want some of that on a salad?

Fresh Tomato Salad

 Serves:
4

1 pt. grape tomatoes, halved, or 2 large fresh tomatoes, chopped into 1-in. chunks	1 cup fresh small mozzarella balls, cut in half
½ cup (about 10 large leaves) fresh basil, chopped, or 1 tsp. dried	3 TB. extra-virgin olive oil
	Salt
	Black pepper

1. In a large bowl, combine tomatoes, basil, and mozzarella, and distribute to serving plates.

2. Drizzle with extra-virgin olive oil, season with salt and pepper, and serve.

 MINUTE MORSEL

Mozzarella cheese comes in many varieties. When it comes to eating it in salads, however, nothing tops fresh mozzarella for flavor. Fresh mozzarella, found in the deli or cheese section of your grocery stores, comes packed in brine in small balls called ciliegine (about the size of cherry tomatoes) or large balls called ovoline (about the size of an egg). Fresh mozzarella is a rich, creamy cheese with a mild flavor that melds perfectly with fresh tomatoes.

Warm Asparagus-Artichoke Salad with Prosciutto and Pine Nuts

20   **Serves:**
4

3 TB. olive oil

1 TB. chopped garlic

1 lb. fresh asparagus, top 4 inches cut into 1-in. sections for salad and remainder reserved for another use

1 (9-oz.) pkg. frozen artichoke hearts, thawed

½ cup diced prosciutto

¼ cup toasted pine nuts

2 TB. *balsamic vinegar*

¼ cup shredded Parmesan cheese

Salt

Black pepper

1. In a large skillet over medium heat, heat olive oil. Add garlic and asparagus, and cook, stirring, for 3 minutes or until asparagus is tender-crisp. Add artichoke hearts, and heat for 1 minute.

2. Turn off heat, and stir in prosciutto and pine nuts.

3. Distribute warm salad to serving plates, drizzle with balsamic vinegar, sprinkle with Parmesan cheese, and season with salt and pepper.

DEFINITION

Balsamic vinegar is produced primarily in Italy, from the juice of the Trebbiano grape, and aged in wood barrels. It's heavier, darker, and more flavorful than most vinegars.

Three-Bean Salad

 Serves:
6

1 lb. cut fresh green beans or 1 lb. frozen, thawed

1 (15-oz.) can white beans, drained and rinsed

1 (15-oz.) can chickpeas, drained and rinsed

1 red bell pepper, ribs and seeds removed, and chopped into ¼-in. pieces

¼ large sweet onion (about ½ cup), diced

¼ cup sweetener (optional)

⅓ cup olive oil

⅓ cup red wine vinegar

½ tsp. dill

½ tsp. celery seed

½ tsp. salt

½ tsp. black pepper

1. In a container with a lid, mix green beans, white beans, chickpeas, red bell pepper, sweet onion, sweetener (if using), olive oil, red wine vinegar, dill, celery seed, salt, and pepper.

2. Cover and refrigerate for several hours or all day, if possible. Serve in small bowls alone or as a tasty side dish.

ON THE CLOCK

I recommend you chill this salad to allow the flavors to mend, so maybe keep this salad in your "make ahead" file.

Chickpea Salad

10	**Serves:** 6

1/3 cup olive oil

2 TB. freshly squeezed lemon juice

2 anchovies

1/2 tsp. black pepper

2 (5-oz.) cans chunk white chicken meat, drained

1 (15-oz.) can chickpeas, drained and rinsed

2 celery stalks, cut into 1/4-in. pieces

1 large red bell pepper, ribs and seeds removed, and chopped into 1/4-in. pieces

1 cup chopped fresh parsley

1/2 cup sweet onion, minced

1/2 cup shredded Parmesan cheese

1. In a blender, purée olive oil, lemon juice, anchovies, and pepper.

2. In a salad bowl, arrange chicken, chickpeas, celery, red bell pepper, parsley, and sweet onion. Drizzle with dressing, and toss to coat.

3. Distribute salad to serving plates, and sprinkle each serving with Parmesan cheese.

Variation: For **Presto Pesto Chickpea Salad,** omit the chicken and anchovies, and replace with 1/4 cup prepared pesto sauce and 3 tablespoons toasted pine nuts.

Jean's Oriental Cabbage Salad

10	**Serves:** 4 to 6

6 TB. wine vinegar

1/2 cup canola oil

6 TB. sugar

Spice packet from 1 (3-oz.) pkg. ramen noodle soup mix (oriental flavor)

6 cups shredded cabbage

Noodles from soup mix

1 cup peanuts

6 TB. sesame seeds

1. In a small bowl, mix wine vinegar, canola oil, sugar, and spice packet, and set aside.

2. In a large bowl, place cabbage, and crumble dry noodles over top. Add peanuts, and lightly mix.

3. Pour dressing over salad, add sesame seeds, toss salad thoroughly, and serve.

Pear and Walnut Salad

 20

Serves:
4

½ cup walnuts

6 TB. walnut oil

2 TB. sherry vinegar

1 tsp. Dijon mustard

1 TB. sherry

2 tsp. runny honey (heated for 10 seconds in microwave if necessary)

Black pepper

1 pkg. mesclun salad

½ cup crumbled blue cheese

1 pear, sliced thinly

1. Preheat the oven to 350°F.

2. Arrange walnuts on a single layer on a baking sheet, and bake for 10 minutes, or until toasty. Remove them before they turn dark.

3. Meanwhile, in a small bowl, combine walnut oil, sherry vinegar, Dijon mustard, sherry, honey, and pepper.

4. Arrange mesclun in a serving bowl. Pour dressing over salad, and toss well. Add blue cheese, arrange pear slices on top, and sprinkle with toasted walnuts.

 ON THE CLOCK

In a hurry? Many fresh vegetables can be served with a minimum of preparation. Carrots and cucumbers need only to be scraped, sliced, and served with salt and pepper, vinegar, or salad dressing to be a tasty, nutritious snack or side dish. Broccoli, cauliflower, and even beans can be washed, cut, and served with a dip or dressing as well.

Spinach Salad

20   **Serves:**
     4 to 6

¼ lb. bacon	¼ lb. fresh mushrooms, sliced
1 (10-oz.) pkg. baby spinach	Oil-based dressing
2 hard-boiled eggs, peeled and sliced	1 cup your favorite croutons

1. In a large skillet over medium heat, cook bacon until crispy. Remove bacon to a paper towel–lined plate, drain off most of fat, and crumble into ½-inch pieces.

2. In a large bowl, combine spinach, eggs, mushrooms, and bacon.

3. Drizzle dressing over top, and toss to coat. Top with croutons, and serve.

Smoked Salmon Salad

10   **Serves:**
     2

4 large romaine lettuce leaves	2 TB. chopped chives
8 oz. smoked salmon, cut into ½-in. pieces	1 tsp. lemon juice
½ cup sliced almonds, toasted	Pinch black pepper
2 TB. olive oil	2 lemon wedges

1. Set 1 romaine leaf on each of 2 serving plates.

2. Chop remaining 2 romaine leaves, and mix in a bowl with smoked salmon, almonds, olive oil, chives, lemon juice, and pepper.

3. Divide salmon salad between 2 intact romaine leaves, and serve, garnished with 1 lemon wedge each.

Variation: Other salmon variations will also work, even canned salmon.

Barry's Taco Salad

 20 **Serves:**
4

1 lb. ground beef
1 (15-oz.) can creamed corn
1 (1.25-oz.) envelope taco
    seasoning mix

1 (10-oz.) bag tortilla chips
2 cups shredded cheddar cheese
$\frac{1}{2}$ head shredded iceberg lettuce
1 large tomato, chopped

1. In a large frying pan over medium heat, brown ground beef. Drain fat, and turn off heat.

2. Mix creamed corn and taco seasoning mix in with beef.

3. In a large bowl, layer, in order, tortilla chips (crushed by hand), ground beef mixture, cheddar cheese, iceberg lettuce, and tomatoes. Repeat layers until all ingredients are used (usually 2 or 3 layers), and serve.

 MINUTE MORSEL

This salad is delicious garnished with sour cream, black olives, and salsa, and served with—what else?—a good Mexican beer (like Dos Equis).

Piquant Ham Salad in Iceberg Bowls

 10 **Serves:**
2

1 small (about 5-in.) head crisp
    iceberg lettuce
$\frac{1}{2}$ lb. ham, chopped into $\frac{1}{4}$-in.
    pieces
1 celery stalk, trimmed and
    chopped into $\frac{1}{4}$-in. pieces
$\frac{1}{2}$ cup chopped fresh parsley

$\frac{1}{2}$ cup toasted pine nuts
2 TB. mayonnaise
2 TB. balsamic vinegar
Salt
Black pepper
Dash hot pepper sauce

1. Cut head of lettuce in half lengthwise, and remove inner leaves to form 2 bowls. (Reserve removed lettuce for another use.)

2. In a large bowl, combine ham, celery, parsley, pine nuts, mayonnaise, balsamic vinegar, salt, pepper, and hot pepper sauce.

3. Divide salad between 2 lettuce bowls.

 ON THE CLOCK

Many grocery stores sell ham steaks, a convenient cut of cooked meat that can be quickly chopped for this salad. You might also find packages of ready-chopped ham in the same area.

Tuna-Cannellini Salad

10   **Serves:**
6

2 (6-oz.) cans chunk white tuna, drained

1 (15-oz.) can white beans, drained and rinsed

1 celery stalk, cut into $\frac{1}{4}$-in. pieces

1 crisp Granny Smith apple, cored and chopped into $\frac{1}{4}$-in. pieces

2 cups fresh arugula, stems removed, and chopped

$\frac{1}{2}$ cup sweet onion, minced

$\frac{1}{2}$ cup vinaigrette or Italian dressing

$\frac{1}{2}$ cup shredded Parmesan cheese

1. In a salad bowl, combine tuna, white beans, celery, apple, arugula, and sweet onion.

2. Drizzle vinaigrette over salad, and toss to coat.

3. Distribute to serving plates, and sprinkle each serving with Parmesan cheese.

Tuna Broccoli Pasta Salad

 Serves:
4

½ lb. pasta shells

1 bunch broccoli

3 medium tomatoes, cubed

1 (6-oz.) can solid white water-packed tuna, drained

¼ cup red wine vinegar

¼ cup olive oil

2 tsp. dried basil

1 tsp. dried oregano

Salt

Black pepper

1. Cook pasta shells according to package directions, drain, and rinse under cold water. Set aside.

2. Meanwhile, chop broccoli into bite-size florets about 1 inch long. In a vegetable steamer or large saucepan with 1 inch boiling water, steam broccoli for 5 to 8 minutes or until crisp-tender. Drain and rinse under cold water.

3. In a large bowl, combine pasta, broccoli, tomatoes, and tuna.

4. In a small bowl, whisk red wine vinegar, olive oil, basil, and oregano.

5. Pour dressing over salad, and toss to coat. Season with salt and pepper.

Endive Stuffed with Piquant Tuna Salad

10   **Serves:**
4

1 (6-oz.) can chunk white tuna in water, drained

½ celery stalk, chopped into ¼-in. pieces

¼ cup mayonnaise

1 TB. small capers, drained and rinsed

1 tsp. lemon juice

1 tsp. fresh dill or ¼ tsp. dried

Dash hot pepper sauce

Pinch black pepper

2 heads *Belgian endive*

Parsley (optional)

1. In a salad bowl, mix tuna, celery, mayonnaise, capers, lemon juice, dill, hot pepper sauce, and pepper. Place the bowl on a serving platter.

2. Break Belgian endive into leaves, and arrange leaves around the bowl of tuna salad. Serve with a spreading knife or a spoon, placing a generous spoonful of tuna salad in each endive cup and garnishing with parsley (if using).

Variation: This salad is delicious served immediately, but it also packs well. To carry with you, place Belgian endive leaves in a separate container from tuna salad, store in the fridge, and combine at lunchtime.

DEFINITION

Belgian endive is a crisp, slightly astringent green that resembles a small bullet-shape head of romaine lettuce. Endives are popular dippers for appetizers. The individual leaves can be broken off and used as crisp scoops for all kinds of fillings. The big outside leaves are the most useful for stuffing, so buy the largest endives you can. Save the smaller core leaves to slice and use in a salad.

Anya's Turkey Salad

 10   **Serves:**
4

1½ lb. white turkey meat, cubed

2 TB. olive oil

2 TB. sherry

1 TB. sugar

2 TB. low-fat or fat-free sour cream

½ tsp. salt

½ lb. seedless grapes, cut in half

1 cup walnut pieces

1. Place turkey pieces in a salad bowl.

2. In a small bowl, combine olive oil, sherry, sugar, sour cream, and salt, and pour over turkey.

3. Gently stir in grapes and walnuts.

Italian Turkey-Pecan Chef Salad

10   **Serves:**
2

¼ cup pecans, toasted or raw

1 (6-oz.) can turkey meat, drained

½ (16-oz.) bag salad mix

½ crisp apple, rinsed, chopped

⅓ cup shredded mozzarella cheese

¼ cup Italian dressing

1. In a salad bowl, mix pecans and turkey with a fork, mashing to break up any large turkey chunks.

2. Add salad mix, apple, and mozzarella cheese, and toss to mix.

3. Drizzle with Italian dressing.

Satisfying Soups and Stews

In This Chapter

- Savory vegetable soups
- Quick and hearty chilis
- Rich meat stews
- Irresistible chowders

In this chapter, we explore some of the magic appeal of soups and stews, chilis and chowders. In terms of quick, soups are a natural. And because a big batch of soup or stew will live happily in the fridge for a couple days—tasting better all the time—you'll have several lunches or dinners that only need warming up later.

Soups and stews abound in the cuisines of many cultures. The examples in this chapter use representative ingredients and seasoning to give just a taste of that wondrous variety.

Minestrone

30	**Serves:** 10

2 TB. olive oil

1 large onion, chopped into ½-in. pieces

2 TB. chopped garlic

4 (14.5-oz.) cans chicken broth (about 8 cups)

1 (14.5-oz.) can chopped tomatoes with juice

2 (15-oz.) cans white beans, drained and rinsed

¼ small head cabbage sliced into thin, ½×2-in. pieces (about 1½ cups)

2 large carrots, peeled and cut into ¼-in. slices

2 large celery stalks, including leaves, cut into ¼-in. slices

¼ cup fresh basil leaves, coarsely chopped, or 1 tsp. dried

2 tsp. fresh oregano or 1 tsp. dried

¼ tsp. crushed red pepper flakes

1 tsp. salt

1 (10-in.) zucchini squash, ends removed, halved lengthwise, and cut into ½-in. slices

Black pepper

Shredded Parmesan cheese

1. In a large stockpot over medium heat, heat olive oil. Add onion, and cook, stirring, for 4 minutes. Add garlic, and cook for 1 more minute.

2. Add chicken broth, tomatoes, white beans, cabbage, carrots, celery, basil, oregano, crushed red pepper flakes, and salt, and cook for 10 minutes.

3. Add zucchini squash, and cook for 3 minutes or until zucchini squash, carrots, and celery are tender. Serve in bowls, seasoning with pepper and sprinkling with Parmesan cheese.

Chicken, Spinach, and Rice Soup

This version is simple but hearty—a meal in a bowl. A big bowl.

 20

Serves:
4 to 6

2 TB. olive oil

1 medium onion, chopped

1 (10-oz.) pkg. frozen chopped spinach

1 cup cooked chicken, chopped into $\frac{1}{2}$-in. pieces

1$\frac{1}{2}$ cups cooked rice

$\frac{1}{2}$ tsp. crushed red pepper flakes

$\frac{1}{2}$ tsp. dried oregano

$\frac{1}{2}$ tsp. salt

$\frac{1}{4}$ tsp. black pepper

6 cups chicken broth

1. In a large skillet over medium heat, heat olive oil. Add onion, and sauté onion for 5 minutes.

2. Meanwhile, thaw spinach in the microwave by heating on defrost for 5 minutes or until thawed. (Defrost times vary depending on the power of your microwave, so adjust accordingly.)

3. When onion has cooked, add spinach, chicken pieces, rice, crushed red pepper flakes, oregano, salt, and pepper to the skillet, and cook, stirring, for 1 minute.

4. Add chicken broth, heat to a low boil, and simmer for 10 minutes. Serve with crusty bread for a "comfort food 101" meal.

 MINUTE MORSEL

There's something homey and comfortable about all soups, but for many people, chicken soup is where those feelings start. It wards off everything from colds to evil spirits, and it appeals to our practical sensibilities; most ingredients, from the broth to the rice and chicken, can be from leftovers.

Quick Turkey Vegetable Soup

20 **Serves:** 4

2 (14.5-oz.) cans chicken broth

2 (5-oz.) cans chunk turkey meat, drained

1 (16-oz.) pkg. frozen broccoli, green beans, pearl onions, and red pepper mix

1 (1.4-oz.) pkg. vegetable soup mix

Salt

Black pepper

1. In a large microwave-safe bowl, combine chicken broth, turkey, frozen veggie mix, and vegetable soup mix, and microwave on high for 5 to 8 minutes, stirring twice. (Cook time will vary according to microwave power.)

2. Stir and serve, seasoning with salt (if necessary—there's salt in the soup mix) and pepper.

Variation: Other canned meats, such as chicken or even diced ham, also work well in this soup.

ON THE CLOCK

I always recommend fresh vegetables, but for speed and convenience, don't ignore frozen vegetables, especially in winter when fresh local produce isn't in season. Add that to a few choice canned items from the pantry, and you're on your way to a terrific soup.

🍎 Cream of Spinach Soup

20   **Serves:**
4

2 (10-oz.) pkg. frozen chopped
spinach, thawed

3 cups chicken broth

2 tsp. sweet paprika

$\frac{1}{2}$ tsp. salt

$\frac{1}{2}$ tsp. black pepper

$\frac{1}{2}$ cup heavy cream

$\frac{1}{4}$ tsp. ground nutmeg

1. Bring a large saucepan of water to a boil over high heat, add spinach, and cook for 4 minutes. Drain in a colander.

2. In a blender or food processor, working in batches, process spinach and some chicken broth (to aid in processing) to a smooth consistency with visible pieces of leaves to add appealing texture.

3. Return creamed spinach and any remaining broth to the saucepan over medium heat, and stir in sweet paprika, salt, and pepper. Heat for 5 minutes, stirring.

4. Stir in heavy cream, heat for 1 minute, and serve in big bowls, each garnished with a pinch of nutmeg.

Butternut Squash Soup

This soup is the definition of richness and the antidote for a cold winter's day.

30   **Serves:**
4

1 butternut squash

$\frac{1}{4}$ cup water

1 (16-oz.) can vegetable broth

1 cup sour cream

2 egg yolks

Salt

Black pepper

1. Slice squash in half lengthwise, and scrape out seeds and threads with a spoon. Place squash face down in a microwave-safe baking dish, add water, cover with plastic wrap (poke some steam holes on top), and microwave on high for 8 to 10 minutes.

2. When squash has cooked and is soft, spoon flesh out of skin and place in a food processor or blender. Add some vegetable broth, and purée.

3. Pour squash into a large saucepan with the rest of broth, and bring to a boil over high heat. Reduce heat to medium.

4. In a small bowl, whisk together sour cream and egg yolks, and pour mixture into the saucepan, stirring. Cook for 1 minute.

5. Season with salt and pepper, pour into soup bowls, and top with dollop of sour cream, fresh chives or scallions, and a few toasted seeds.

Potato and Leek Soup

This hearty soup will last for several meals.

20	**Serves:** 6 to 8

5 (14.5-oz.) cans vegetable broth	¼ cup sour cream
4 TB. butter	½ tsp. cumin
1 bunch leeks, white parts only, sliced thin and rinsed	1 (4-oz.) pkg. fresh baby spinach
	Salt
4 medium all-purpose potatoes, peeled and chopped	Black pepper

1. In a large saucepan over medium-high heat, bring vegetable broth to a boil.

2. Meanwhile, in a large skillet over medium heat, melt butter. Add leeks, and cook for 5 minutes.

3. Add leeks and potatoes to boiling broth, and cook for 10 minutes or until potato is soft.

4. Add sour cream and cumin, and cook for 5 minutes. Mix in the baby spinach, season with salt and pepper, and serve.

ON THE CLOCK

For dishes that call for vegetable broth, you can also use vegetarian vegetable bouillon, available in most grocery stores.

Miso Soup with Scallions, Tofu, and Carrots

 Serves:
4

2 (14-oz.) cans vegetable broth

1 large carrot, peeled and sliced on the diagonal into $\frac{1}{16}$- to $\frac{1}{8}$-in.-thick ovals

$\frac{1}{4}$ cup *miso*

4 scallions, roots and dark green parts removed, cut into $\frac{1}{4}$-in. rings

$\frac{1}{4}$ (16-oz.) pkg. soft tofu, drained and cut into $\frac{1}{4}$-in. chunks

2 TB. soy sauce (optional)

1. In a saucepan or stockpot over medium-high heat, bring vegetable broth to a boil. Add sliced carrots, reduce heat to low, cover, and cook for 5 minutes.

2. Remove $\frac{1}{2}$ cup broth to a heat-safe measuring cup, and stir in miso until well blended. Pour miso and broth back into soup, stirring to blend.

3. Add scallions and tofu, season with soy sauce (if using), and serve.

Variation: Use 4 cups water and 2 vegetable bouillon cubes in place of canned vegetable broth. For an interesting variation in texture and flavor, use adzuki beans in place of tofu.

DEFINITION

Miso is a fermented, flavorful soybean paste and is a key ingredient in many Japanese dishes. You'll find it in larger grocery stores and stores specializing in Asian foods.

Crunchy Watercress-Crab Soup

20   **Serves:**
4

3 TB. sesame or olive oil

1 small onion, chopped into ½-in. pieces

1 TB. chopped garlic

1 (10-in.) zucchini squash, ends trimmed, quartered lengthwise, cut into ¼-in. pieces

1 TB. sesame seeds

1 tsp. crushed red pepper flakes

2 (14-oz.) cans vegetable broth

2 (4.5-oz.) cans crabmeat, drained and picked over to discard shell fragments

1 tsp. dried lemongrass (optional)

1½ cups watercress, stems removed and coarsely chopped

Salt

Black pepper

1. In a large skillet or saucepan over medium heat, heat sesame oil. Add onion, and cook, stirring, for 4 minutes.

2. Add garlic, zucchini squash, sesame seeds, and crushed red pepper flakes. Cover and cook for 4 minutes, uncovering to stir several times.

3. Add vegetable broth, crabmeat, and lemongrass (if using), and heat for 4 more minutes or until just beginning to bubble. Stir in watercress, and serve, seasoning with salt if necessary (there's salt in vegetable broth) and pepper.

MINUTE MORSEL

As these recipes show, seasonings bring with them a wealth of cultural context. Sesame oil, sesame seeds, and lemongrass are all traditional ingredients in Asian dishes. Cinnamon, cloves, and saffron evoke an entirely different image. Basil, oregano, rosemary, and other herbs found in Italian seasoning, although nominally Italian, are common to many Mediterranean cuisines.

Mushroom Mélange Soup

 20

Serves:
4

4 strips bacon

1 medium onion, chopped into ¹⁄₂-in. pieces

1 (8-oz.) pkg. sliced portobello mushrooms

1 TB. chopped garlic

2 TB. whole-wheat flour

3 (15-oz.) cans chicken broth

¹⁄₂ cup white wine

1 (4-oz.) pkg. shiitake mushrooms, stemmed, wiped with a damp paper towel, and sliced

1 (8-oz.) pkg. sliced white mushrooms

2 tsp. fresh thyme

¹⁄₂ tsp. black pepper

¹⁄₂ cup heavy cream

Salt

1. In a large skillet over medium heat, cook bacon for 2 minutes per side or until crisp. Remove bacon to a paper towel–lined plate to drain.

2. Drain off most fat from the skillet, leaving just enough to coat the bottom of the pan. Add onion, and cook, stirring, for 5 minutes.

3. Add portobello mushrooms and garlic, sprinkle mushrooms with whole-wheat flour, and cook, stirring, for 4 minutes.

4. While bacon is cooking, in a large stockpot over medium heat, add chicken broth, white wine, shiitake mushrooms, white mushrooms, thyme, and pepper. Cook for 5 minutes, stirring. Add portobello mushrooms from the skillet, and cook, stirring, for 5 more minutes.

5. Stir in heavy cream, and serve in bowls, garnishing with crumbled bacon and seasoning with salt.

Variation: For a delicious cream soup, process half of the soup in a blender or food processor to a creamy consistency and return it to the pot with the rest of the soup. To save on cleaning, cook bacon in the same pot before the soup. This will add to the total time of preparation.

 DEFINITION

Mélange is French for a mixture or blend—in this case, of mushrooms. Next time you make dinner with leftovers, don't call it *leftovers,* call it a *mélange.* There, doesn't that taste better?

Hearty Chili

20	**Serves:** 6

2 TB. olive or canola oil

1 medium onion, chopped into ½-in. pieces

1 lb. ground beef

1 (15.5-oz.) can red kidney beans, drained and rinsed

2 (14.5-oz.) cans diced tomatoes with juice

1 (4.5-oz.) can chopped green chiles

1 (4.25-oz.) can chopped ripe olives, drained

2 TB. chili powder

2 TB. unsweetened baking chocolate, chopped, or chocolate chips

2 TB. Worcestershire sauce

1 TB. ground cumin

1. In a large skillet over medium heat, heat olive oil. Add onion and ground beef, and cook, stirring, for 5 minutes or until meat is browned.

2. Add kidney beans, tomatoes, green chiles, olives, chili powder, chocolate, Worcestershire sauce, and cumin, and cook, stirring, for 10 minutes. Serve in big bowls.

Variation: Substitute bittersweet chips for unsweetened chocolate.

 MINUTE MORSEL

Chocolate doesn't always have to be associated with sweet flavors or dessert. In other parts of the world, chocolate is used in all kinds of sweet and savory dishes. The use of chocolate here adds authentic richness and depth.

Vegetarian Chili

20	**Serves:** 8

3 TB. olive oil

1 large onion, coarsely chopped

1 (28-oz.) can plum tomatoes, with juice, roughly chopped

1 (15-oz.) can black beans, drained and rinsed

1 (15-oz.) can fat-free refried beans

1 (8-oz.) pkg. sliced white mushrooms

2 TB. chili powder

1 TB. ground cumin

1 TB. chopped fresh cilantro (optional)

1 tsp. salt

$\frac{1}{2}$ tsp. black pepper

Sour cream (optional)

1. In a large skillet over medium heat, heat olive oil. Add onion, and cook, stirring, for 5 minutes.

2. Add tomatoes, black beans, refried beans, mushrooms, chili powder, cumin, cilantro (if using), salt, and pepper, and stir to mix. If chili is too thick, add a little water. Cook, stirring, for 10 minutes.

3. Serve in bowls, topping with a dollop of sour cream (if using).

ON THE CLOCK

A dose of Beano in bean-intensive dishes such as chili helps prevent a gas crisis.

Lightning Chicken Stew

20 **Serves:**
4

1 (10-oz.) can chunk white chicken meat, drained

1 (10.75-oz.) can "healthy" condensed cream of mushroom soup (don't add extra water)

1 (14.5-oz.) can cut green beans, drained

1 (6-oz.) can sliced mushrooms, drained

1 cup milk

½ tsp. black pepper

Dash hot pepper sauce

1. In a large microwave-safe dish with a lid, combine chicken, cream of mushroom soup, green beans, mushrooms, milk, pepper, and hot pepper sauce. Put on the lid (leaving it loose to allow steam to escape), and microwave for 4 minutes or until stew is hot, stirring once or twice. (If your microwave does not have a turntable, stir a couple times to ensure even cooking.)

2. Ladle stew into bowls, and serve.

DEFINITION

A **dash** refers to a few drops, the amount (usually of a liquid) released by a quick shake of, for example, a bottle of hot sauce.

Chicken, White Bean, and Vegetable Stew

This stew is reminiscent of Italian farmhouse dishes, rich with vegetables, herbs, and nutrition. Leftovers will taste even better the next night.

30

Serves:
4 to 6

4 TB. olive oil

1½ lb. boneless, skinless chicken breasts, chopped into ½-in. cubes

¾ tsp. salt, plus more as needed

Pinch black pepper, plus more as needed

1 onion, chopped

1 TB. chopped garlic

2 large carrots, scraped and cut into ¼-in. rounds

4 large celery sticks, cut into ¼-in. slices

½ tsp. dried basil

½ tsp. dried oregano

4 cups fat-free chicken broth

1 (16-oz.) can cannellini beans, drained

1 cup 20-Minute Tomato Sauce (recipe in Chapter 24), or 1 cup crushed tomatoes

Parmesan cheese

1. In a large skillet over medium-high heat, heat 2 tablespoons olive oil. Sprinkle chicken pieces with ¼ teaspoon salt and pepper, and cook for 6 minutes or until done, turning once. Remove chicken from the skillet, place on a plate, and cover with foil to keep warm.

2. Add remaining 2 tablespoons olive oil to the skillet, add onion, and cook for 2 minutes. Add garlic, carrots, and celery, and cook for 2 more minutes.

3. Add basil, oregano, chicken broth, cannellini beans, remaining ½ teaspoon salt, 20-Minute Tomato Sauce, and cooked chicken. Cook, stirring, for 14 minutes. Serve in large bowls topped with Parmesan cheese, and season with salt and pepper.

Quick Vegetable-Beef Stew

20

Serves:
6

3 TB. olive or canola oil

1 medium onion, chopped into
   ½-in. pieces

1½ lb. steak tips, cut into ½-in.
   pieces

Pinch salt

½ tsp. black pepper

1 (16-oz.) pkg. frozen green beans
   and pearl onions mixture

2 TB. tomato paste

1 (14.5-oz.) can beef broth

1 (14.5-oz.) can diced tomatoes
   with juice

2 TB. Worcestershire sauce

1. In a large skillet over medium heat, heat olive oil. Add onion and steak tips, and cook, stirring, for 5 minutes or until done. Season steak tips with salt and pepper as it cooks.

2. Meanwhile, in a microwave-safe bowl, thaw frozen green beans and pearl onions in the microwave.

3. In a small bowl, whisk tomato paste into 1 cup beef broth. Add tomatoes to the skillet along with broth and tomato paste mixture, thawed green beans and pearl onions, and Worcestershire sauce. Mix thoroughly, and cook, stirring, for 10 minutes.

ON THE CLOCK

For the vegetable enthusiast, substitute fresh vegetables or other interesting mixes from the freezer section such as broccoli, cauliflower, carrots, and bell peppers, or cauliflower, carrots, and peapods.

Quick Seafood Vegetable Stew

 20

Serves:
8

5 TB. olive oil

1 medium onion, chopped into ½-in. pieces

2 large carrots, peeled and cut into ¼-in. pieces

2 TB. chopped garlic

2 tsp. *Italian seasoning*

½ tsp. crushed red pepper flakes

1 cup arugula, rinsed, stemmed, and coarsely chopped

1 (15-oz.) can white beans, drained and rinsed

1 (14.5-oz.) can vegetable broth

1 cup water

1 cup dry white wine

1 lb. cod, haddock, or other whitefish, rinsed in cold water, patted dry with paper towels, and cut into 1-in. chunks

½ lb. bay scallops or quartered sea scallops, rinsed

Salt

Black pepper

1. In a large skillet or stockpot over medium heat, heat olive oil. Add onion and carrots, and cook, stirring, for 5 minutes.

2. Add garlic, Italian seasoning, and crushed red pepper flakes, and cook for 1 more minute. Add arugula, white beans, vegetable broth, water, and white wine, and bring to a low boil.

3. Add fish, and cook for 2 minutes. Add scallops, and cook for 4 more minutes or until fish and scallops are just done. Serve in big bowls, seasoning with salt and pepper.

 DEFINITION

Italian seasoning, the ubiquitous grocery store blend including oregano and thyme, is a useful seasoning for quick flavor that evokes the "Old Country."

Spicy Shrimp Stew

20   **Serves:**
6

4 strips bacon

1 large onion, chopped into ½-in. pieces

1 tsp. garlic

½ tsp. crushed red pepper flakes

½ tsp. ground cumin

½ tsp. ground thyme

2 (15-oz.) cans chicken broth

¼ tsp. black pepper, plus more as needed

Dash hot pepper sauce

1 bunch (about 1 lb.) asparagus, chopped into 1-in. segments, bottom 2 in. discarded

1 lb. (31 to 40 count) medium cooked shrimp, tail off

¼ cup Madeira or sherry

Shredded Parmesan cheese

Salt

1. In a large skillet over medium heat, cook bacon for 4 minutes or until crisp. Remove bacon to a paper towel–lined plate.

2. Drain most of fat from skillet, leaving enough to coat the bottom. Add onion, garlic, crushed red pepper flakes, cumin, and thyme, and cook, stirring, for 4 minutes.

3. Meanwhile, in a large saucepan or stockpot over medium heat, heat chicken broth, ¼ teaspoon pepper, and hot pepper sauce. Add asparagus, and cook for 8 minutes or until asparagus is crisp-tender.

4. Stir in cooked onion and garlic from the skillet, add shrimp and Madeira, and cook for 3 minutes. Serve topped with crumbled bacon, Parmesan cheese, salt, and more pepper.

TIME WASTER

Many of these recipes use canned chicken or vegetable broth for a base. You have some choices here, particularly between low-sodium and regular broth. If you use the regular, higher-salt version, taste the result before adding any additional salt. You might not need it.

Middle Eastern Vegetable Stew

 20

Serves:
4

3 TB. olive oil

1 medium onion, chopped into ½-in. pieces

2 celery stalks, chopped into ½-in. pieces

2 TB. chopped garlic

3 (15-oz.) cans chicken broth

1 (10-in.) zucchini squash, ends trimmed, halved lengthwise, and chopped into ½-in. pieces

1 (15-oz.) can chickpeas, drained and rinsed

1 (14-oz.) can plum tomatoes with juice, coarsely chopped

2 tsp. ground cinnamon

2 tsp. sweet paprika

1 tsp. fennel seed

1 tsp. ground cumin

1 tsp. salt

½ tsp. black pepper

½ tsp. turmeric

¼ tsp. ground cloves

Pinch saffron

½ cup plain yogurt

1. In a large stockpot over medium heat, heat olive oil. Add onion, and cook, stirring, for 4 minutes.

2. Add celery and garlic, and cook for 1 more minute. Add chicken broth, zucchini squash, chickpeas, tomatoes with juice, cinnamon, sweet paprika, fennel seed, cumin, salt, pepper, turmeric, cloves, and saffron, and cook, stirring, for 10 minutes.

3. Serve in big bowls with a dollop of yogurt, and watch the sun set over the Sahara.

Quick Fish Chowder

20	**Serves:** 6

1½ lb. flounder, cod, haddock, sole, tilapia, or other whitefish

3 slices bacon

1 medium onion, chopped into ½-in. chunks

2 cups milk

½ cup light cream

½ cup fresh parsley, finely chopped (optional)

Salt

Black pepper

1. Thoroughly rinse fish in cold water, and pat dry with paper towels. Set aside.

2. In a large saucepan or skillet over medium heat, cook bacon until crispy and fat is rendered. Remove bacon and save it on a paper towel–lined plate.

3. Drain most of fat from the skillet, leaving just enough to coat the bottom. Add onion, and, stirring, cook for 5 minutes.

4. Add milk, and heat until barely beginning to boil. Add fish, and cook, stirring occasionally, for 3 or 4 minutes until fish is opaque and flakes easily. Add light cream and parsley (if using), and heat for 1 minute, stirring.

5. Ladle into serving bowls, crumble bacon over each bowl, and serve, salting to taste and seasoning generously with pepper.

Variation: Without parsley, this chunky chowder is white and creamy. Parsley adds texture, color, and flavor.

TIME WASTER

Whenever the words *milk* and *boil* appear in the same sentence, that's an alert to watch closely! Milk boils over easily, creating a big, hard-to-clean mess.

Country Potato Chowder

 20

Serves:
4 to 6

1½ lb. baking potatoes, peeled and cut into 1-in. cubes, or new potatoes, skin on, scrubbed, and cut into 1-in. chunks

3 TB. olive oil

1 large onion, sliced thin

1 cup skim milk

1½ cups fat-free chicken broth

¼ cup sherry or cooking wine

2 tsp. salt

Salt

Black pepper

½ cup fat-free or low-fat sour cream

1. Arrange potatoes in a microwave-safe baking dish, and microwave on high for 10 minutes or until soft.

2. Meanwhile, in a large skillet over medium-low heat, heat olive oil. Add onion, and cook until potatoes are finished cooking.

3. Working in batches, add cooked potatoes, cooked onion, a little skim milk, and a little chicken broth to a food processor. Purée until smooth and creamy. If chowder is too thick, add a little more milk and broth.

4. Return chowder to the skillet, add sherry and salt and any remaining skim milk and chicken broth, and cook for 5 minutes. Serve with salt, pepper, and a spoonful of sour cream.

 ON THE CLOCK

For a flavor and visual variation to this chowder, I like to stir in a handful of fresh arugula or spinach, washed and chopped, stems removed, a minute before cooking is finished. This addition makes a big change to the texture of the chowder, however, which is not to everyone's taste!

Lunchbox-Worthy Sandwiches and Wraps

In This Chapter

- Sensational sandwiches
- Making good use of your neighborhood deli
- Maximizing flavor with fresh vegetables
- Wrapping and rolling your way to a delicious lunch

A sandwich is so much more than PB&J. And just because sandwiches and wraps are portable doesn't mean you have to resort to fast-food ingredients. To prove this point, in this chapter we look at sandwiches, wraps, and roll-ups filled with delicious—sometimes unexpected—ingredients. Some may be old friends, and others might just be new to you. Also, pick healthy, tasty fresh bread to give yourself a head start. I often choose 100 percent whole wheat for the rich, nutty taste and high nutrition.

Cucumber and Tomato Cream Cheese Sandwiches

This tasty combination is especially quick because it requires no heating or mixing. Just slice the ingredients, and assemble.

 Serves:
6 to 8

1 cup cream cheese or light cream cheese, softened

8 slices white or whole-wheat bread, crusts removed, and each cut into 4 triangles

1 English-style cucumber, ends removed, *striped,* and sliced into $\frac{1}{8}$-in. rounds

8 grape tomatoes, sliced into $\frac{1}{4}$-in. rounds

2 TB. finely chopped fresh dill

2 TB. finely chopped fresh chives

Kosher salt

1. Spread about 2 teaspoons cream cheese on each slice of bread, and top each with slices of cucumber and tomato. Arrange on a serving tray.

2. Sprinkle a pinch of dill, a pinch of chives, and a few grains of kosher salt on each, and serve.

 DEFINITION

Striped refers to using a vegetable peeler to peel the skin in lengthwise strokes along the cucumber, leaving "stripes" of skin between the peeled sections.

Mom's Open-Faced Bacon and Tomato Sandwiches

Bacon and tomato, a heavenly combination to begin with, is perhaps made just a bit better when added to melted cheese. To reduce the fat, I cook the bacon before adding it to the sandwich.

 20   **Serves:**
4

4 slices thick bacon

4 slices whole-wheat bread

4 slices cheddar cheese (or your favorite)

4 $\frac{1}{2}$-in. fresh tomato slices

1. Preheat the broiler.

2. In a large skillet over medium heat, cook bacon for 6 minutes or until crisp. Remove bacon to a paper towel–lined plate.

3. Meanwhile, arrange bread on a baking sheet. Broil for 2 minutes, flip over pieces, and broil other side for 2 more minutes or until bread begins to brown.

4. Top each piece of bread with 1 slice cheddar cheese, and broil for 2 minutes until cheese begins to melt.

5. Top each piece of bread with 1 slice tomato and 1 piece bacon, folded in a V shape. Broil for 4 minutes or until cheese around edge of tomato begins to bubble.

 ON THE CLOCK

With open-faced sandwiches, the challenge is to reach that balance between crispness and moisture, which is why these recipes call for toasting each side of a piece of bread before adding the feature ingredients.

Tomato and Fresh Mozzarella Sandwiches

This sandwich is simple, juicy, and flavorful and sings a summer song.

 Serves:
4

8 slices fresh whole-wheat bread	½ lb. fresh mozzarella cheese, thinly (¼ in.) sliced
¼ cup shredded or grated Parmesan cheese	Salt
4 large tomato slices, ¼ in. thick	Black pepper

1. Assemble each sandwich as follows: 1 slice bread, 1 tablespoon Parmesan cheese spread evenly across bread, 1 slice tomato, 1 slice mozzarella cheese, and a sprinkling of salt and pepper.

2. Cover with 1 slice of bread, and serve with a glass of white wine on your vine-covered terrace.

Mini Tomato and Toast Sandwiches

If the season is right, these little delights are the ultimate treatment for ripe, juicy tomatoes.

 Serves:
4 to 6

6 slices white or whole-wheat sandwich bread, crusts removed	1 large ripe tomato, cut into ¼-in. slices
3 TB. mayonnaise	12 small (1-in.) fresh basil leaves

1. Preheat the broiler.

2. Arrange bread on a baking sheet, and broil for about 1 minute per side or until lightly browned.

3. Spread 1 tablespoon mayonnaise on 3 slices, top each with 1 slice tomato and 4 basil leaves, and cover with another piece of toast.

4. Cut each sandwich on the diagonal to form 4 small triangular sandwiches. Place 2 or 3 small sandwiches on each small plate, and serve.

Grilled Chicken and Sweet Onion Sandwiches

This sandwich is a compelling reason to make extras when grilling. This next-day dish is practically instant ... and also disappears practically instantly.

 Serves:
4

4 TB. mayonnaise	Black pepper
8 slices fresh whole-wheat bread	4 very thin slices ($\frac{1}{8}$ in.) sweet onion, such as Vidalia
$1\frac{1}{2}$ cups thinly ($\frac{1}{4}$ in.) sliced cooked chicken	4 pieces crisp lettuce
Salt	

1. Spread 1 tablespoon mayonnaise on 4 pieces of bread.

2. Distribute chicken among bread, and sprinkle with salt and pepper.

3. Add 1 slice sweet onion and 1 piece lettuce, top with 1 slice bread, and devour.

Italian Turkey and Sprout Sandwiches

 Serves:
4

4 slices whole-wheat bread

4 slices deli turkey

1½ cups alfalfa sprouts

4 slices cheddar cheese (or your favorite)

1. Arrange bread on a baking sheet, and broil for 2 minutes. Flip over bread, and broil other side for 2 minutes or until bread begins to turn a light brown.

2. Top each piece of toasted bread with 1 slice turkey, ¼ of alfalfa sprouts, and 1 slice cheddar cheese.

3. Broil for 4 minutes or until cheese melts and begins to bubble.

Variation: For **Smoked Ham and Sprout Sandwiches,** replace the turkey with slices of smoked deli ham, add your choice of mustard, and omit the cheese.

 TIME WASTER

Eat sandwiches with moist ingredients immediately so, for example, water from a juicy tomato slice doesn't soak the bread.

Tuna Melts

 Serves:
4

4 slices low-carb bread

1 (6-oz.) can chunk white tuna in water, drained

3 TB. mayonnaise

½ cup finely chopped celery

½ tsp. dried dill

4 slices cheddar cheese

1. Preheat the broiler.

2. Lay bread in a single layer on a baking tray and broil for 1 minute or until just beginning to crisp.

3. In a medium bowl, combine tuna, mayonnaise, celery, and dill. Spread an equal amount of tuna mixture on each slice of toasted bread.

4. Top each with 1 slice cheddar cheese, and broil for 3 minutes or until cheese is melted. Distribute to plates, and serve.

Variation: For **Pesto Tuna Melts,** reduce the mayonnaise to 2 tablespoons and replace the celery, dill, and cheddar cheese with 3 tablespoons prepared pesto sauce, 2 tablespoons toasted *pine nuts,* and 4 slices sharp provolone or regular provolone cheese.

DEFINITION

Pine nuts are edible nuts grown on pine trees. They're rich, flavorful, and a bit pine-y. Pine nuts are a traditional component of pesto and are one of those irresistible flavor boosters that add interest to a dish. A bag of pine nuts in your pantry (or in your freezer, if you tend to use them slowly) will come in handy for many recipes in this book.

Turkey, Arugula, and Almond Roll-Ups

 Serves:
2

½ lb. thickly sliced deli turkey (6 to 8 slices)

3 TB. mayonnaise

¼ cup sliced almonds

1 cup fresh arugula leaves, stems removed, washed, and dried (about 12 big leaves)

Salt

Black pepper

1. Spread each turkey slice with mayonnaise, and sprinkle with sliced almonds. Lay several arugula leaves over turkey, season with salt and pepper, and roll turkey over filling to form a bulky cylinder.

2. Set rolls on a serving plate if you're serving right away. To take them with you, pack rolls in a sandwich bag or a small rectangular plastic container with a lid.

Variation: Toasted almonds add delicious flavor. Other fresh savory greens, such as watercress, can be used in place of the arugula.

 ON THE CLOCK

When you're looking for convenient cuisine, take advantage of the deli. Turkey, chicken, and roast beef are all good candidates. Sliced ham and meat salads can also be terrific.

Roast Beef and Watercress Roll-Ups

10	**Serves:** 2

½ lb. lean thickly sliced roast beef (about 6 to 8 slices)

2 TB. prepared horseradish

2 cups watercress leaves, stemmed, washed, and dried, about 8 sprigs

Salt

Black pepper

1. Spread each roast beef slice with horseradish, and arrange several watercress leaves so they'll be rolled lengthwise. Season with salt and pepper.

2. Roll roast beef over watercress to form a cylinder, and bind with toothpicks if necessary.

3. Serve immediately, or store in a rectangular plastic container with a lid for a portable lunch.

 ON THE CLOCK

Some wraps and roll-ups, such as those made with deli meats, don't need much help to hold together. Others, such as those where lettuce is the wrap, are best held together with a couple toothpicks and carried in a plastic container with a lid. If I have them in the fridge, I use a couple extra-long scallion leaves as a wrapper. Another option (sort of the "maximum-hold styling gel" for your lunch) is to bind them in squares of aluminum foil.

Cheddar Chicken Wrap

 10   **Serves:**
1

1 large low-carb soft tortilla

¼ lb. sliced deli chicken or 1 cup thinly sliced cooked leftover chicken

2 TB. mayonnaise

¼ cup shredded cheddar cheese

Salt

Black pepper

2 large romaine or iceberg lettuce leaves, crushed flat to facilitate rolling

1. Top tortilla with chicken, mayonnaise, and cheddar cheese, and season with salt and pepper. Arrange romaine leaves on top.

2. Tuck in sides of tortilla to enclose filling, and roll firmly but gently from one side. Cut in half on the diagonal. Store in a plastic container with a lid or a large plastic food storage bag.

 ON THE CLOCK

Crunchy lettuce leaves tend to break upon rolling. To solve this, lay them on a flat surface and crush them with the heel of your hand. Then they should roll (lengthwise) just fine.

Tuna Salad Wraps

10   **Serves:**
2

1 (6-oz.) can chunk white tuna in water, drained

1 celery stalk, chopped into ¼-in. pieces

2 TB. mayonnaise

1 TB. Dijon-style mustard

¼ tsp. dried dill

Salt

Black pepper

6 large romaine or iceberg lettuce leaves, washed and dried

1. Scoop tuna into a medium bowl, and break up any large chunks. Mix in celery, mayonnaise, Dijon-style mustard, dill, salt, and pepper.

2. Distribute tuna salad among romaine leaves, roll leaves lengthwise to form long cylinders, and pin with 2 or 3 toothpicks.

 ON THE CLOCK

Tuna is a top choice when it comes to light lunches: great flavor, lots of protein, a good source of healthy fat, and affordable, too. That's not bad for a brown-bag lunch!

Smoked Salmon Asparagus Wraps

10 **Serves:**
4

1 (4-oz.) pkg. thinly sliced smoked salmon, cut into 2×3-in. pieces

$\frac{1}{2}$ lb. thin (about $\frac{1}{3}$ in. across) asparagus spears, bottom half removed, top 3 inches *blanched* for 1 minute

2 TB. freshly squeezed lemon juice

Salt (optional)

$1\frac{1}{2}$ tsp. fresh dill or $\frac{1}{2}$ tsp. dried

Lemon twists

1. Wrap 1 strip smoked salmon around 1 asparagus spear, and secure with a toothpick.

2. Arrange spears on a serving plate, drizzle with lemon juice, and sprinkle with salt (if using) and dill. Garnish with lemon twists, and serve.

 DEFINITION

To **blanch** something is to quickly submerge it in boiling water and then just as quickly submerge it in cool water. Blanching many vegetables enhances color and flavor.

Vegetarian Wrap

10   **Serves:**
1

¼ cup fresh *chevre,* softened

1 large low-carb soft tortilla

¼ cup sliced almonds

1½ cups mixed-greens salad mix, chopped into ¼-in. pieces

Salt

Black pepper

2 TB. Italian or vinaigrette dressing

1. Spread softened chevre on tortilla, top with almonds and salad mix, and sprinkle with salt and pepper.

2. Tuck in sides of tortilla to enclose filling, and roll tortilla, firmly but gently, from one side. Cut in half on the diagonal.

3. Store in a plastic container with a lid or a large plastic food storage bag. Pour Italian dressing into a small plastic container alongside and dress just before eating.

Variation: For more flavor, toast the almonds in a 350°F oven for 5 minutes before adding to the wrap.

DEFINITION

Fresh **chevre,** or goat's milk cheese, is a creamy-salty soft cheese that looks like cream cheese but has a richer, slightly tangy flavor. Chevres vary in style from mild and creamy to aged, firm, and flavorful. Artisanal chevres are usually more expensive and sold in smaller quantities; these are often delicious by themselves. Other chevres produced in quantity are less expensive and often more appropriate for combining with fruit or herbs.

Satisfying Snacks and Appetizers

Part 4

Snacks and appetizers tantalize the taste buds—one reason why these small bites often carry such big flavor. Whether we're talking about starting a party, a meal, or a social gathering, appetizers are the multitaskers of the kitchen. They help satisfy those urgent before-meal hunger pangs. Served at a party or social gathering, they set the tone for whatever is to come. You can even make a whole meal out of several appetizers.

The recipes in Part 4 fill so many needs. From quick "popper" bites, to dips and spreads, to fruity finds, the following chapters offer a buffet of snacks and appetizers you and your guests won't be able to resist!

And if you're looking for quick and healthy snacks, I've included a chapter just for you.

Quick Bites

In This Chapter

- Quick, surefire snacks
- Creative pairings and creative presentation
- Familiar friends and new faces
- Simple, savory bites

Of all the snacks out there, among the simplest and neatest are those self-contained flavor explosions all wrapped up and ready to eat with no additional seasoning, dipping, or heating. These morsels bites are, as a rule, easy to carry. They're perfect for any occasion, from bringing to someone else's party to unveiling at your own soirée.

Is it any wonder these bites are the topic of their own chapter?

Avocado Swiss Bites

Avocado lovers, this is for you.

---

(10)   **Serves:**
4

---

1 ripe avocado $\frac{1}{2}$ lb. Swiss cheese, cut into $\frac{1}{2}$-in.
2 TB. fresh lemon juice   chunks

                                        Salt

1. Cut avocado in half, and remove pit by embedding the blade (not the tip) of a sharp knife into it. Turn the knife slowly to release pit.

2. Cut avocado flesh into $\frac{1}{2}$-inch squares, drop in a bowl, and drizzle with lemon juice to delay browning.

3. On a toothpick, spear 1 piece Swiss cheese and 1 piece avocado. Repeat with remaining cheese and avocado. Arrange on a platter and serve, inviting guests to sprinkle each piece with salt if they desire.

Stuffed Dates

These rich, sweet morsels are a traditional snack at winter holiday gatherings.

---

(10)   **Serves:**
4

---

1 (10-oz.) pkg. pitted dates $\frac{1}{2}$ cup whole almonds
$\frac{1}{4}$ cup sugar

1. With a sharp knife, slit each date lengthwise to form small pockets.

2. Pour sugar into a shallow bowl.

3. Insert 1 almond into each date, roll date in sugar to coat, and arrange dates on a serving plate.

Variation: Instead of almonds, stuff dates with cream cheese. You'll need about $\frac{1}{2}$ cup for a 10-ounce package of dates. These are also delicious without sugar.

Asiago-Chicken Bites

 Serves:
6

½ lb. sliced deli chicken breast, cut
   into 1×2-in. pieces

4 oz. Asiago cheese, cut into
   ¼×¼×1-in. pieces

Black pepper

1. Arrange chicken pieces on a work surface in a single layer, and place 1 piece Asiago cheese in center of each.

2. Wrap ends of each chicken piece inward over cheese, and fasten with toothpicks.

3. Arrange on a platter, sprinkle with pepper, and serve.

Chicken, Mozzarella, and Roasted Pepper Bites

These are sort of like a gourmet deli sandwich, rolled up and bite-size.

 Serves:
6

1 lb. thin slices deli roast chicken
   (or turkey), cut in half

1 (8-oz.) pkg. fresh mozzarella balls,
   cut into ¼-in.-thick pieces

½ cup roasted red peppers, sliced
   into ½-in.-wide pieces

Salt

Black pepper

1. Place 1 slice chicken on a work surface. Arrange mozzarella pieces on it in a line about 1 inch in from the longest edge of chicken slice. Top mozzarella with roasted red pepper slices.

2. Working from the longest edge, roll chicken over mozzarella and peppers to form a cylinder. Insert toothpicks at ½-inch intervals along length of roll.

3. Using a sharp knife, cut through the roll at the midpoint between each toothpick. Repeat with remaining chicken, mozzarella, and peppers. Arrange on a serving plate, season with salt and pepper, and serve.

Variation: Sun-dried tomatoes are also delicious instead of the roasted red peppers.

Turkey with Apricot and Walnuts

10 **Serves:**
6 to 8

¼ cup chopped walnuts

1 cup cream cheese or light cream cheese, softened

½ cup apricot preserves

1 lb. thin slices deli turkey breast, cut in half

1. Preheat the broiler.

2. Spread walnuts in a single layer on a baking sheet, and broil on the high rack for 2 minutes, watching closely to prevent any blackening. Stir and broil for 1 more minute.

3. In a medium bowl, combine cream cheese, apricot preserves, and walnuts.

4. Place 1 piece turkey on a work surface. Spread about 1 tablespoon cream cheese mixture to form a line along one side of slice about 1 inch in from side closest to you. Working from this side, roll turkey over cheese to form a cylinder. Insert toothpicks at ½-inch intervals.

5. Using a sharp knife, cut at the midpoint between each toothpick. Repeat with remaining turkey and cream cheese mixture. Arrange bites on a plate, and serve.

Roast Beef and Endive Bites

Adapted from notable cook Anne-Marie Kott, this recipe brings a welcome heartiness to the starter lineup.

🕙 **10**	**Serves:** 4 to 6

2 heads Belgian endive	3 sprigs chopped fresh dill (about 2 TB.)
½ lb. thin slices rare roast beef, cut into 1×2-in. pieces	¼ cup prepared horseradish
2 TB. capers, drained	¼ cup Russian dressing

1. Arrange Belgian endive leaves on a serving platter. Top each with 1 piece roast beef, and sprinkle with capers and dill.

2. Serve with small bowls of horseradish and Russian dressing.

Corned Beef Cornucopias

I like to use packaged corned beef for this, rather than having the deli staff slice it for me, because the packaged corned beef is squared off and can be cut to form triangles. Thanks to Nancy Woods for this elegant version of a snack classic.

🕙 **10**	**Serves:** 10

3 cups cream cheese or light cream cheese, softened	1 (2.5-oz.) pkg. corned beef slices, cut in half diagonally to form triangles
5 heaping TB. prepared horseradish	1 tsp. dried dill

1. In a small bowl, combine cream cheese and horseradish.

2. Place 1 corned beef triangle on a work surface so the corner that forms a 90-degree angle (the larger one of the three) faces you. Spoon 1 teaspoon cream cheese mixture on this corner, and fold other corners inward over cheese to form a cone.

3. Arrange on a platter, sprinkle with dill, and serve.

Prosciutto-Wrapped Asparagus

 Serves:
8 to 12

1 (15-oz.) can asparagus spears,
drained

8 oz. thin slices prosciutto, cut into
3×3-in. squares

1. Wrap each asparagus spear in a prosciutto square.

2. Arrange wrapped spears on a serving plate, tips pointing out like sunrays, and
serve.

Variation: Sliced ham works well in place of prosciutto in this recipe.

Pepperoni-Spinach Rolls

 Serves:
4 to 6

½ lb. pepperoni slices

24 to 30 baby spinach leaves, each
about 1×2 in.

1. Place 1 pepperoni slice on each spinach leaf, roll to form a cylinder, and fasten
with a toothpick.

2. Arrange on a platter, and serve.

Variation: Serve surrounding a small bowl of mustard dip or softened cream cheese.

 ON THE CLOCK

Where a recipe calls for a certain number of, for example, spinach leaves, obviously you're not going to go to the grocery store and buy that number. ("Excuse me, could I buy 24 spinach leaves please?") Buy a package of baby spinach, and count out how many you need, picking out the prettiest leaves of the right size and shape. Use the rest for a salad or another snack.

Salami, Watercress, and Cream Cheese Bites

The cool crispness of the *watercress* is a great counterpoint to spicy salami.

 Serves:
4 to 6

½ lb. thin slices salami, cut in half

½ cup cream cheese or light cream cheese, softened

1 cup watercress sprigs

1. Place 1 piece salami on a work surface. Spread cream cheese along one side of salami, place 1 sprig watercress in center, and roll loosely to form a cone, with watercress sticking out the top like a feather in a pointed hat. If necessary, fasten with a toothpick.

2. Repeat with remaining salami, cream cheese, and watercress. Arrange standing in a circle on a platter, and serve.

Variation: Use other crisp greens, such as spinach or even *arugula*, in place of the watercress.

 DEFINITION

Watercress is a crunchy, peppery-tasting plant popular in salads and sandwiches and as a garnish. **Arugula** is a spicy-peppery garden plant with leaves that resemble a dandelion. Its distinctive and very sharp flavor is delicious to some people (I love it), but for others, it might take some getting used to. Don't mistake it for lettuce!

Spinach-Wrapped Bacon and Parmesan Bites

The fresh taste of baby spinach leaves lends a welcome freshness and springtime feel to this simple dish. Pick spinach leaves that are large enough to completely surround the filling to avoid spillage.

 Serves:
4

¾ cup (about 6 oz.) cream cheese or light cream cheese, softened	18 to 24 baby spinach leaves (use the larger ones)
⅓ cup shredded Parmesan cheese	1 TB. extra-virgin olive oil
3 TB. real bacon bits	Kosher salt

1. In a small bowl, combine cream cheese, Parmesan cheese, and bacon bits. Place about 2 teaspoons cheese mixture onto each spinach leaf, wrap leaf around cheese, and fasten with a toothpick.

2. Arrange on a serving plate, drizzle with extra-virgin olive oil, sprinkle with kosher salt, and serve.

Chevre, Toasted Pecans, and Ham

 Serves:
4

¼ cup chopped pecans	4 oz. fresh chevre (goat's milk cheese), softened
½ lb. thin slices smoked ham, cut in half	

1. Preheat the broiler.

2. Spread pecans in a single layer on a baking sheet, and broil on the high rack for 2 minutes, watching closely to prevent any blackening. Stir and broil for 1 more minute.

3. Meanwhile, place 1 slice ham on a work surface. Spread about 1 tablespoon chevre in a line along one side of slice, about 1 inch in from the side closest to you.

4. Spread about $\frac{1}{2}$ tablespoon toasted pecans over cheese. Starting from this side, roll ham over cheese and nuts to form a cylinder. Insert toothpicks at $\frac{1}{2}$-inch intervals.

5. Cut at the midpoint between each toothpick. Repeat with remaining ham, cheese, and nuts. Arrange bites on a plate, and serve.

Ham Salad Crostini

Serves:
6 to 8

4 pieces bread, crusts removed, each cut into 4 triangles

$\frac{1}{2}$ lb. deli ham salad

$\frac{1}{4}$ cup shredded Parmesan cheese

2 TB. finely chopped fresh parsley

1. Preheat the broiler.

2. Arrange bread on a baking sheet, and broil for about 1 minute on each side until lightly browned. Remove from the oven.

3. Spread about 1 tablespoon ham salad on each triangle, sprinkle with Parmesan cheese, and arrange on a serving tray.

4. Sprinkle a pinch of parsley on each, and serve.

Smoked Ham and Asparagus

 Serves:
4

¼ cup cream cheese or light cream cheese, softened

2 TB. Dijon-style mustard

½ lb. thin slices smoked ham, cut in half

1 (15-oz.) can whole asparagus spears, drained

1. In a small bowl, combine cream cheese and Dijon-style mustard.

2. Place 1 piece ham on a work surface. Place 1 piece asparagus on top, about 1 inch in from the longest edge. Spread asparagus with cream cheese mixture. Working from that edge, roll ham over asparagus to form a cylinder.

3. Repeat with remaining ham, asparagus, and cream cheese mixture. Arrange pieces on a serving plate, and serve.

Variation: Rare roast beef works well in place of the ham. If you've got the time, fresh asparagus, blanched for 1 minute in boiling water, is delicious instead of the canned version.

Ham Stuffed with Ricotta, Pine Nuts, and Garlic

 Serves:
4 to 6

½ lb. deli ham, thinly sliced

½ cup ricotta cheese

¼ cup pine nuts

½ tsp. garlic salt

1. Place 1 ham slice on a work surface. Spoon a line of ricotta cheese along one side of ham, about 1 inch in from the side closest to you. Sprinkle with pine nuts and a pinch of garlic salt. Starting from this side, roll ham over filling to form a cylinder. Insert toothpicks at ½-inch intervals.

2. Cut through roll at the midpoint between each toothpick. Repeat with remaining ham and filling. Arrange bites on a platter, and serve.

ON THE CLOCK

This snack is great as is but even better if the pine nuts are toasted. I think just about any recipe that calls for nuts could benefit from a toasting.

Endive with Herbed Sausage and Apricot Preserves

This hearty sweet and savory spread is unlike so many of the creamy spreads.

 Serves:
4

$\frac{1}{2}$ lb. cooked spicy sausage meat

1 cup apricot preserves

1 scallion, dark green leaves removed, cut into $\frac{1}{2}$-in. pieces

Belgian endive leaves

1. In a food processor fitted with a metal blade, process sausage, apricot preserves, and scallion pieces until spreadable but still chunky.

2. Scrape spread into a serving bowl, and place the bowl on a platter surrounded by Belgian endive leaves.

Sausage Rounds with Mustard Dip

 Serves:
4

½ cup whole-grain mustard

½ cup mayonnaise

½ lb. cooked sausage, such as knockwurst or herbed chicken sausage

1. In a small bowl, combine whole-grain mustard and mayonnaise, and place bowl in the center of a serving platter.

2. Slice sausage into ½-inch rounds, insert a toothpick into each, arrange on a platter surrounding mustard dip, and serve.

Variation: To serve the sausage warm, heat it in the microwave for 1 minute.

Miso Shrimp Bites

Sharp, savory miso adds an Asian element to this shrimp dish.

 Serves:
4 to 6

¼ cup miso

½ lb. (51 to 70 count, about 30) cooked shrimp, peeled, deveined, and tails removed

40 baby spinach leaves

1. Spread about ½ teaspoon miso on 1 shrimp, place shrimp in the center of 1 leaf spinach, roll leaf over filling, and fasten with a toothpick.

2. Repeat with remaining spinach, miso, and shrimp. Arrange shrimp bites on a platter, and serve.

Variation: Serve with a small bowl of soy sauce for dipping.

Swiss Shrimp Bites

Swiss cheese is good with ingredients from the orchard to the sea.

 Serves:
4

½ lb. Swiss cheese, cut into ½-in. cubes

½ lb. (31 to 40 count, about 18) cooked shrimp, peeled, deveined, and tail removed

4 lemon wedges

1. With a toothpick, pierce 1 chunk Swiss cheese and 1 shrimp. Repeat with remaining shrimp and cheese.

2. Arrange on a serving platter, garnish with lemon wedges, and invite guests to squeeze a few drops of lemon juice on each bite.

Shrimp with Lemon Cream Cheese

Light, tasty seafood and flavors of citrus and creamy cheese beg to be accompanied with a tasty Sauvignon Blanc.

 Serves:
4 to 6

Shaved ice

½ cup cream cheese, softened

1 TB. prepared horseradish

1 TB. fresh lemon juice

¼ cup minced sweet onion (about ½ medium)

½ lb. (31 to 40 count, about 18) cooked shrimp, peeled and deveined

Lemon wedges

1. Mound shaved ice in a large (12-inch) bowl so ice comes up almost to the top.

2. In a small (4-inch) bowl, combine cream cheese, horseradish, lemon juice, and sweet onion. Nestle this bowl in the center of ice.

3. Arrange shrimp on top of shaved ice around the bowl, garnish with lemon wedges, and serve with a knife for guests to spread a dab of cream cheese on shrimp.

Quick Crab Balls

Crab cakes are delicious, and these tiny, quick versions preserve that rich flavor.

10	**Serves:** 6

¼ cup canola oil	½ tsp. celery seed
¼ cup breadcrumbs	Dash hot pepper sauce
1 egg	Pinch salt
1 TB. mayonnaise	1 (6-oz.) can crabmeat
1 tsp. Worcestershire sauce	Lemon wedges

1. In a 12-inch skillet over medium heat, heat canola oil.

2. In a medium bowl, combine breadcrumbs, egg, mayonnaise, Worcestershire sauce, celery seed, hot pepper sauce, and salt. Mix in crabmeat, and, using your hands, form into balls about 1 inch across. As you make the balls, carefully place them into the skillet.

3. Cook crab balls for about 2 minutes per side or until browned and cooked through the center. Remove crab balls to a serving platter, garnish with lemon wedges, and serve with toothpicks.

Healthful Snacks

In This Chapter

- Good-for-you snacks
- Versatile vegetable snacks
- Flavorful hummus and spreads
- Delicious dips

Some people feel bad about their desire to snack, but that desire is a natural one. Our distant ancestors likely survived by foraging for little bits of food at a time. Of course, today, eating every bit of food we come across (sort of "foraging in the kitchen") can get us into trouble. Those distant relatives didn't also have three full meals a day.

Although snacking is okay, the challenge is to avoid the unhealthy snacks that surround us. It helps to control portion size. If I have a pound of almonds with me, guess how much I'll end up eating. Instead, pack a reasonable snack in a container or zipper bag. Portion sizes vary according to the food. Nuts are a very concentrated source of both calories and nutrition—a little goes a long way. Vegetables, on the other hand, are largely water, so you can eat a lot more of them to get to a similar nutritional place. Fresh vegetables have great texture and flavor and require minimum preparation to make a quick snack.

With some smart choices, the possibilities for delicious, nutritious snacks are almost limitless.

Sliced Cucumber Sandwiches

Perhaps one of the most famous "finger sandwiches," this refreshing, bite-size morsel is a great snack.

 Serves:
4 to 6

1 TB. chopped fresh dill	1 English-style cucumber, striped and very thinly sliced
2 TB. light margarine, softened	Salt
8 slices white or whole-wheat sandwich bread, crusts removed	$\frac{1}{2}$ tsp. black pepper

1. In a small bowl, combine dill and margarine.

2. Spread dill margarine over 4 slices of bread. Top each slice with a layer of thinly sliced cucumber, sprinkle with salt and pepper, top with bread, and cut on the diagonal to create small triangular sandwiches. Arrange on a serving platter, and serve.

 TIME WASTER

Many vegetables, such as cucumbers, contain a lot of water. To prevent your snack sandwiches from becoming "sogwiches," prepare them just before serving.

Quick and Cool Cukes

Now this is a great hot-weather snack! When I was a kid, my mom used to serve these before dinner. My brothers and I could never get enough.

 Serves:
4

2 small cucumbers, striped and
sliced into ¼-in. sections

½ cup cold water

½ cup red wine vinegar

½ tsp. dried dill or 1 TB. fresh

Ice cubes

1. Arrange cucumbers in a 12-inch shallow bowl or pie plate. Pour cold water and red wine vinegar over cucumbers, sprinkle with dill, and add a few ice cubes.

2. Pass the bowl, and serve cucumber slices on a plate to eat with a fork.

Fresh Jicama Sticks

 Serves:
4

1 lb. *jicama*, peeled and sliced into
½x½x4-in. sticks

Juice of 1 lime

Dash hot pepper sauce (optional)

1. Place jicama sticks in a container with a tightly fitting lid.

2. Toss with lime juice and hot pepper sauce (if using), and serve.

 DEFINITION

Jicama is a juicy, crunchy, sweet, Central American vegetable that's eaten both raw and cooked. It's available in many large grocery stores as well as from specialty vendors.

Sautéed Snap Peas

Take these pods for a "quick wok," and you've got an irresistible crunchy snack.

 Serves:
4

2 TB. olive oil	1 lb. fresh sugar snap peas
¼ cup soy sauce	¼ tsp. kosher salt
1 tsp. chopped garlic	

1. In a wok or 10-inch skillet over medium-high heat, heat olive oil.

2. Pour soy sauce into a small bowl, and place the bowl in the center of a serving platter.

3. Add garlic and sugar snap peas to the wok, and cook, stirring, for 1 minute. Arrange pea pods on the serving plate around the bowl, sprinkle with kosher salt, and serve, inviting guests to dip pea pods into soy sauce.

Variation: This works well with snow peas (flat pod peas), fresh snap beans, and other vegetables, too.

 # Grape Tomatoes with Feta and Oil

 Serves:
2

1⅓ cups grape tomatoes, each cut in half	½ tsp. Italian seasoning
2 TB. olive oil	Pinch salt
6 TB. crumbled feta cheese	Pinch black pepper

1. Place tomato halves in a container with a lid.

2. Drizzle olive oil over top; sprinkle with feta cheese, Italian seasoning, salt, and pepper; and toss to coat.

Variation: Use your favorite Italian or vinaigrette dressing in place of the olive oil, salt, and Italian seasoning.

 ON THE CLOCK

Grape tomatoes are the only store-bought tomatoes I've found to have reliable fresh flavor when purchased out of tomato season.

Broiled Mushroom Caps with Fresh Mozzarella

 10   **Serves:**
6

1 (8-oz.) pkg. small white mushrooms, stems removed and wiped with damp paper towels

3 TB. olive oil

1 cup fresh small mozzarella balls (about 4 oz.), each ball cut in half, or larger balls cut into $\frac{1}{2}$-in. pieces

$\frac{1}{2}$ tsp. Italian seasoning

$\frac{1}{2}$ tsp. salt

$\frac{1}{4}$ tsp. black pepper

1. Preheat the broiler.

2. Arrange mushroom caps, cap up, on a baking tray, and brush caps with about 1 tablespoon olive oil. Broil for 2 minutes on the high rack.

3. Remove the tray from the broiler, and flip caps. Insert $\frac{1}{2}$ mozzarella ball into each mushroom cap cavity. Drizzle mushrooms with remaining 2 tablespoons olive oil, and sprinkle with Italian seasoning, salt, and pepper. Broil for 3 minutes or until filling is beginning to bubble.

4. Arrange stuffed mushrooms on a platter, and serve.

Heart of Palm and Mushroom Skewers

 Serves:
6

1 (14-oz.) can hearts of palm, drained and cut into 1-in. segments

1 (8-oz.) pkg. fresh button mushrooms, halved through the cap and stem

¼ cup light Italian salad dressing (your favorite)

Salt

Black pepper

1. Spear 1 heart of palm through side of heart and 1 mushroom piece with a toothpick. Repeat with remaining hearts of palm and mushrooms.

2. Arrange bites on a serving plate; drizzle with Italian dressing, salt, and pepper; and serve.

Prosciutto-Artichoke Bites

10 **Serves:**
6

1 (14-oz.) can artichoke bottoms (about 6 bottoms), drained

⅓ cup diced prosciutto

⅓ cup shredded Parmesan cheese

1 TB. olive oil

½ tsp. dried oregano

1. Preheat the broiler.

2. Arrange artichoke bottoms on a baking tray, concave side up, and distribute diced prosciutto among artichoke bottoms, spreading prosciutto to cover. Distribute Parmesan cheese over prosciutto. Drizzle each artichoke with olive oil, and dust with a pinch of oregano. Broil on the high rack for 3 minutes or until cheese begins to melt and oil bubbles.

3. For a sit-down snack, serve 1 artichoke bottom on a plate with a knife and fork. For a stand-up snack, cut each artichoke bottom into quarters, and serve on a platter with toothpicks.

ON THE CLOCK

Prosciutto (Italian-style salt-cured ham) is commonly sold in thin slices. A number of grocery stores, however, also sell diced prosciutto, which is often less expensive than the sliced version.

Lean Ham and Sweet Red Pepper Bites

The soft, savory ham and the crisp sweet pepper make for a crunchy, tasty snack.

 10 **Serves:**
6

1 TB. prepared mustard	½ lb. thinly sliced lean ham
1 TB. low-fat sour cream	2 large sweet red peppers, ribs and seeds removed, and cut lengthwise into ¼-in. slices
½ tsp. salt	

1. In a small bowl, combine mustard, sour cream, and salt.

2. Spread a thin line of mustard mixture along one side of a slice of ham about 1 inch in from the edge. Place a slice of sweet red pepper over mustard, and roll ham over pepper to create a cylinder.

3. Slice each cylinder in half, arrange in a circle like the spokes in a wheel, and serve.

Garden Salsa

Serves:
6

2 large tomatoes, seeded and chopped into $\frac{1}{4}$-in. pieces

$\frac{1}{2}$ cup sweet onion, such as Vidalia, chopped into $\frac{1}{4}$-in. pieces

1 (4.5-oz.) can chopped green chiles, drained

$\frac{1}{4}$ cup chopped fresh cilantro

2 TB. lime juice

2 TB. red wine vinegar

1 tsp. kosher salt

$1\frac{1}{2}$ tsp. fresh oregano or $\frac{1}{2}$ tsp. dried

$\frac{1}{4}$ tsp. hot pepper sauce

$\frac{1}{2}$ (6-oz.) bag multigrain tortilla chips (about 15 chips per person)

1. In a serving bowl, combine tomatoes, sweet onion, green chiles, cilantro, lime juice, red wine vinegar, kosher salt, oregano, and hot pepper sauce.

2. Serve with tortilla chips. This is also a good topping on other Mexican-style dishes and will last in the fridge for a day or two.

ON THE CLOCK

When in season, use fresh local tomatoes in this salsa for the best flavor.

Salsa Verde

The texture of this Salsa Verde is like fresh salsa, but the flavor is quite different because of the unique, piquant *tomatillo*.

Serves:
4 to 6

½ lb. tomatillos, papery peel removed and flesh chopped into ¼-in. dice or smaller

½ cup sweet onion such as Vidalia, chopped into ¼-in. dice or smaller

½ can green chiles, drained and chopped

¼ cup chopped fresh cilantro

1 TB. fresh lime juice

1 tsp. kosher salt

Tortilla chips

1. In a serving bowl, combine tomatillos, sweet onion, green chiles, cilantro, lime juice, and kosher salt.

2. Serve with tortilla chips. This is also a good topping on other Mexican-style dishes.

DEFINITION

The **tomatillo,** available in specialty and large grocery stores, looks like a green tomato with a papery skin but is actually a closer botanical relative to the gooseberry. It's a small, round fruit with a distinctive spicy flavor and is a traditional component of many south-of-the-border dishes.

Guacamole

10	**Serves:** 6

2 ripe avocados	1 tsp. chopped garlic
¾ cup sour cream	½ tsp. salt
1 small fresh tomato, seeded and chopped into ¼-in. pieces	¼ tsp. hot pepper sauce
3 TB. lemon juice	½ (6-oz.) bag low-carb tortilla chips (about 15 chips per person)

1. Cut avocados in half lengthwise, and discard pits. Scoop out flesh into a bowl.

2. Add sour cream, tomato, lemon juice, garlic, salt, and hot pepper sauce, and mix with a fork to a chunky consistency.

3. Serve with tortilla chips.

Variation: For **Guacamole Salsa Swirl,** add 1 (12-ounce) jar salsa and stir a few times to create a swirl effect.

Quick Tapenade

10	**Serves:** 6

1 cup pitted *kalamata olives*	1 tsp. chopped garlic
1 cup pitted green olives	1 tsp. fresh lemon juice
¼ cup olive oil	Dash hot pepper sauce
2 scallions, cut into 1-in. segments	Pinch black pepper

1. In a food processor fitted with a steel blade, coarsely process kalamata olives, green olives, olive oil, scallions, garlic, lemon juice, hot pepper sauce, and pepper.

2. Scrape mixture into a bowl (with a lid if it will be transported). Scoop with celery, carrot, and Belgian endive as dippers.

> **DEFINITION**
>
> **Kalamata olives,** traditionally from Greece, are a medium-small, long black olive with a smoky, rich flavor—very different from run-of-the-mill canned black olives. Try them, and you'll be hooked.

Olive Spread

10   **Serves:**
6

1 (6-oz.) can pitted ripe black olives, drained	¼ cup chopped fresh parsley
¼ cup chopped walnuts or pine nuts (toasted if possible)	1 TB. chopped garlic
¼ cup shredded Parmesan cheese	½ tsp. salt
¼ cup olive oil	¼ tsp. black pepper
	4 heads Belgian endive, broken into leaves

1. In a food processor fitted with a steel blade, process black olives, walnuts, Parmesan cheese, olive oil, parsley, garlic, salt, and pepper just enough to pulverize olives but leaving plenty of texture.

2. Scrape spread into a serving bowl, and serve surrounded by Belgian endive leaves (and surrounded by images in your mind of the Tuscan countryside).

Quick Homemade Hummus

10   **Serves:**
2

1 (15-oz.) can chickpeas, drained and rinsed	1 tsp. salt
1 TB. chopped garlic	2 TB. olive oil
Juice of 1 lemon (about 3 TB.)	¼ cup tahini

1. In a food processor fitted with a steel blade, process chickpeas, garlic, lemon juice, salt, olive oil, and tahini until texture is fine and creamy.

2. If hummus is too thick, add more olive oil.

Variation: For a flavor shortcut, consider purchasing a jar of chopped or minced garlic (in the vegetable section of the grocery store). The flavor sacrifice is minimal, and you'll save a lot of time. Serve with cucumber sticks, baby carrots, and celery stalks, and you've got a tasty, easy-to-carry lunch.

Endive with Hummus and Arugula

Arugula brings a sharp freshness to this vegetable dish.

	Serves:
10	4

1 cup hummus

2 cups chopped fresh arugula

3 heads Belgian endive, leaves separated

¼ cup shelled pistachios

1. In a large bowl, combine hummus and arugula.

2. Spread about 1 tablespoon hummus on stem end of 1 Belgian endive leaf, and arrange leaves on a serving plate.

3. Sprinkle a few pistachios on each, and serve.

ON THE CLOCK

In just about every recipe that calls for nuts—such as pistachios, sliced almonds, or chopped walnuts—the dish will taste even better if the nuts are toasted. Toasting is easy—just roast for 3 minutes under the broiler.

Grilled Hummus Triangles

 Serves:
6 to 8

1 cup hummus

1 TB. chopped garlic

3 pita breads, each sliced into
    8 wedges

2 TB. shredded Parmesan cheese

2 TB. olive oil

1. Preheat the broiler.

2. In a small bowl, combine hummus and garlic. Spread about 1 teaspoon hummus on each piece of pita bread. Sprinkle each with a pinch of Parmesan cheese.

3. Arrange pita pieces on a baking sheet in a single layer, and broil for about 1 minute or until pita begins to brown and cheese begins to glisten.

4. Remove from the broiler, arrange on a serving plate, decorate with a very thin swirl of olive oil around the plate that touches each piece of hummus, and serve.

Lemon-Pepper Dipping Sauce

 Serves:
4 to 6

2 TB. honey

2 TB. extra-virgin olive oil

2 tsp. fresh lemon juice

1 tsp. peeled and grated fresh
    ginger

$\frac{1}{2}$ tsp. black pepper

Salt

1. Pour honey into a microwave-safe serving bowl, and microwave for 10 seconds.

2. Add extra-virgin olive oil, lemon juice, ginger, pepper, and salt, and mix thoroughly.

3. Serve with fresh vegetable dippers.

Tzatziki (Greek Cucumber Dip)

 Serves:
2

1 cup plain yogurt

1 cucumber, half peeled and finely chopped and half cut into sticks

1 TB. chopped garlic

1 TB. olive oil

2 tsp. lemon juice

½ tsp. black pepper

½ tsp. salt

1 cup crisp raw snow pea pods, stems removed and cut into pieces

1 large celery stalk, rinsed, trimmed, and cut into sticks

1. In a small container with a lid, combine yogurt, cucumber, garlic, olive oil, lemon juice, pepper, and salt.

2. Serve Tzatziki along with cut snow pea pods and celery.

Chutney and Cottage Cheese Dip

This dip is a lower-fat, but no less flavorful, version of the cream cheese spreads.

 Serves:
4 to 6

1 cup low- or nonfat cottage cheese

1 (9-oz.) jar Major Grey's Chutney

Crusty bread or apple slices

1. In a serving bowl, combine cottage cheese and ½ of Major Grey's Chutney.

2. Spread remaining Major Grey's Chutney on top of cottage cheese, and serve with wedges of crusty bread or crunchy apple slices and a spreading knife.

Variation: For added zing, mix 1 teaspoon aged balsamic vinegar into the spread.

Delicious Dips and Spreads

In This Chapter

- Satisfying dips
- Thick, savory spreads
- Versatile dipping vehicles

Dips and spreads exist on a continuum. For the purposes of this book, let's call a dip a creamy, flavorful appetizer that varies from almost fluid to almost solid but is always soft enough to be scooped with something edible—the other component that makes the appetizer complete. If something is too thick to be scooped, I call it a spread, more appropriate for use with a knife.

On the continuum of formality, spreads are perhaps a bit higher than dips. With dips, you use your fingers and stick food right into the bowl. Spreads are served with a spreading knife, and often guests will hold a serving plate with several hors d'oeuvres. The overall effect is to set the tone just a bit higher but still have fun.

The Dip Is a Passenger—but What Is the Vehicle?

In a simple sense, appetizers such as dips and spreads are all about passengers and vehicles. The passenger is the focus of your attention (the dip), and the vehicle is the means by which you get that passenger to your mouth. Choose vehicles carefully to either complement the dip (crisp, salty chips with creamy dip) or to serve primarily as transportation.

The more fluid the dip, the lighter the "dipper" you should use to pick it up—think of a potato chip for a yogurt-based dip as opposed to a sturdy bread stick or carrot stick with a thicker, cream cheese–based dip. Vehicles for spreads should be strong enough to stand up to the pressure of a knife pressing down on them with a thick substance. Good candidates are toasts, thick crackers, fruits, and vegetables. Thin crackers and chips might crack under pressure.

Good choices for dippers include Belgian endive leaves; breadsticks; potato chips; slices of baguette or other crusty bread; tortilla chips and chips made from other types of bread such as pita or even bagel "chips"; vegetables such as broccoli, carrots, celery, cauliflower, radishes, green beans, and blanched asparagus; and wedges of pita bread or store-bought pita crisps.

TIME WASTER

I've often chastised my children about "double dipping"—dipping a chip in dip, biting off part of the chip, and reinserting that same chip back in, with all the germ-spreading implications. I try to prevent the double-dipping syndrome by serving dip with small dippers that don't encourage a second trip.

When serving dips with crisp dippers such as chips and crisps, avoid the temptation to artfully arrange them in the dip for guests to take. In just a few minutes, those pita crisps will become pita *sogs*. Serve dip in a bowl on a platter surrounded by your dippers or with the dippers *alongside* instead of *in*.

Warm Artichoke Dip

	Serves:
	6

1 (14-oz.) can artichoke hearts or pieces, broken into 1-in. pieces

½ cup mayonnaise

½ cup sour cream or light sour cream

1 cup shredded Swiss cheese

2 scallions, roots and dark green leaves removed, and minced

Dash hot pepper sauce

4 Belgian endive heads, broken into leaves

1. In a microwave-safe bowl, mix together artichoke hearts, mayonnaise, sour cream, Swiss cheese, scallions, and hot pepper sauce. Microwave on high for 2 minutes or until dip begins to bubble and cheese is melted.

2. Stir and serve with Belgian endive leaves.

MINUTE MORSEL

Warm dips are the epitome of comfort food and are always a hit at parties, especially during cold weather. Be sure to serve warm dips *warm*. Prepare and serve them for immediate consumption using a heat source such as an electric hot pad/tray or a heatproof container suspended over special candles or canned heat such as Sterno. A small slow cooker works well, too.

Warm Blue Cheddar Dip with Slivered Almonds

 10 | **Serves:**
4 to 6

½ cup crumbled blue cheese	2 TB. *Madeira* or other sweet dessert wine
⅔ cup shredded mild cheddar cheese	⅓ cup slivered almonds
½ cup sour cream	Wheat crackers or Belgian endive leaves
½ cup cream cheese or light cream cheese, softened	

1. In a microwave-safe serving dish, combine blue cheese, cheddar cheese, sour cream, and cream cheese. Microwave on high for about 2 minutes or until mixture begins to bubble.

2. Stir in Madeira, top with slivered almonds, and serve with wheat crackers or Belgian endive leaves.

DEFINITION

Madeira is a fortified wine, similar to port and sherry, with sweet flavors of caramel, nuts, and honey.

Warm Crab Dip with Scallions, Ricotta, and Cheddar

 Serves:
6

1 (6-oz.) can flaked crabmeat

1 cup part-skim ricotta cheese

¼ cup shredded cheddar cheese

¼ cup mayonnaise

1 scallion, dark green leaves removed, sliced into ½-in. pieces

Pita or tortilla chips

1. In a food processor fitted with a metal blade, process crabmeat, ricotta cheese, cheddar cheese, mayonnaise, and scallion until smooth.

2. Scrape dip into a microwave-safe serving bowl, and microwave on high for 90 seconds or until dip just begins to bubble.

3. Stir and serve with pita or tortilla chips.

Warm Cheddar-Bacon Dip

 Serves:
4 to 6

4 slices bacon, or 1 (3-oz.) jar real bacon bits

2 cups shredded mild cheddar cheese

1 cup cream cheese or light cream cheese, softened

¼ cup Madeira

3 scallions, sliced into ¼-in. pieces (about ⅓ cup)

Thin slices of baguette

1. In a 10-inch skillet over medium heat, cook bacon until crispy. Remove bacon from the skillet, drain on a paper towel–lined plate, and crumble into small pieces.

2. Meanwhile, in a microwave-safe serving dish, combine cheddar cheese, cream cheese, and Madeira. Microwave on high for 90 seconds or until bubbly.

3. Stir in bacon, top with scallions, and serve with thin slices of baguette.

Buffalo Chicken Dip

| **10** | **Serves:** 8 to 10 |

1 (16.5-oz.) can chicken, drained

1 cup chunky blue cheese salad dressing

1 cup hot sauce

Bagel or pita crisps

1. In a serving bowl, place chicken and break up larger chunks with a spoon. Pour in blue cheese dressing and hot sauce, and toss to combine.

2. Serve with bagel or pita crisps or another sturdy grain-based dipper.

Variation: For a warm dip, heat in the microwave for 2 minutes.

Chicken-Parmesan Dip

This creamy and satisfying dip raises the question: is it a dip, or is it a meal? I like using shredded Parmesan cheese for the texture, but grated cheese can also be used.

| **10** | **Serves:** 6 to 8 |

1 (12.5-oz.) can chunk white chicken meat, broken up in the bowl with a spoon

1 cup sour cream or light sour cream

$\frac{1}{2}$ cup mayonnaise

1 cup shredded Parmesan cheese

$\frac{1}{2}$ tsp. garlic salt

$\frac{1}{2}$ tsp. black pepper

Dash hot pepper sauce

Chopped scallion pieces (optional)

Tortilla chips

1. In a serving bowl, place chicken and break up larger pieces with a spoon. Add sour cream, mayonnaise, Parmesan cheese, garlic salt, pepper, and hot pepper sauce, and mix thoroughly.

2. Top with scallion pieces (if using), and serve with tortilla chips.

Crab Ricotta Dip with Roasted Red Peppers

 Serves:
6

1 (6-oz.) can flaked crabmeat

1 cup ricotta cheese

½ (5-oz.) jar roasted red or piquillo peppers, drained

⅓ cup shredded cheddar cheese

½ tsp. garlic salt

2 TB. chopped fresh chives (optional)

Pita crisps or tortilla chips

1. In a food processor fitted with a metal blade, process crabmeat, ricotta cheese, roasted red peppers, cheddar cheese, and garlic salt until smooth.

2. Scrap dip into a microwave-safe serving bowl, and microwave on high for 90 seconds or until dip begins to bubble.

3. Stir, top with chives (if using), and serve with pita crisps or tortilla chips.

Red Pepper–Parmesan Dip

This colorful, piquant, and cheesy dish will get the party started on the right foot.

 Serves:
6 to 8

½ (5-oz.) jar roasted red peppers, drained

1 cup sour cream

1 cup cream cheese or light cream cheese, softened

½ cup shredded Parmesan cheese

Dash hot pepper sauce

Thinly sliced scallions

Tortilla chips

1. In a food processor fitted with a metal blade, process roasted red peppers, sour cream, cream cheese, Parmesan cheese, and hot pepper sauce until almost smooth.

2. Scrape dip into a bowl, and serve topped with sliced scallions and surrounded by tortilla chips.

Quick Spinach-Parmesan Dip

10   **Serves:**
           6

1 (10-oz.) pkg. frozen chopped
  spinach, thawed and squeezed
  dry

1 cup light sour cream

½ cup fat-free small curd cottage
  cheese

½ cup shredded Parmesan cheese

½ tsp. garlic salt

Dash hot pepper sauce

4 Belgian endive heads, broken
  into leaves

1. In a serving bowl, combine spinach, sour cream, cottage cheese, Parmesan cheese, garlic salt, and hot pepper sauce.

2. Serve with Belgian endive leaves.

TIME WASTER

To my taste, fat-free cottage cheese is a good alternative to regular cottage cheese. Light cream cheese, light sour cream, and light mayonnaise are also good options—note these are *reduced* fat, not *no* fat. The taste (and texture) of the totally fat-free versions are so different I don't recommend them.

Hot Cheddar-Onion Dip

A classic, this dip is so easy to prepare and is perfect alongside a light red wine.

Serves:
4

2 cups shredded sharp cheddar
cheese

¼ cup finely chopped *sweet onion*

¾ cup mayonnaise

¼ tsp. black pepper

Tortilla chips, crackers, or crusty
bread

1. In a microwave-safe serving dish, combine cheddar cheese, sweet onion, mayonnaise, and pepper. Microwave on high for 3 minutes or until bubbling.

2. Stir, and serve with tortilla chips, good crackers, or crusty bread.

DEFINITION

Regular table onions have plenty of that tart, eye-watering quality that requires ample cooking to reduce. **Sweet onions** are an important ingredient in quick appetizers because they're not quite so sharp and can be used uncooked (in moderation) in recipes. Vidalia and Spanish are two popular sweet onions.

Cheesy Salsa Dip

Serves:
6 to 8

1 (12-oz.) jar prepared salsa

1 cup cream cheese or light cream
cheese, softened

1 cup shredded Monterey Jack or
Mexican-style cheese

Tortilla chips

1. In a serving bowl, combine salsa and cream cheese.

2. Top with shredded Monterey Jack cheese, and serve with tortilla chips.

Jean's Mexican Dip

 Serves:
8

½ (1.25-oz.) pkg. taco seasoning

1 cup sour cream

1 (17-oz.) can refried beans

1 cup guacamole

2 cups shredded Mexican cheese

3 small tomatoes, chopped

3 scallions, dark green parts removed, chopped

1 (8-oz.) can sliced black olives, drained

Tortilla chips

1. In a small bowl, combine taco seasoning and sour cream.

2. In a quiche pan or pie plate, layer ingredients, starting with refried beans on the bottom, then taco seasoning–sour cream mixture, guacamole, Mexican cheese, tomatoes, scallions, and ending with black olives on top.

3. Serve with tortilla chips for dipping.

Dill-Tarragon Dip

 Serves:
4 to 6

1 cup sour cream or light sour cream

1 cup cream cheese or light cream cheese, softened

3 scallions, dark green leaves removed, finely chopped, plus more as needed (optional)

2 tsp. dried dill weed

½ tsp. dried tarragon

½ tsp. garlic salt

Cucumber slices

1. In a serving bowl, combine sour cream, cream cheese, 3 scallions, dill weed, tarragon, and garlic salt. If possible, refrigerate for 1 hour or more.

2. Stir, garnish with additional scallion pieces (if using), and serve with cucumber slices for a match made in heaven—or rather, a match made in the garden.

Ricotta Dip with Sun-Dried Tomatoes

 Serves:
6

1 cup part-skim milk ricotta cheese

½ cup oil-packed sun-dried tomatoes, drained, 2 TB. oil reserved

¼ tsp. garlic salt

Dash hot pepper sauce

1 TB. chopped chives (optional)

2 large carrots, peeled and cut into 4-in. sticks

2 small cucumbers, peeled and cut into 4-in. sticks

1. In a food processor fitted with a steel blade, process ricotta cheese, sun-dried tomatoes, reserved 2 tablespoons oil, garlic salt, and hot pepper sauce until almost smooth but with visible tomato pieces remaining.

2. Scrape dip into a serving bowl, sprinkle with chives (if using), and serve surrounded by carrot and cucumber sticks.

Chickpea and Sun-Dried Tomato Dip

A close cousin of hummus, this rich, savory dip is so tasty. You can use the oil from the sun-dried tomatoes as a nice replacement for an equal amount of the olive oil.

 Serves:
6

1 (15.5-oz.) can chickpeas, drained

⅔ cup oil-packed sun-dried tomatoes, oil reserved

½ cup olive oil or oil from sun-dried tomatoes

Juice of ½ lime

Pita bread

1. In a food processor fitted with a metal blade, process chickpeas and sun-dried tomatoes until smooth.

2. While the machine is running, slowly add olive oil and process until mixture reaches a creamy consistency.

3. Scrape dip into a serving bowl, stir in lime juice, blend thoroughly, and serve with pita bread.

Variation: Add ½ to 1 cup nonfat plain yogurt for a creamier, slightly milder dip.

ON THE CLOCK

Chickpeas (also known as garbanzo beans), the base ingredient in the Middle Eastern dip hummus, are high in fiber and low in fat, making them both a delicious and healthy component of many appetizers.

Derek's Curry Ball

This unusual, flavorful appetizer benefits from being made ahead. It's also delicious right away if you can't wait!

 Serves:
30   4 to 6

1 cup cream cheese or light cream cheese, softened	½ cup raisins (optional)
2 TB. sour cream	Dried or flaked coconut
2 tsp. curry powder	1 cup chutney such as Major Grey's Mango
½ cup chopped scallions	Wheat crackers
½ cup coarsely chopped dried peanuts	

1. In a large bowl, combine cream cheese and sour cream. Blend in curry powder, and add chopped scallions, peanuts, and raisins (if using).

2. Mix thoroughly, form into a ball, and chill.

3. To serve, roll ball in coconut, pour chutney over top, and serve with wheat crackers.

Spicy Thai Peanut and Chicken Spread

This spread is tailor-made for pairing with wines with a bit of residual sweetness, such as a German Riesling or Gewürztraminer.

 Serves:
6 to 8

1 (8-oz.) jar peanut dipping sauce

1 (12-oz.) can chunk chicken

¼ cup sesame oil

2 scallions, dark green parts removed, and chopped

2 TB. shelled peanuts

Fresh vegetable sticks or crusty bread

1. In a food processor fitted with a metal blade, process peanut sauce, chicken, sesame oil, and scallions until almost smooth.

2. Scrape spread into a serving bowl, scatter peanuts on top, and serve with fresh vegetable sticks or crusty bread.

Warm Dijon-Ham Spread

If you have leftover ham, this spread is the perfect destination for it. If you don't have leftovers, head for the deli for the honey ham.

 Serves:
6 to 8

½ lb. sliced honey ham

1 cup shredded mild cheddar cheese

¼ cup Dijon-style mustard

Wheat crackers

1. In a food processor fitted with a metal blade, process ham and cheddar cheese until ham is reduced to small pieces.

2. Scrape mixture into a microwave-safe serving bowl, and heat on high power for 1 minute or until cheese begins to bubble.

3. Stir in Dijon-style mustard, and serve with wheat crackers. Sighs of appreciation will follow.

Apple and German Sausage Spread

 10

Serves:
6 to 8

½ lb. cooked German sausage
    such as bratwurst, cut into ½-in.
    sections
½ cup shredded Swiss cheese
1 crisp Granny Smith apple, sliced
2 tsp. prepared mustard

1 tsp. fresh lemon juice
Dash hot pepper sauce
Salt
Black pepper
Belgian endive leaves or *toast
    points*

1. In a food processor fitted with a metal blade, process German sausage, Swiss cheese, Granny Smith apple, mustard, lemon juice, hot pepper sauce, salt, and pepper until almost smooth.

2. Scrape into a microwave-safe serving bowl, heat on high power for 2 minutes, stir, and serve with Belgian endive leaves or toast points.

DEFINITION

Toast points are quick and easy to make. They are, quite simply, pieces of bread with the crusts removed and toasted for about a minute on each side. Cut on the diagonal from each corner, one piece of bread results in four triangle pieces.

Salmon Spread with Roasted Red Peppers

	Serves:
10	6

1 (6-oz.) can pink salmon, drained, skin and bones discarded, if necessary

1 (8-oz.) pkg. cream cheese, softened

1/2 cup roasted red peppers, rinsed and patted dry on paper towels

1/4 cup minced fresh chives, plus more as needed (optional)

2 TB. olive oil

1 tsp. lemon juice

4 heads Belgian endive, broken into leaves

1. In a food processor fitted with a steel blade, process salmon, cream cheese, roasted red peppers, 1/4 cup chives, olive oil, and lemon juice to a creamy consistency.

2. Scrape spread into a serving bowl, and garnish with additional chives (if using). Place spread in the center of a plate or platter.

3. Arrange Belgian endive leaves around the bowl, all pointing outward to create a flower pattern. Serve with a knife to spread.

Variation: Whole-wheat crackers are delicious with this spread.

Cream Cheese and Chive Spread

 Serves:
6 to 8

1 bunch fresh chives, finely chopped, or 1 (.25-oz.) jar dried chives	Assorted fresh vegetables cut into finger-food size or assorted baby vegetables
2 cups cream cheese or light cream cheese, softened	Crisp wheat crackers

1. If you are using fresh chives, set aside 1 tablespoon for garnish.

2. In a serving bowl, combine cream cheese and remaining chives.

3. Sprinkle reserved fresh chives on top as a garnish if using. Serve with an assortment of fresh vegetables or crisp wheat crackers.

Variation: Although this spread will taste good immediately, an hour or more in the fridge will make it taste even better.

Ginger-Lemon Chevre

Here's a delicate, elegant spread for your summer cocktail party out under your spreading oak.

 Serves:
6

1 (8-oz.) pkg. fresh chevre (goat's milk cheese), softened	¼ cup chopped walnuts
2 TB. extra-virgin olive oil	¼ cup raisins or other chopped dried fruit such as cranberries
2 tsp. fresh lemon juice	Belgian endive leaves or wheat crackers
1 tsp. peeled, chopped fresh ginger	

1. In a serving bowl, combine chevre, extra-virgin olive oil, lemon juice, and ginger. If possible, refrigerate for an hour or two or even all day.

2. Top with a single layer of chopped walnuts, followed by raisins, and serve surrounded with Belgian endive leaves or wheat crackers.

Blue Cheese and Chopped Pecan Spread

 10

Serves:
4 to 6

1 cup cream cheese or light cream
   cheese, softened

1 cup crumbled blue cheese

1 cup chopped pecans

Belgian endive leaves

Sliced pears

Wheat crackers

1. In a serving bowl, combine cream cheese, blue cheese, and $^2/_3$ cup chopped pecans.

2. Top with remaining $^1/_3$ cup pecans, and serve surrounded by a combination of Belgian endive leaves, pear slices (rub with lemon juice if setting out in advance), and/or wheat crackers.

Variation: For **Chunky Blue Cheese Spread with Apple and Walnuts,** replace the pears and pecans with 1 tart Granny Smith apple, cut into $^1/_4$-inch cubes, and $^1/_2$ cup chopped walnuts. Reduce the blue cheese to $^1/_2$ cup. Cut the apples just before serving.

Crunchy Creamy Vegetable Spread

If you have the time, make this in the morning and let the flavors meld in the fridge for a few hours.

10

Serves:
4 to 6

1 stick celery

1 large carrot, peeled

2 scallions, dark green leaves
   removed, 1 TB. finely chopped
   green leaves reserved for
   garnish

1 cup cream cheese, softened

$^1/_2$ cup light sour cream

$^1/_2$ cup shredded Parmesan cheese

Dash hot pepper sauce (optional)

Crunchy breadsticks or pita bread
   wedges

1. In a food processor fitted with a shredder wheel, shred celery, carrot, and scallions.

2. In a serving bowl, combine shredded vegetables with cream cheese, sour cream, Parmesan cheese, and hot pepper sauce (if using).

3. Sprinkle remaining 1 tablespoon chopped scallions over top, and serve with crunchy breadsticks or pita bread sliced into pie-shape wedges.

Variation: For a lower-fat recipe, use nonfat cottage cheese instead of cream cheese.

White Bean Salad Spread

 Serves:
4 to 6

1 (15-oz.) can cannellini beans, drained	1 TB. red wine vinegar
1 cup fresh basil leaves	1 TB. olive oil, plus more as needed
¼ cup chopped sweet onion such as Vidalia	½ tsp. kosher salt
	Fresh vegetables or crusty wheat bread

1. In a blender or food processor fitted with a metal blade, process cannellini beans, basil leaves, sweet onion, red wine vinegar, olive oil, and kosher salt to the consistency of a thick, chunky paste. If necessary, add a little more olive oil to achieve the right consistency.

2. Scrape spread into a serving bowl, and serve with fresh vegetables or crusty wheat bread.

 ON THE CLOCK

In some recipes where I've called for olive oil to assist processing, other high-moisture ingredients such as nonfat yogurt can also do the trick—but use it only where the inherent yogurt flavor won't conflict with the rest of the ingredients.

Roasted Red Pepper Spread

Chickpeas make a hearty, rich base for this spread.

 10

Serves:
6 to 8

1 (15.5-oz.) can chickpeas, drained	¼ tsp. salt
1 cup nonfat plain yogurt	Dash hot sauce
½ cup roasted red peppers, drained and cut into 1-in. pieces	1 TB. fresh lemon juice
2 TB. olive oil, plus more as needed	1 TB. chopped fresh chives (optional)
1 tsp. chopped garlic	Pita crisps

1. In a food processor fitted with a metal blade, process chickpeas, yogurt, roasted red peppers, olive oil, garlic, salt, and hot sauce until almost smooth. If necessary, add a little more olive oil to achieve a smooth consistency.

2. Scrape spread into a serving bowl, stir in lemon juice, sprinkle chives on top (if using), and serve with pita crisps.

Fish and Seafood Appetizers

In This Chapter

- Fish-based dips and spreads
- Sensational shrimp appetizers
- Delicious crab-based hors d'oeuvres
- Calling on clams

For many people, seafood, and especially fish, form the flavor backbone for appetizers. If there's a table with several choices, one of which is a fish dish, that's the one they visit first. Distinctive seasonings, color, and texture all contribute to making these hors d'oeuvres favorites.

Salmon, with its distinctive pinkish color and pleasingly rich seafood flavor, is a welcome component in many unique appetizers, as is tuna. Shrimp is perhaps one of the most used seafood ingredients. And recipes containing crab produce a rich, buttery flavor, while clams supply a meaty heartiness. But one thing all seafood appetizers have in common is that distinctive umame—the rich tang of the sea.

In this chapter, I give you some of my favorites.

Spicy Mayonnaise

This mayo is delicious as a spread for smoked salmon!

10 | **Serves:**
4 to 6

½ cup mayonnaise

2 TB. Worcestershire sauce

2 TB. Dijon mustard or brown mustard

1 tsp. hot pepper sauce

1 tsp. paprika

¼ tsp. black pepper

Juice of 1 lemon

1. In a small bowl, whisk together mayonnaise, Worcestershire sauce, Dijon mustard, hot pepper sauce, paprika, pepper, and lemon juice.

2. Use as a spicy condiment for on seafood, from appetizers to seafood steaks.

Creamy Seafood Dip

This is the place for imitation crabmeat (actually fish). Real crabmeat and canned salmon will also work.

10 | **Serves:**
6 to 8

½ lb. imitation crabmeat

1 cup sour cream

½ cup mayonnaise

2 scallions, dark green leaves removed, cut into ½-in. pieces

1 TB. fresh lemon juice

1 tsp. dried dill

Dash hot pepper sauce

Belgian endive leaves and/or pita crisps

1. In a food processor or blender, process imitation crabmeat, sour cream, mayonnaise, scallions, lemon juice, dill, and hot pepper sauce to a slightly coarse consistency. (I like to leave a bit of texture.)

2. Serve in a bowl surrounded by Belgian endive leaves and/or pita crisps.

Smoked Salmon and Cream Cheese Wheels

 Serves:
6 to 8

1 (8-oz.) pkg. smoked salmon, thinly sliced	2 TB. chopped fresh chives (optional)
1 cup cream cheese or light cream cheese, softened	

1. Arrange salmon slices on a work surface in a single layer, with narrow ends facing you. Spread each with a thin layer ($\frac{1}{4}$ inch or less) of cream cheese. Working from one end, roll salmon evenly over cream cheese. When salmon is completely rolled, insert toothpicks spaced at $\frac{1}{2}$-inch intervals along roll.

2. Using a very sharp knife, slice roll at the midpoint between each toothpick. Repeat with other pieces of salmon.

3. Arrange finished wheels on a serving plate, and sprinkle with chives (if using).

 ON THE CLOCK

Canned salmon is a quick and convenient starting point for salmon dips and spreads. Smoked salmon, packaged in flat, thin slices, is also perfect as a topping and for rolling those wheels.

Teriyaki Salmon Dip

This dip marries ingredients from East and West: Japanese-style teriyaki sauce and the dairy products prized in Western cuisines. The result is delicious.

 Serves:
4

1 (6-oz.) can boneless, skinless pink salmon, drained	1 TB. teriyaki sauce
¾ cup sour cream	1 tsp. fresh lemon juice
¼ cup cream cheese or light cream cheese, softened	2 TB. chopped fresh chives
	Wheat crackers

1. In a food processor fitted with a metal blade, process salmon, sour cream, cream cheese, teriyaki sauce, and lemon juice until smooth.

2. Scrape into a serving bowl, sprinkle with chives, and serve with wheat crackers.

Variation: For a chunky, farmhouse-style spread, mix with a spoon instead of a food processor.

Salmon and Sun-Dried Tomato Spread

The rich, sunny taste of tomatoes blends beautifully with salmon, and the red and green colors are so cheerful.

 Serves:
4 to 6

1 (6-oz.) can boneless, skinless pink salmon, drained	2 TB. olive oil, plus more as needed
½ cup cream cheese or light cream cheese, softened	1 tsp. fresh lemon juice
⅔ cup chickpeas	1 sliced scallion
½ cup oil-packed sun-dried tomatoes, drained and oil preserved	Pita bread wedges or crisps

1. In a food processor fitted with a metal blade, process salmon, cream cheese, chickpeas, sun-dried tomatoes, olive oil, and lemon juice until smooth. If necessary, add a little more olive oil to achieve a thick, smooth consistency.

2. Scrape spread into a serving bowl, top with scallion slices, and serve with pita bread wedges or pita crisps.

Variation: If possible, chill this spread for an hour or so before serving to let the flavors meld.

 ON THE CLOCK

If your sun-dried tomatoes are packed in a relatively healthful oil such as sunflower oil, use that oil in your recipe instead of olive oil. Not only do you make efficient use of good ingredients, but this oil is infused with all that wonderful tomato flavor—a boost for your spread!

Salmon with Cucumber and Dill

 Serves:
6 to 8

1 cup fresh, mild chevre (goat's milk cheese), softened	1 (8-oz.) pkg. thinly sliced smoked salmon, cut into 1-in. squares
2 TB. plus ¼ tsp. chopped fresh dill or 2 tsp. dried dill	Kosher salt
1 English-style cucumber, ends removed, striped, and sliced into ⅛-in. rounds	Lemon wedges

1. In a small bowl, combine chevre and 2 tablespoons fresh or 2 teaspoons dried dill.

2. Spread about 2 teaspoons chevre mixture on each cucumber slice, top each with 1 piece salmon, and arrange on a serving platter.

3. Sprinkle remaining ¼ teaspoon fresh dill (if using) and a few grains of kosher salt on each, and serve with lemon wedges for guests to squeeze a few drops on each bite.

Quick Tuna Dip

 Serves:
6

1 (6-oz.) can white tuna packed in water, drained

1 cup light sour cream

1 (.53-oz.) pkg. vegetable soup mix

1 TB. lemon juice (fresh, if possible)

Pinch black pepper

4 heads Belgian endive, broken into leaves

1. In a serving bowl, and using a fork, combine tuna, sour cream, vegetable soup mix, lemon juice, and pepper, breaking up any large tuna chunks. If possible, chill for 1 hour or so to allow the flavors to blend.

2. Serve with Belgian endive leaves as dippers.

Variation: Use canned salmon, skin and bones removed if necessary, in place of tuna.

 ON THE CLOCK

No time to chill this dip? With soup-mix recipes, put the mix into a microwave-safe serving bowl, add 2 tablespoons water, mix, and microwave on high for 15 to 20 seconds. Then add the rest of your dip ingredients, mix, and serve. This quick heat softens the ingredients and accelerates the flavor spreading.

Spicy Anchovy Pâté

 Serves:
4

1 (6.5-oz.) can skinless, boneless pink salmon

2 anchovies

½ cup plain breadcrumbs

¼ cup cream cheese or light cream cheese, softened

2 TB. olive oil, plus more as needed

2 scallions, dark green parts removed, cut into ½-in. sections

1 tsp. fresh lemon juice

1 tsp. dried dill

Dash hot pepper sauce

4 slices white or whole-wheat bread, crusts removed, cut on the diagonal to form triangles

1. In a food processor fitted with a metal blade, process salmon, anchovies, breadcrumbs, cream cheese, olive oil, scallions, lemon juice, dill, and hot pepper sauce until smooth. If necessary, add a little more oil to achieve a thick, smooth consistency.

2. Scrape mixture into a serving bowl and, if possible, chill for several hours.

3. Preheat the broiler.

4. Arrange bread on a baking sheet, and broil for 1 minute on each side until lightly browned.

5. Serve pâté with toast triangles.

> **TIME WASTER**
>
> Many fish-based appetizers are quick and easy to make, but unless the recipe calls for chilling, make them just before you need them. Old fish tastes like, well, old fish.

Sardine, Olive, and Sun-Dried Tomato Spread

 10

Serves:
4 to 6

1 (3.75-oz.) can sardines, drained

1 cup cream cheese or light cream cheese, softened

½ cup oil-packed sun-dried tomatoes, drained, oil reserved

½ cup pitted kalamata olives, drained

2 TB. olive oil (or oil from tomatoes), plus more as needed

1 TB. fresh lemon juice

1 sprig parsley

Crisp wheat crackers

1. In a food processor fitted with a metal blade, process sardines, cream cheese, sun-dried tomatoes, kalamata olives, olive oil, and lemon juice until blended but still chunky. If necessary for processing, add a little more olive oil.

2. Scrape mixture into a serving bowl, garnish with parsley, and serve with crisp wheat crackers.

Shrimp Spread

The whole shrimp studding this savory spread make for a tasty yet attractive appetizer.

 Serves:
4

½ cup cream cheese or light cream cheese, softened

½ cup mayonnaise

2 scallions, dark green parts removed, cut into ½-in. pieces, plus 1 scallion (optional)

1 TB. chopped fresh dill or 1 tsp. dried dill

2 tsp. fresh lemon juice

½ tsp. dried thyme

Dash hot pepper sauce

1 (6-oz.) can tiny cocktail shrimp, drained

Melba toast or sturdy wheat crackers

1. In a food processor fitted with a metal blade, process cream cheese, mayonnaise, 2 scallions, dill, lemon juice, thyme, and hot pepper sauce until almost smooth.

2. Scrape spread into a serving bowl, and stir in shrimp.

3. Sprinkle with remaining scallion pieces (if using), and serve with melba toast or sturdy wheat crackers.

Shrimp Balls

These are very popular at parties. If you do take them, wait to roll the balls in corn-flakes just before serving to help the flakes keep their crunch.

 Serves:
4 to 6

1 cup crushed cornflakes

1 cup cream cheese or light cream cheese, softened

¼ cup mayonnaise

2 TB. prepared mustard

2 TB. onion flakes

1 tsp. dried dill

1 tsp. fresh lemon juice

1 (6-oz.) can tiny cocktail shrimp, drained

25 (3-in.) pretzel sticks

1. Spread crushed cornflakes on a plate.

2. In a medium bowl, combine cream cheese, mayonnaise, mustard, onion flakes, dill, and lemon juice. Gently mix in shrimp, and using your hands, form mixture into small balls about $\frac{1}{2}$ inch in diameter or about the size of a large marble.

3. Roll each ball in cornflakes to coat, skewer with pretzel stick, and set out on a serving plate.

Shrimp with Sweet Pineapple Onion Relish

 10   **Serves:**
6

1 (8-oz.) can pineapple chunks in juice, drained

$\frac{1}{3}$ cup honey

1 TB. fresh lemon juice

$\frac{1}{4}$ cup chopped sweet onion (about $\frac{1}{2}$ medium)

$\frac{1}{2}$ lb. (51 to 70 count, or about 30) cooked shrimp, peeled, deveined, and tail removed

1. In a food processor fitted with a metal blade, pulse pineapple, honey, lemon juice, and chopped sweet onion to relish consistency.

2. Scrape relish into a serving bowl, place the bowl on a plate or platter, and surround with shrimp. Serve using shrimp as dippers.

 ON THE CLOCK

When it comes to mincing onion, I save time by using either a grater (using the large-hole section) for small quantities such as half an onion, or a food processor fitted with the larger piece wheel when I have larger quantities to mince.

Jicama, Shrimp, and Cream Cheese Bites

 10

Serves:
6

½ lb. (51 to 70 *count,* or about 30) cooked shrimp, peeled, deveined, and tail removed

1 TB. fresh lime juice

½ cup cream cheese or light cream cheese, softened

8 oz. jicama, peeled and cut into 1×2-in. pieces about ½-in. thick

2 TB. chopped fresh chives

Black pepper

Lime wedges

1. In a large bowl, toss shrimp and lime juice to coat.

2. Spread about 1½ teaspoons cream cheese on each piece of jicama, top each with 1 shrimp, and arrange on a serving plate.

3. Sprinkle with chives, season with a few twists of pepper, garnish with lime wedges, and serve.

 DEFINITION

On shrimp packaging, you'll often see a reference to the **count.** This refers to the size of the shrimp according to how many compose a pound. Many of the recipes in this chapter call for 51 to 70 count (51 to 70 make up a pound), which are perfect for an appetizer.

Shrimp Macadamia Rafts

10

Serves:
6 to 8

½ cup cream cheese or light cream cheese, softened

1½ TB. freshly grated ginger

1 (6-oz.) box plain wheat crackers

1 lb. (51 to 70 count, or about 30) cooked shrimp, peeled, deveined, and tail removed

⅔ cup macadamia nuts (about 18)

Lime wedges

Kosher salt

1. In a small bowl, combine cream cheese and ginger.

2. Spread about $1\frac{1}{2}$ teaspoons cream cheese mixture on a wheat cracker, top each with 1 shrimp, and nestle 1 macadamia nut inside curled shrimp.

3. Arrange on a platter, drizzle with a few drops of lime juice, sprinkle with kosher salt, and serve.

MINUTE MORSEL

Fresh ginger—straight from the ginger root—is an unforgettable, piquant, savory-sweet seasoning with a better flavor than the powdered stuff in the spice rack. Buy a piece of ginger root, peel it, and keep it in the freezer in a freezer-proof bag or container. When you need some, simply grate off what you need and pop the rest back in the deep freeze for next time.

Crab Spread

 10   **Serves:**
6 to 8

1 (6-oz.) can crabmeat	1 TB. fresh lemon juice
1 cup cream cheese or light cream cheese, softened	$\frac{1}{2}$ tsp. dried dill
2 scallions, dark green parts removed, cut into $\frac{1}{2}$-in. pieces	$\frac{1}{4}$ tsp. black pepper
	Dash hot pepper sauce
1 TB. Madeira or other sweet dessert-style wine	Wheat crackers

1. In a food processor fitted with a metal blade, process crabmeat, cream cheese, scallions, Madeira, lemon juice, dill, pepper, and hot pepper sauce until smooth.

2. Scrape into a serving bowl, and serve with wheat crackers.

Variation: For a chunky spread, mix with a spoon instead of a food processor. For a simple but savory **Crab and Romano Spread,** combine the crabmeat with $\frac{1}{2}$ cup softened cream cheese or light cream cheese, $\frac{1}{2}$ cup mayonnaise, $\frac{1}{2}$ cup shredded Romano cheese, and 2 teaspoons fresh lemon juice. Serve with pita crisps or pieces of fresh, crusty bread.

ON THE CLOCK

For a fun alternative in serving spreads, use them as a filling in small sandwiches. For example, prepare bread or toast triangles, and use Crab Spread as filling, along with a piece of arugula or watercress. What a sandwich!

Hot Crab Dip

 Serves:
6 to 8

2 (6-oz.) cans crabmeat	2 tsp. fresh lemon juice
1 cup sour cream	¼ tsp. garlic salt
½ cup cream cheese or light cream cheese, softened	Dash hot pepper sauce
½ cup shredded Parmesan cheese	Chopped scallion (optional)
	Tortilla chips

1. In a microwave-safe bowl, combine crabmeat, sour cream, cream cheese, Parmesan cheese, lemon juice, garlic salt, and hot pepper sauce. Microwave on high for 2 minutes or until bubbling, remove from the oven, and stir.

2. Top with sliced scallion pieces (if using), and serve with tortilla chips.

Three-Layer Spicy Crab Spread

Super cook Betty Frankenfield inspired this recipe. Isn't "simple" the kind of secret this book is all about?

 Serves:
4 to 6

1 cup cream cheese or light cream cheese, softened

1 (6-oz.) can crabmeat

½ cup chili sauce

4 pieces white or wheat bread, crusts removed, cut on the diagonal to form triangles

1. Place cream cheese in a shallow serving dish, and spread to an even depth.

2. Pour crabmeat over cream cheese, and spread into a uniform depth.

3. Pour chili sauce over all, spreading again to a uniform depth.

4. Shortly before you're ready to serve, preheat the broiler.

5. Arrange bread on a baking sheet, and broil for 1 minute on each side until lightly browned.

6. Serve with a knife to spread over crisp toast.

Savory Clam Dip

 Serves:
6 to 8

1 (6.5-oz.) can clams (minced or whole), drained

1 cup sour cream

1 cup cream cheese or light cream cheese, softened

3 scallions, dark green parts removed, cut into ½-in. pieces, plus 1 chopped scallion for garnish (optional)

1 tsp. fresh lemon juice

1 tsp. steak sauce or Worcestershire sauce

Tortilla or sturdy ridged chips

1. In a food processor fitted with a metal blade, pulse clams, sour cream, cream cheese, 3 scallions, lemon juice, and steak sauce to an almost-smooth consistency.

2. Scrape dip into a serving bowl, garnish with remaining chopped scallion (if using), and serve with tortilla or sturdy ridged potato chips.

Variation: If you have the time to make this and chill it for later in the day, do so. The extra time will improve the flavors.

Bacon Clam Spread

This spread has great clam and bacon flavor paired with the sharpness of horseradish.

 Serves:
6 to 8

1 (6.5-oz.) can chopped or minced clams, drained	1 TB. prepared horseradish
½ cup sour cream	1 tsp. fresh lime juice
1 cup cream cheese or light cream cheese, softened	1 (3-oz.) jar real bacon bits, 1 TB. reserved
½ cup shredded Parmesan cheese	1 (6-oz.) pkg. pita crisps

1. In a food processor, process clams, sour cream, cream cheese, Parmesan cheese, horseradish, and lime juice.

2. Scrape spread into a serving bowl, and stir in bacon bits. Sprinkle reserved bacon bits over top, and serve surrounded by pita crisps.

 ON THE CLOCK

Canned clams come packed in flavorful juice. If you choose to use this liquid in your recipe, know that it augments flavor but also adds to the liquid. To compensate for this additional liquid, use a little extra of the more solid ingredients such as cream cheese and Parmesan cheese.

Sautéed Scallops with Warm Lemon-Dill Dipping Sauce

These buttery, rich scallops cook quickly and are a terrific candidate for a fast appetizer.

	Serves:
10	4 to 6

⅓ cup butter	½ tsp. dried dill
1 lb. fresh sea scallops	1½ TB. fresh lemon juice
2 TB. chopped fresh parsley	½ cup sour cream

1. In a large (12-inch) skillet over medium-high heat, heat butter. Add scallops, and cook for about 1 minute per side or until flesh just turns white. Remove scallops with a slotted spoon to a serving plate, and sprinkle with parsley.

2. Add dill and lemon juice to the skillet, stir, and turn off the heat. Stir in sour cream until butter, lemon juice, and dill are thoroughly mixed.

3. Scrape sauce into a serving bowl, and serve with scallops, giving guests toothpicks to pick up scallops and dip them in dipping sauce.

ON THE CLOCK

Cook scallops just until they turn white in the center. Scallops are perfect for appetizers because they cook so quickly; if they cook too long, they get tough. Nobody wants an ornery scallop.

Scallops and Bacon

Crisp bacon and creamy scallops are a dream combination.

	Serves:
	6

1 lb. fresh sea scallops

½ lb. bacon slices, cut into 1×4-in. pieces

1. Preheat the broiler.
2. Wrap each scallop in 1 piece bacon, and fasten with a toothpick. Place bacon-wrapped scallops on a baking sheet, and broil for 2 minutes per side or until bacon begins to crisp and scallops are cooked.
3. Serve with small plates and plenty of napkins!

Veggie Appetizers

In This Chapter

- Naturally flavorful veggie hors d'oeuvres
- Terrific tomato appetizers
- Crisp and crunchy veggie snacks
- Fresh-from-the-garden appetizers

From artichokes to zucchini, this chapter is all about vegetables.

A wealth of flavor can be found in the garden. From sweet summer tomatoes, still warm from the sun, to crisp carrots and cool cucumbers, vegetables offer a range of flavors and textures that work magic even without much preparation effort from you. Dishes that make use of fresh vegetables offer several benefits, including terrific taste with a minimum of preparation, high nutrition, and that tantalizing fresh appearance.

The recipes in this chapter explore myriad ways to present vegetables raw, crunchy, and tasty, and others that benefit from quick cooking.

Fast Spinach and Artichoke Dip

 Serves:
6 to 8

2 cups fresh baby spinach leaves

1 (14-oz.) can artichokes, drained

1 cup shredded Parmesan cheese

½ cup light cream cheese, softened

½ cup low-fat mayonnaise

½ cup nonfat plain yogurt

¼ cup shredded mozzarella cheese

½ tsp. chopped garlic

Dash hot pepper sauce

Tortilla chips or wheat crackers

1. In a food processor fitted with a metal blade, process spinach, artichokes, Parmesan cheese, cream cheese, mayonnaise, yogurt, mozzarella cheese, garlic, and hot pepper sauce until thoroughly combined but still very chunky.

2. Scrape mixture into a microwave-safe serving dish, and microwave on high for 2 minutes or until bubbling.

3. Stir and serve with tortilla chips or wheat crackers.

 ON THE CLOCK

Artichokes are available fresh, frozen, and preserved in cans or jars.

Artichoke Hearts with Fried Sage and Garlic

 Serves:
4

3 TB. olive oil

2 tsp. chopped garlic

4 fresh sage leaves or ½ tsp. dried sage

1 (12-oz.) pkg. frozen artichoke hearts, thawed

¼ cup shredded Parmesan cheese

Kosher salt

1. In a 10- to 12-inch skillet over medium-high heat, heat olive oil. Add garlic and sage, and cook for 3 minutes or until garlic sizzles. Using a spatula or fork, carefully remove sage leaves to a paper towel–lined plate. If you used dried sage, leave it in the skillet to mix with next ingredients.

2. Add artichoke hearts, cover, and cook for 3 minutes.

3. Transfer artichoke hearts to a serving platter, sprinkle each with pinch Parmesan cheese and kosher salt. If you used fresh sage leaves, place them in an X in the middle of your serving platter as a whimsical garnish. Serve with toothpicks.

Grilled Artichokes with Chevre Caps

Although a bit messy, these taste so good they're worth the napkins.

10	Serves: 4

3 TB. olive oil

1 TB. chopped garlic

$\frac{1}{2}$ tsp. dried oregano

1 (9-oz.) pkg. frozen artichoke hearts, thawed

1 (8-oz.) pkg. fresh chevre (goat's milk cheese)

1. In a 12-inch skillet over medium heat, heat olive oil, garlic, and oregano. Add artichoke hearts, and sauté, stirring occasionally, for about 2 minutes per side.

2. Transfer artichokes to a serving plate, reserving cooking liquid. Top each artichoke heart with about 2 teaspoons chevre. Drizzle reserved garlic and oil over top, and serve with toothpicks.

Mushroom Caps with Sun-Dried Tomato–Chevre Spread

Fresh white mushroom caps are the key to that crisp mushroom texture.

 Serves:
4 to 6

1 (8-oz.) pkg. fresh chevre, softened

½ cup oil-packed sun-dried tomatoes, drained and finely chopped

½ tsp. garlic salt

1 (8-oz.) pkg. white button mushrooms, stems removed

2 TB. chopped fresh chives

1. In a large bowl, combine chevre, sun-dried tomatoes, and garlic salt.

2. Spoon about 1 tablespoon chevre mixture into each mushroom cap, and arrange caps cheese side up on a platter.

3. Sprinkle with chives, and serve.

Portobello-Garlic Crostini

 Serves:
4 to 6

5 slices white or wheat sandwich bread, crusts removed, cut into 4 triangles per slice

2 or 3 TB. olive oil

1 tsp. crushed garlic

1 (6-oz.) pkg. sliced portobello mushrooms, cut into 1-in. pieces

20 fresh baby spinach leaves

2 TB. shredded Parmesan cheese

Kosher salt

1. Preheat the broiler.

2. Arrange bread on a baking sheet in a single layer, and broil for about 1 minute per side or until lightly browned.

3. Meanwhile, in a 10-inch skillet over medium heat, heat olive oil and garlic. Add portobellos, and sauté, shaking the pan frequently, for about 2 minutes.

4. Arrange toast triangles on a serving platter, and place 1 spinach leaf and mushroom piece on each. Arrange crostini on a serving plate, sprinkle with a pinch of Parmesan cheese and kosher salt, and serve.

Variation: For added zing, drizzle with balsamic vinegar and/or use arugula in place of spinach.

Roasted Red Pepper, Chevre, and Spinach Bites

 Serves:
6 to 8

About 24 fresh baby spinach leaves, each about 2½×1½ in.

6 oz. fresh chevre

¾ cup roasted red peppers, drained and cut into ¼×1½-in. strips

1 tsp. kosher salt

1. In the middle of each spinach leaf, add about 1½ teaspoons chevre and 1 strip roasted red pepper. Roll spinach leaves around filling, and fasten with toothpicks.

2. Arrange spinach bites on a serving platter, sprinkle with kosher salt, and serve.

 ON THE CLOCK

If you find large red, yellow, or green (or all three!) fresh sweet peppers at the store, cut them in half lengthwise, clean out the ribs and seeds, and place the halves on a platter. Fill each one with your assembled Roasted Red Pepper, Chevre, and Spinach Bites, surrounding the pepper halves with the rest.

Mozzarella, Almond, and Spinach Wraps

 Serves:
4 to 6

4 (8-in.) whole-wheat or white flour tortillas	2 cups shredded mozzarella cheese
2 cups baby spinach leaves	$\frac{1}{2}$ cup plus 1 TB. sliced almonds
	1 cup sour cream

1. Place 1 tortilla on a work surface. Arrange a line of spinach leaves about 1 inch in from tortilla side closest to you. Top with $\frac{1}{2}$ cup mozzarella cheese and 2 tablespoons almonds. Starting from the side closest to you, roll tortilla over spinach and cheese to form a cylinder. If necessary, fasten with a toothpick.

2. Repeat with remaining tortillas and filling, place rolls on a microwave-safe plate, and heat for 1 minute or until cheese begins to melt.

3. Spoon sour cream into a small bowl, sprinkle remaining 1 tablespoon almonds on top, and place the bowl in the center of a serving platter.

4. Cut tortillas in half, and arrange on the platter around sour cream like the spokes on a wheel, and serve.

Sun-Dried Tomato Spread

This spread is creamy, hearty, and flavorful.

 Serves:
4 to 6

1 (15-oz.) can chickpeas, drained	$\frac{1}{4}$ cup olive oil, plus more as needed
1 cup oil-packed sun-dried tomatoes, oil reserved	$\frac{1}{2}$ tsp. salt
$\frac{3}{4}$ cup plain nonfat yogurt	Baked tortilla chips

1. In a blender or food processor fitted with a metal blade, process chickpeas, sun-dried tomatoes, yogurt, olive oil, and salt until spread achieves the consistency of a thick paste. If necessary, add a little more olive oil to achieve the right consistency.

2. Scrape spread into a serving bowl, and serve with baked tortilla chips.

Variation: If you want, you can add some of the oil from the sun-dried tomatoes in place of the olive oil.

Summer Tomato Platter

 Serves:
4

2 large fresh tomatoes, sliced about ½ in. thick

1 handful fresh basil leaves

½ lb. fresh mozzarella cheese (comes in brine), sliced in ¼-in. medallions

Good-quality extra-virgin olive oil

Kosher salt

1. Arrange tomato slices in a single layer on a large platter.

2. Place 1 basil leaf on each tomato slice, and top with 1 slice mozzarella cheese.

3. Drizzle platter with extra-virgin olive oil, sprinkle with kosher salt, and serve.

 MINUTE MORSEL

This is even better—and a meal in itself—with fresh Italian bread. Use it to mop up extra juice on the platter.

Sweet Pepper and Tomato Bites

This treat gives a flavor burst from sweet peppers and tomatoes. Grape tomatoes are easier to work with in this colorful mélange, but chunks of larger tomatoes can be used.

 Serves:
6 to 8

½ pt. (about 12) grape tomatoes, halved

2 large yellow sweet peppers, ribs and seeds removed, and cut into ¾-in. squares

¼ cup low-fat or light Italian dressing

1 TB. chopped fresh basil leaves or 1 tsp. dried

Salt

1. Slide each grape tomato half onto a toothpick, and follow with 1 yellow sweet pepper square.

2. Arrange bites on a platter, drizzle with Italian dressing, sprinkle with basil and salt, and serve.

 ON THE CLOCK

Tomato-reliant recipes are best for the late summer, when fresh tomatoes are available in spades. These tomatoes bring sweet, juicy flavor infinitely better than any others imported from far away.

Bacon and Chevre-Stuffed Tomatoes

Make these in minutes; they disappear in seconds.

 Serves:
4 to 6

4 oz. fresh chevre, softened

3 TB. real bacon bits

¼ tsp. salt

¼ tsp. black pepper

1 pt. (about 24) grape or cherry tomatoes, halved

1. In a small bowl, combine chevre, bacon bits, salt, and pepper.

2. Spread about 1 teaspoon chevre mixture on cut side of 1 grape tomato, and top with another tomato half. Continue with remaining tomato halves.

3. Arrange on a platter, and serve.

Cucumber-Dill Dip

Refreshing and cool, this dip is perfect for summer parties.

 **10**	**Serves:** 6 to 8

½ English-style cucumber
½ cup plain yogurt
½ cup light cream cheese, softened
2 tsp. chopped garlic
1½ tsp. dried dill

1 tsp. fresh lemon juice
Double dash hot pepper sauce
Baby carrots, zucchini slices, cucumber strips, celery sticks, or tortilla chips

1. In a food processor fitted with a shredding attachment, shred cucumber. (You can also use a hand grater.)

2. In a serving bowl, combine cucumber, yogurt, cream cheese, garlic, dill, lemon juice, and hot pepper sauce.

3. Surround bowl with baby carrots, zucchini slices, cucumber strips, celery sticks, or tortilla chips, and serve.

 TIME WASTER

When it comes to the hot pepper sauce, start with one dash first. Then, if the dip needs more, add the second dash. You won't be able to remove that extra dash after the fact.

Crisp Snow Peas with Dill Dip

Crunchy and cool, this is the ideal dish to enjoy in the late spring when the peas are in season.

| (10) | **Serves:** |
| | 4 to 6 |

¾ cup low-fat sour cream

½ cup low-fat mayonnaise

3 scallions, dark green leaves removed, and finely chopped

1 tsp. dried dill

1 tsp. fresh lemon juice

½ tsp. salt

1 lb. fresh snow peas, washed and stems removed

1. In a serving bowl, combine sour cream, mayonnaise, scallions, dill, lemon juice, and salt. If possible, chill dip for several hours to allow the flavors to meld.

2. Serve surrounded by snow peas as dippers.

 TIME WASTER

This is a terrific recipe for in-season, crisp, fresh snow peas. When they're out of season, however, consider another crisp vegetable such as snap beans, blanched asparagus, or baby carrots. Droopy pea pods just don't set the stage for a tasty appetizer.

Fried Parmesan Zucchini

These delicious morsels are cooked just enough to make the outside crisp while keeping the squash crunchy inside.

 10

Serves:
4 to 6

¼ cup olive oil

½ cup breadcrumbs

½ cup shredded Parmesan cheese

¼ tsp. ground red pepper

1 egg

2 small (each about 1 in. in diameter and 6 inches long) zucchini, ends removed, sliced into ¼-in.-thick medallions

Salt

Black pepper

1. In a 10-inch skillet over medium heat, heat olive oil.

2. Meanwhile, in a small bowl, combine breadcrumbs, Parmesan cheese, and red pepper.

3. In a separate small bowl, beat egg. Set next to the bowl containing Parmesan-breadcrumb mixture.

4. Using a fork, dip each zucchini piece in egg, turn to coat, and dip in Parmesan-breadcrumb mix, and turn to coat. Carefully place coated zucchini into the skillet, being careful not to spatter hot oil. Cook for about 1 minute per side, remove to a serving plate, and season with salt and pepper.

5. Serve with toothpicks.

Grilled Zucchini

A summertime favorite with a glass of dry white wine, this is also tasty as a side dish.

	Serves:
10	4 to 6

3 small zucchini, sliced lengthwise into $\frac{1}{4} \times \frac{1}{2}$-in. pieces

$\frac{1}{3}$ cup olive oil

2 tsp. chopped garlic

2 tsp. dried basil

Salt

Black pepper

1. Heat the grill.

2. Put zucchini slices in a small container with a lid (or a zipper-lock plastic bag).

3. In a small bowl, combine olive oil and garlic, and pour over zucchini. Seal zucchini container securely, and shake to coat.

4. Sprinkle with basil, salt, and pepper.

5. Place zucchini pieces on the grill at right angles to the grill grates to minimize the risk of a piece slipping through. Cook for 2 minutes per side, brush with remaining oil mixture, and serve.

TIME WASTER

When grilling any vegetables, be sure you've applied plenty of oil or oil-based marinade (olive oil and so on) and watch grilling vegetables closely to be sure they don't dry out.

Tofu Salad Spread

Thanks to Marci Goldberg, a good friend and a terrific cook, for this tasty addition.

10	**Serves:** 4 to 6

1 (15-oz.) pkg. firm *tofu,* drained	1 TB. miso
½ cup light mayonnaise	Pita wedges
2 large carrots, peeled and shredded	

1. To get as much liquid as possible out of tofu (and avoid a soupy consistency), slice tofu into thick slices, place on several thicknesses of paper towels, cover with more paper towels, and press.

2. In a serving bowl, combine tofu, mayonnaise, carrots, and miso.

3. Serve with pita wedges.

DEFINITION

Tofu is a cheeselike substance made from soybeans and soy milk. Flavorful and nutritious, tofu is an important component of foods across the globe, especially those from the Far East.

Balsamic-Pesto Spread

(10)	**Serves:** 4 to 6

1 cup cottage cheese

2 or 3 TB. prepared pesto

1 TB. balsamic vinegar

Crisp wheat crackers

1. In a serving bowl, combine cottage cheese, pesto, and balsamic vinegar.

2. Serve surrounded with crisp wheat crackers.

Variation: Instead of cottage cheese, use $\frac{1}{2}$ cup cream cheese and $\frac{1}{2}$ cup sour cream.

Curried Pineapple Bites

These bites are spicy and sweet.

(10)	**Serves:** 4 to 6

$\frac{1}{4}$ cup honey

1 TB. sesame oil

$\frac{1}{2}$ tsp. curry powder

$\frac{1}{4}$ cup coconut flakes

2 (8-oz.) cans pineapple chunks, drained

1. In a small bowl, combine honey, sesame oil, and curry powder.

2. Spread coconut flakes on a small plate.

3. Insert a toothpick into each pineapple chunk, dip into honey-curry mixture, and dredge in coconut flakes to coat.

4. Arrange pineapple chunks on a platter with their toothpicks intact, and serve.

Variation: If you really like curry flavor, use more than the $\frac{1}{2}$ teaspoon called for.

Cheese- and Bread-Based Bites

In This Chapter

- Classic cheese appetizers
- Pairing cheese with fruits, nuts, and other flavors
- Bread soul mates
- Great grain-based appetizers

From one everyday ingredient—milk—comes something new, different, and exciting: cheese. Cheese comes in hundreds of varieties and textures, each representative of its region of origin, and each offering a tremendous opportunity to explore and learn. Pairing your favorite cheeses with fruits, nuts, bread, and other ingredients gives you a new perspective on your old friends. The quick cheese-based hors d'oeuvres in this chapter take advantage of the familiar rich, creamy texture of cheese but take enjoyment to whole new levels.

And then there's bread. I'm not talking about the mass-market sliced stuff, but hearty bread baked in long loaves you cut into thick, crusty slices or wedges. The crunchy, savory, bread-based canapés and crostini in this chapter are classy and irresistible. Although the base is bread, the toppings are limited only by your imagination. Are there slightly unusual toppings that will add fun and interest? Try them out!

Baby Brie and Apples

This is a classic. If the sliced apples will be out for long, rub them with the cut side of a lemon half to delay browning.

 Serves:
8 to 10

1 (13-oz.) wheel baby Brie, at room temperature

4 crisp Granny Smith apples (or another tart, crisp variety), cored and each cut into 8 to 10 slices

1. Unwrap Brie and place it at the center of a serving platter.
2. Surround with freshly sliced apples, and serve with a knife so guests can spread cheese on each slice.

Variation: Fresh, crisp pear slices or wheat crackers are also tasty serve-withs.

 MINUTE MORSEL

Soft cheeses, like Brie, come to a wonderful spreadable consistency and a richer mouthfeel when served at room temperature. Just take the cheese out of the fridge an hour or so before you plan to serve it. You can also serve Brie warm by heating it in a warm oven for a few minutes or in the microwave for about 10 seconds. Be very careful not to overheat, or you'll end up with hot liquid Brie.

Herbed Cheese Spread

This classic cheese spread is simple to make and tasty as a spread for appetizers or on sandwiches.

 Serves:
4 to 6

8 oz. cream cheese, softened

$\frac{1}{2}$ tsp. garlic salt

$\frac{1}{2}$ tsp. dried dill

$1\frac{1}{2}$ tsp. Italian seasoning

$\frac{1}{4}$ tsp. black pepper

Dash hot pepper sauce

Crisp pita crackers or melba toasts

1. In a serving bowl, combine cream cheese, garlic salt, dill, Italian seasoning, pepper, and hot pepper sauce. If possible, chill for several hours to allow the flavors to meld.

2. Serve with crisp pita crackers or melba toasts.

Hard Cheese and Chutney

 Serves:
6 to 8

¾ lb. aged flavorful hard cheese, such as Asiago, aged gouda, or sharp cheddar

1 (7- to 9-oz.) pkg. wheat crackers
1 (9-oz.) jar Major Grey's *Chutney*

1. Arrange cheese and wheat crackers on a cutting board with a sharp cheese knife.

2. Scoop Major Grey's Chutney into a serving bowl.

3. Prepare several wheat crackers topped with cheese and a scant spoonful of Major Grey's Chutney to get people used to the idea.

Variation: Try your favorite marmalade in place of chutney.

DEFINITION

Usually the consistency of relish, **chutney** is a combination of sweetened fruits and spices that originated on the Indian subcontinent. It's somewhat unusual in this country but pairs beautifully with many cheeses. You'll find it in most large grocery stores.

Olive and Cheese Ball

 Serves:
4 to 6

8 oz. cream cheese, softened

1 cup crumbled blue cheese

1 cup pitted black olives

3 scallions, dark green leaves removed, and chopped coarsely

1 TB. fresh lemon juice

¼ tsp. black pepper

Parsley

Crisp wheat crackers

1. In a food processor, place cream cheese, blue cheese, black olives, scallions, lemon juice, and pepper, and process until just coarsely blended.

2. Scrape out cheese, and form into a ball. Chill to set.

3. Garnish with parsley, and serve with crisp wheat crackers and a sturdy spreading knife.

 ON THE CLOCK

Although you can buy lemon and lime juice bottled, there's just no flavor comparison with fresh, and not much time saved. When it comes to appetizers, where flavor and quality is critical, that freshness is essential. Do a taste test, and you'll see what I mean.

Cream Cheese and Prosciutto

This is easy and classy. The saltiness of the cured ham is a nice contrast to the cream cheese.

 Serves:
6 to 8

8 slices white or wheat bread, crusts removed, cut into 4 triangles per slice

1 cup cream cheese or light cream cheese, softened

1 cup diced prosciutto

2 TB. finely chopped fresh parsley

1. Preheat the broiler.

2. Arrange bread slices in a single layer on a baking sheet, and broil for about 1 minute on each side or until lightly browned.

3. Meanwhile, in a medium bowl, combine cream cheese and prosciutto.

4. Remove toast points from the broiler. Spread about 1 tablespoon cream cheese–prosciutto mixture on each, and arrange on a serving tray.

5. Sprinkle 1 pinch parsley on each, and serve.

Variation: Use diced ham or other meat in place of the prosciutto. Or even thin slices of roast beef.

 ON THE CLOCK

To save time, take a close look at your grocery store shelves. Some stores sell pro-sciutto already diced, and—*shh*—it's usually cheaper than the full-size version.

Chevre and Cherry Tomatoes

You'll love the beautiful colors and textures of this cheese and tomato appetizer.

	Serves:
	6 to 8

8 slices white or whole-wheat bread, crusts removed, cut into 4 triangles per slice	½ pt. (about 12) cherry tomatoes, halved
1 cup fresh chevre (goat's milk cheese)	2 TB. finely chopped fresh chives

1. Preheat the broiler.

2. Arrange bread in a single layer on a baking sheet, and broil for about 1 minute on each side until lightly browned.

3. Remove the baking sheet from the oven, and arrange toast points on a work surface. Spread about 2 teaspoons chevre on each, and top each with 1 cherry tomato half, cut side down.

4. Arrange on a serving tray, sprinkle 1 pinch chives on each, and serve.

Mozzarella-Stuffed Plum Tomatoes

This is a recommendation from Italo, my barber and Italian food consultant.

	Serves:
	6

12 fresh small mozzarella balls, drained

3 TB. extra-virgin olive oil

1 TB. chopped fresh basil or 1 tsp. dried basil

6 ripe plum tomatoes, sliced in half lengthwise, seeds removed

½ tsp. kosher salt

1. In a medium bowl, drizzle mozzarella balls with extra-virgin olive oil, sprinkle with basil, and gently turn to coat.

2. Arrange tomatoes in a single layer on a serving platter, hollow side up, and place 1 mozzarella ball into each tomato, reserving oil used from marinating cheese.

3. Drizzle platter with reserved oil, sprinkle with kosher salt, and serve.

TIME WASTER

Some appetizers are good candidates for advance preparation and refrigeration, but dishes with fresh tomatoes are not among them. Refrigeration causes tomatoes to lose their fresh flavor and texture.

Quick Grilled Chevre on Toast Points

 Serves:
4

8 slices white or whole-wheat
bread, crusts removed, cut into
4 triangles per slice

1 cup fresh chevre
¼ tsp. garlic salt
¼ tsp. paprika

1. Preheat the broiler.

2. Arrange bread on a baking sheet, and broil for about 1 minute on each side until lightly browned. Remove from the oven.

3. Spread toast points with about 2 teaspoons chevre each, sprinkle with garlic salt and paprika, and broil for 1 more minute or until chevre begins to melt and bubble.

4. Arrange on a serving tray, and serve.

Crostini with Apple and Fontina

The simple combination of apple with delicious cheese and crisp toast makes for a tasty starter.

 Serves:
4 to 6

6 slices white or whole-wheat
sandwich bread, crusts
removed, cut on the diagonal to
form triangles
3 Granny Smith or similarly tart
apples

½ lb. Italian Fontina d'Aosta
cheese, sliced into ¼-in.-thick
pieces, slightly smaller than
bread slices

1. Preheat the broiler.

2. Arrange bread in a single layer on a baking sheet, and broil for 1 minute on each side or until lightly browned. Remove from the oven.

3. Cut 2 apples lengthwise into 8 to 10 slices each, removing core and seeds. Place 1 piece Italian Fontina d'Aosta cheese and 1 slice apple on each toast triangle.

4. Arrange toasts on a platter surrounding remaining whole apple to set the mood, and serve.

DEFINITION

Crostini is toasted bread spread with pastes traditionally made of chicken liver, olives, or artichokes. Modern chefs have adapted crostini to hold all kinds of flavorful toppings.

Toasted Grilled Pita with Parmesan

These are a slightly softer cousin of the popular crisps you can buy at the grocery store, but, of course, they're much better served hot from the oven.

10	**Serves:** 4

2 *pita breads,* sliced into 8 wedges each

2 TB. olive oil

2 TB. shredded Parmesan cheese

Coarse salt

Sprig fresh parsley (optional)

1. Preheat the broiler.

2. Arrange pita wedges in a single layer on a baking sheet, drizzle with olive oil, and sprinkle 1 pinch Parmesan cheese on each piece. Broil for about 1 minute or until pita begins to brown and crisp.

3. Remove from the broiler and arrange on a serving platter, season with coarse salt, place parsley sprig (if using) in the center of the platter, and serve.

DEFINITION

Pita bread, also known as Syrian bread, is a flat, hollow wheat bread from the Middle East that can be used for sandwiches or sliced pizza style. Pita bread is terrific soft with dips and baked or broiled as a vehicle for other ingredients.

Garlic-Basil Toasts with Dipping Sauce

I like to use crusty baguette slices cut in half for these toasts. The pointed end is perfect for dipping, and the crust holds up to the sauce.

 10   **Serves:**
4 to 6

⅓ cup olive oil

1 TB. chopped garlic

1 TB. dried basil

1 baguette or slender loaf of crusty bread, sliced crosswise into ½-in. rounds, each piece then cut in half

1½ cups pizza sauce

1 TB. shredded Parmesan cheese (optional)

1. Preheat the broiler.

2. In a small bowl, combine olive oil, garlic, and basil. Brush each piece of bread on both sides with olive oil mixture, and arrange in a single layer on a baking sheet. Broil for 1 minute on each side or until lightly browned.

3. Pour pizza sauce in a small microwave-safe serving bowl, and heat for about 1 minute or until very warm but not boiling, stirring to ensure even temperature.

4. Sprinkle Parmesan cheese (if using) over sauce, place the bowl in the center of a serving platter, and surround with toasted bread arranged pointing outward like spokes on a wheel.

Variation: Instead of garlic and basil, try this with 2 tablespoons prepared pesto.

 TIME WASTER

Many high-quality pasta sauces will also work as a dipping sauce. Feel free to experiment, but avoid those prepared sauces with a lot of added sugar. (Sugar will be near the top on the ingredient list.) These overly sweet sauces could strike an incongruous note in your savory "starter symphony."

Parmigiano and Roasted Piquillo Pepper Canapés

 Serves:
6

1 baguette or long loaf of bread, sliced into $\frac{1}{2}$-in.-thick pieces	6 oz. Parmigiano-Reggiano, cut into flat 1×2×$\frac{1}{4}$-in. pieces
1 (12-oz.) jar roasted piquillo or red peppers, drained and cut into 1×2-in. pieces	$\frac{1}{4}$ cup chopped fresh chives for garnish (optional)

1. Preheat the broiler.

2. Place bread slices in a single layer on a baking sheet, and broil for about 1 minute on each side or until lightly browned.

3. Remove from the oven, and top each piece of toast with 1 piece roasted piquillo pepper and 1 piece Parmigiano-Reggiano. Return to the oven, and broil for about 1 more minute.

4. Remove from the broiler, arrange toasts on a serving platter, top with a sprinkling of chives (if using), and serve.

 TIME WASTER

The broiler is an invaluable tool for the cook in a hurry, but watch your food carefully. Bite-size servings can burn in a matter of seconds.

BBQ Canapés

 Serves:
4 to 6

8 slices white or whole-wheat
   bread, crusts removed, cut into
   4 triangles per slice
¼ cup barbecue sauce

1 cup cream cheese or light cream
   cheese, softened
2 TB. finely chopped fresh chives

1. Preheat the broiler.

2. Arrange bread in a single layer on a baking sheet, and broil for about 1 minute
on each side until lightly browned.

3. Meanwhile, in a small bowl, combine barbecue sauce and cream cheese.

4. Remove the baking sheet from the oven, and arrange toast points on a work
surface. Spread about 2 teaspoons cream cheese mixture on each. Top each with
1 pinch chives, arrange on a serving tray, and serve.

Sun-Dried Tomato Canapés

 Serves:
4

1 baguette or long loaf of bread,
   sliced into ½-in.-thick pieces
2 tsp. crushed garlic
½ cup olive oil
¾ tsp. salt

1 (8-oz.) jar oil-packed sun-dried
   tomatoes, drained and chopped
1 cup shredded mozzarella cheese

1. Preheat the broiler.

2. Arrange bread slices in a single layer on a baking tray.

3. In a small bowl, combine garlic, olive oil, and salt, and brush on each piece of
bread. Broil bread for 2 minutes or until just barely beginning to brown. Turn over
bread, brush again with olive oil mixture, and broil until just turning light brown.

4. Remove tray from oven, distribute sun-dried tomato pieces among slices of bread, and top each piece of bread with 1 pinch mozzarella cheese.

5. Broil for 1 more minute or until cheese is melted. Serve warm *canapés* to guests, and receive warm appreciation.

> **DEFINITION**
>
> **Canapés** are hors d'oeuvres made up of small pieces of bread topped with your favorite ingredients—commonly cheese, vegetables, and herbs—that sometimes are broiled or toasted, sometimes not.

Bagel-Crisp Canapés

 10

Serves:
4

1 (6-oz.) pkg. garlic or herb bagel crisps	3 scallions, thinly sliced
1 (6- to 8-oz.) wedge port, salut, or Brie cheese, sliced into thin pieces slightly smaller than size of bagel crisps	$\frac{1}{2}$ tsp. paprika

1. Preheat the broiler.

2. Arrange bagel crisps in a single layer on a baking sheet. Top each with 1 slice wedge port cheese and 1 pinch scallions. Broil for 1 minute or until cheese begins to melt.

3. Arrange canapés on a serving platter, sprinkle with paprika, and serve.

Variation: Use pita crisps or *melba toast* as the vehicle.

> **DEFINITION**
>
> **Melba toasts** are small pieces of crisp bread available in the cracker section of the grocery store. Avoid the seasoned versions, though, to keep the focus on *your* ingredients.

Around-the-World Appetizers

In This Chapter

- Sunny Southwest-inspired apps
- Fruit and meat matches
- Olive, fig, and fresh fruit apps
- Asian-inspired bites
- Exciting Latin American combos

When it comes to appetizers, we owe a huge flavor debt to the cuisines of the world. Whether you're in the mood for something from the Southwest, a bite inspired by Mediterranean breezes, a little something French, a taste of the Italian countryside, a snack with a Far East influence, or a spicy Indian treat, you've come to the right chapter.

The appetizers in this chapter take your taste buds on a whirlwind world tour—and you don't even have to leave your kitchen!

Four-Layer Bean Dip

 Serves:
10 to 12

1 (15-oz.) can plain refried beans

1 (1.25-oz.) pkg. taco seasoning mix

1 (16-oz.) pkg. guacamole

2 cups sour cream

1 cup tomato salsa

2 cups shredded Mexican-style cheese

Tortilla chips

1. In a medium bowl, combine refried beans and taco seasoning mix in a bowl. Spread mixture evenly over the bottom of a pie plate or similar-size serving dish.

2. Spread guacamole over refried beans.

3. In a medium bowl, combine sour cream and salsa. Spread over guacamole.

4. Sprinkle Mexican-style cheese over sour cream, and serve with tortilla chips.

Variation: For a low-fat version, use fat-free refried beans made without lard.

Mexican Chili Dip

 Serves:
6

1 cup cream cheese, softened

1 cup shredded Mexican-style or Monterey Jack cheese

$\frac{1}{2}$ cup chunky medium salsa

1 TB. fresh lime juice

1 TB. *chili powder*

1 tsp. kosher salt

Dash hot pepper sauce

Tortilla chips

1. In a microwave-safe bowl, combine cream cheese, Mexican-style cheese, salsa, lime juice, chili powder, kosher salt, and hot pepper sauce. Microwave for 2 minutes or until warm.

2. Stir and serve with tortilla chips.

Variation: To vary the intensity of the heat in this dip, increase or reduce the amount of chili powder and hot sauce.

> **DEFINITION**
>
> **Chili powder** is a seasoning blend that includes chili peppers, cumin, oregano, and, in some cases, garlic. Proportions vary among different versions, but they all offer a warm, rich flavor that offers, at least in the imagination, a culinary trip south of the border.

Chili, Chicken, and Lime Quesadillas with Sour Cream

	Serves:
10	6 to 8

3 TB. olive oil	½ lb. thin slices deli chicken or ⅔ (12-oz.) can chicken, drained
6 (6-in.) soft white or whole-wheat flour tortillas	1 TB. fresh lime juice
2 cups shredded Monterey Jack or Mexican-style cheese	½ tsp. chili powder
	Sour cream
	Chopped fresh chives

1. In a 10-inch skillet over medium-high heat, heat olive oil. Working quickly, set 1 tortilla in the skillet, top with about ⅓ cup Monterey Jack cheese, ⅓ of chicken, and another ⅓ cup cheese. Drizzle with 1 teaspoon lime juice, sprinkle with 1 pinch chili powder, and top with another tortilla. Cook for about 1 minute, flip over with a spatula, and cook for 30 more seconds or so until cheese inside is melted sufficiently to bind quesadilla together.

2. Remove quesadilla to a serving plate, slice pie-style into 6 or 8 wedges, and keep warm. Repeat with remaining tortillas and filling ingredients.

3. Serve with sour cream and a spoon for spreading. A sprinkling of chopped fresh chives completes the dish.

 ON THE CLOCK

I've suggested the pan-frying method for quesadillas, but broiling is also an option. Simply brush a bit of oil (or use butter or margarine) on each side of the tortilla and broil on the high rack for about 1 minute per side.

Pineapple, Ham, and Mozzarella Quesadillas

 Serves:
6 to 8

3 TB. olive oil	½ lb. thin slices deli ham
6 (6-in.) soft white or whole-wheat flour tortillas	1 (8-oz.) can crushed pineapple, drained
2 cups shredded mozzarella cheese	½ tsp. salt

1. In a 10-inch skillet over medium-high heat, heat olive oil. Working quickly, set 1 tortilla in the skillet, top with about ⅓ cup mozzarella cheese, ⅓ of ham, ⅓ crushed pineapple, and another ⅓ cup cheese. Sprinkle with 1 pinch salt, and top with another tortilla. Cook for about 1 minute, flip over with a spatula, and cook for another 30 seconds or so until cheese inside is melted sufficiently to bind quesadilla together.

2. Remove to a serving plate, slice pie-style into 6 or 8 wedges, and keep warm. Repeat with remaining tortillas and filling ingredients, and serve.

Bacon and Swiss Tostada

 Serves:
4 to 6

2 (12-in.) soft white or whole-wheat flour tortillas	¼ cup real bacon bits
1 (8-oz.) pkg. shredded Swiss cheese	

1. Preheat the broiler.

2. Place tortillas on a baking sheet, and sprinkle with ½ of Swiss cheese and ½ of bacon bits. Broil for 2 minutes or until cheese is melted and starting to bubble.

3. Slice on a cutting board, and serve pizza style.

Tostada with Fresh Mozzarella and Roasted Peppers

 Serves:
4 to 6

2 (12-in.) spinach tortillas	8 pitted kalamata olives, sliced in half lengthwise
8 fresh mozzarella balls (in brine), drained and cut in half	3 TB. shredded Parmesan cheese
16 roasted red pepper pieces, about 1 in. square	1 TB. olive oil
	Kosher salt

1. Preheat the broiler.

2. Place tortillas on a baking sheet. Arrange 8 mozzarella ball halves equally spaced around the perimeter of each tortilla. Then, working inward from mozzarella halves, place pieces of roasted red pepper and kalamata olive so the result resembles spokes in a wheel.

3. Sprinkle each tortilla with Parmesan cheese, dress with a swirl of olive oil, and broil for about 2 minutes or until tortilla begins to crisp.

4. Sprinkle with kosher salt. Slice, pizza style, making your cuts in between mozzarella/pepper/olive rows. Separate the pieces to form a sort of decorative wreath, and serve.

Variation: Use oil-packed, sun-dried tomato pieces in place of roasted pepper, and dress with oil from the tomatoes.

Cheese, Garlic, and Spinach Wraps

10   **Serves:**
4 to 6

4 (8-in.) soft white or whole-wheat flour tortillas	$\frac{1}{2}$ tsp. garlic salt
2 cups baby spinach leaves	1 cup sour cream
2 cups shredded Monterey Jack or Mexican-style cheese	

1. Place 1 tortilla on a work surface. Arrange spinach leaves in a line about 1 inch in from the side closest to you. Top with $\frac{1}{2}$ cup shredded Monterey Jack cheese and 1 pinch garlic salt. Starting from the side closest to filling, roll tortilla into a cylinder. If necessary, hold it in place with a toothpick. Repeat with other tortillas and filling ingredients.

2. Place wraps on a microwave-safe plate, and heat for 1 minute or until cheese begins to melt.

3. Cut each wrap in half, and arrange pieces on a serving plate like the spokes on a wheel, surrounding a bowl of sour cream for dipping, and serve.

Variation: Instead of cheese, garlic, and spinach, these wraps are also tasty with shrimp and rosemary, chili powder and lime, olives and feta cheese, sautéed onions and mozzarella cheese, or bean sprouts and mozzarella cheese.

Quick-Grilled Shrimp with Chili and Lime

Succulent shrimp is served with a hint of spice and the fresh, cool flavor of lime.

 10   **Serves:**
4 to 6

½ lb. (31 to 40 count, about 18) cooked shrimp, peeled, deveined, and tail removed

3 TB. fresh lime juice

1 tsp. chili powder

2 TB. olive oil

1 tsp. chopped garlic

1. Place shrimp in a large bowl, pour in 2 tablespoons lime juice, and toss to coat. Sprinkle shrimp with chili powder and toss again.

2. In a 12-inch skillet over medium-high heat, heat olive oil and garlic. Add shrimp, and sauté for 2 minutes, turning once.

3. Remove warm shrimp to a serving plate, insert a toothpick in each, *drizzle* with remaining 1 tablespoon lime juice, and serve.

 DEFINITION

To **drizzle** is to lightly sprinkle drops of a liquid over food. Drizzling is often the finishing touch to a dish.

Magic Garlic Mayonnaise Aioli

Traditionally a sauce for main courses, aioli can also be used as a dip or garnish.

 10   **Serves:**
4 to 6

1 cup mayonnaise

1 TB. chopped garlic

1 TB. high-quality olive oil

2 tsp. fresh lemon juice

Toast points or sliced mushrooms

1. In a serving bowl, combine mayonnaise, garlic, olive oil, and lemon juice.

2. Serve with toast points or pieces of sliced mushroom.

Marinated Chicken and Fig Spears

The savory flavor of marinated chicken with the sweetness of a bite of fig is a memorable flavor sensation.

 Serves:
6

1 (12-oz.) can chicken, drained and cut into ¾-in.-square chunks	5 ripe figs, sliced in quarters lengthwise
½ cup Greek-style or Italian dressing	1 or 2 TB. chopped fresh chives

1. In a medium bowl, combine chicken and Greek-style dressing, and turn to coat.

2. Spear 1 piece chicken and 1 fig quarter on a *skewer* or toothpick. Repeat with remaining chicken and figs, using 1 piece of each per skewer.

3. Place skewers on a serving platter, arranging them so food is at one side of the plate and the handles are on the other. Sprinkle with chopped chives, and serve.

 DEFINITION

Skewers are thin wooden or metal sticks, usually about 8 inches long, perfect for assembling kebabs, dipping things into hot liquid, or serving single-bite food items with a bit of panache.

Pepperoni and Olive Bites

 Serves:
6 to 8

18 to 24 pitted kalamata or medium black olives	18 to 24 thin pepperoni slices
	1 TB. olive oil

1. Wrap each kalamata olive with 1 pepperoni slice, and fasten with a toothpick. (Pepperoni will not completely surround olive.)

2. Arrange bites, olive side up, on a serving platter, drizzle with olive oil, and serve.

Warm Herbed Cheese (Boursin) with Endive

 Serves:
4

1 cup cream cheese or light cream cheese, softened

3 TB. butter, softened

1 TB. chopped garlic

2 tsp. Italian seasoning

$\frac{1}{2}$ tsp. kosher salt

$\frac{1}{2}$ tsp. black pepper

Belgian endive leaves or sliced crusty bread

1. In a microwave-safe serving bowl, combine cream cheese, butter, garlic, Italian seasoning, kosher salt, and pepper. Microwave on high heat for 60 seconds or until warm.

2. Stir, and serve with Belgian endive leaves or sliced crusty bread.

Cognac Cream Shrimp

Creamy and just slightly sweet, this shrimp dish is very unusual.

 Serves:
4 to 6

1 TB. butter

1 tsp. chopped garlic

½ lb. (31 to 40 count, or about 18) cooked shrimp, peeled, deveined, with tail on

1½ TB. cognac

¼ cup heavy cream

½ tsp. salt

¼ tsp. black pepper

1. In a 12-inch skillet over medium-high heat, heat butter and garlic for about 30 seconds or until garlic begins to soften. Add shrimp, and sauté for 1 minute, stirring, until shrimp is pink.

2. Add cognac, and heat for 1 more minute.

3. Remove warm shrimp to a serving platter.

4. Increase heat under the skillet to high, add heavy cream, and heat for about 30 seconds or until bubbling. Remove from heat.

5. Drizzle shrimp with cognac cream, sprinkle with salt and pepper, insert a toothpick in each, and serve.

Quick Cannellini Dip

Cannellini beans bring a rich texture to spreads without dairy products.

 Serves:
4 to 6

1 (8-oz.) can cannellini beans, drained

⅓ cup shredded Parmesan cheese

¼ cup olive oil

1½ TB. chopped garlic

½ tsp. salt

½ tsp. dried oregano

Sliced crusty bread or toast

1. In a food processor fitted with a metal blade, process cannellini beans, Parmesan cheese, olive oil, garlic, salt, and oregano just enough to pulverize beans but leave plenty of chunky texture.

2. Scrape dip into a serving bowl, surround with sliced crusty bread or toast, and serve.

Quick-Sautéed Tortellini with Dipping Sauce

If your deli knew it was making this appetizer so easy for you, it would probably start charging more. Note that this recipe makes use of prepared pasta. Pasta that requires cooking might push you over the 10-minute mark.

10	**Serves:** 4 to 6

¼ cup olive oil	1 (15-oz.) can pizza sauce
1 TB. chopped garlic	3 TB. Parmesan cheese
1 lb. (16 oz.) prepared fresh deli tortellini	Salt

1. In a large (12-inch or larger) skillet over medium heat, heat olive oil and garlic. Add tortellini in a single layer, and heat for 2 or 3 minutes, turning once.

2. Meanwhile, in a microwave-safe serving bowl, heat pizza sauce for 2 minutes or until warm. Stir sauce, and sprinkle with 1 tablespoon Parmesan cheese.

3. Transfer pasta to a serving plate, sprinkle with remaining 2 tablespoons Parmesan cheese, insert toothpicks, and serve to guests, with salt if desired, inviting them to dip tortellini in accompanying sauce.

Variation: Fresh ravioli or other fun cooked pastas are perfect for this recipe.

Olivada with Toast Points

 Serves:
4

1 (6-oz.) can pitted ripe black
   olives, drained

¼ cup olive oil

1 tsp. fresh lemon juice

¾ tsp. black pepper

4 slices white or whole-wheat
   sandwich bread, crusts
   removed, cut on the diagonal to
   form triangles

1. Preheat the broiler.

2. In a food processor fitted with a metal blade, process black olives, olive oil, lemon juice, and pepper until almost smooth. Scrape into a serving bowl.

3. Arrange bread on a baking sheet in a single layer, and broil for 1 minute on each side or until lightly browned. Remove from oven, and serve spread surrounded by toast triangles.

 DEFINITION

Olivada is a simple combination of olives, oil, and black pepper that carries a wealth of flavor without the pretension.

Toasted Prosciutto and Provolone

 Serves:
6

⅓ cup olive oil

1 baguette or slender loaf crusty
   bread, cut into ½-in. slices

8 oz. thin slices prosciutto, cut into
   2-in.-square pieces, or roughly
   corresponding to size of bread
   slices

4 oz. provolone cheese, thinly
   sliced and cut in pieces roughly
   corresponding to size of bread
   slices

1. Preheat the broiler.

2. Brush a bit of olive oil on both sides of each piece of bread, and arrange bread in a single layer on a baking sheet. Broil on the high rack for 1 minute per side until lightly browned.

3. Remove from the oven, arrange bread on a serving tray, top each with 1 piece prosciutto and 1 piece provolone cheese, and serve.

Variation: To melt the cheese, broil the completed toast-prosciutto-provolone combination for 1 more minute.

> **DEFINITION**
>
> **Prosciutto**—a dry, salt-cured ham—is salty, rich, and evocative of Italy. It's popular in many simple dishes in which its unique flavor is allowed to shine.

Teriyaki Shrimp, Pineapple, and Baby Spinach Bites

 10 **Serves:** 8

½ lb. (31 to 40 count, about 18) cooked shrimp, peeled and deveined with tail on	18 large (about 1×2½-in.) baby spinach leaves
1 (8-oz.) can pineapple chunks in juice, drained	1 or 2 TB. teriyaki sauce

1. Wrap 1 shrimp and 1 pineapple chunk in 1 spinach leaf with shrimp tail sticking out (this allows diners to avoid biting the tail), and fasten with a toothpick. Repeat with remaining ingredients.

2. Arrange bites on a serving platter, drizzle with teriyaki sauce, and serve.

Variation: Use "tail-off" shrimp for convenience rather than visual appeal.

Pineapple Shrimp Skewers

If you like the combination of shrimp and pineapple, try this warm version.

 Serves:
4 to 6

3 TB. canola oil	1 TB. sesame seeds
½ lb. (31 to 40 count, about 18) cooked shrimp, tail on	½ tsp. *chili oil*
1 (8-oz.) can pineapple chunks in juice, drained	Salt

1. In a wok or 10-inch skillet over medium-high heat, heat canola oil. Add shrimp, and heat for 1 minute, stirring. Add pineapple chunks, and heat for 1 additional minute.

2. Pierce 1 pineapple chunk and 1 shrimp on a bamboo skewer. Repeat with remaining shrimp and pineapple pieces.

3. Arrange skewers on a serving plate, with shrimp at the center and the handles extending out in a circle like the spokes on a wheel. Sprinkle shrimp with sesame seeds, drizzle with chili oil, season with salt, and serve.

 DEFINITION

Chili oil is a fiery, hot pepper–infused oil popular in many Asian dishes, and it's not a bad accompaniment to non-Asian heat-loving dishes, either. Find it in most grocery and specialty food stores.

Hoisin Chicken Dip

 Serves:
6 to 8

1 (16.5-oz.) can chicken, drained, and larger pieces broken up

1 cup cream cheese or light cream cheese, softened

½ cup mayonnaise

¼ cup hoisin sauce

3 TB. onion flakes

2 scallions, dark green leaves removed, and finely chopped

Pita crisps or tortilla chips

1. In a medium bowl, combine chicken, cream cheese, mayonnaise, hoisin sauce, and onion flakes.

2. Scrape dip into a serving bowl, top with chopped scallions, and serve surrounded by sturdy dippers such as pita crisps or tortilla chips.

Ginger Shrimp Sticks

Fresh ginger and shrimp is another one of those "perfect pairs."

 Serves:
4

3 TB. olive oil

1 tsp. chopped garlic

½ lb. (31 to 40 count, about 18) cooked shrimp, peeled, deveined, with tail on

1 TB. soy sauce

1 tsp. peeled, grated fresh ginger

1. In a 10- to 12-inch skillet over medium-high heat, heat olive oil and garlic for about 30 seconds. Add shrimp, and heat thoroughly, stirring, for 1 or 2 minutes.

2. Add soy sauce, and heat for an additional 30 seconds, stirring.

3. Remove shrimp to a serving plate, sprinkle with ginger, insert toothpicks, and serve.

Coconut Shrimp

If you have a sweet tooth, these little morsels have your name all over them.

 Serves:
4

½ lb. (31 to 40 count, about 18) cooked shrimp, peeled, deveined, with tail on	½ cup duck sauce ¾ cup shredded coconut

1. In a medium bowl, combine shrimp and pour duck sauce, and turn shrimp to coat.

2. Place coconut into a small bowl.

3. Spear 1 shrimp with a toothpick, and dredge in coconut, coating all sides. Repeat with remaining shrimp.

4. Arrange coated shrimp on a serving platter, each with its own toothpick, and serve.

Tandoori Chicken Bites

 Serves:
4

2 TB. canola oil	¼ tsp. tandoori *masala* or *garam masala*
½ lb. chicken breast cut into pieces about ¾-in. square	Salt
½ tsp. ground ginger	Black pepper
½ tsp. ground garlic	1 tsp. fresh lemon juice

1. In a wok or 12-inch skillet over medium-high heat, heat canola oil. Add chicken, ginger, garlic, tandoori masala, and salt, and cook, stirring, for about 3 minutes or until chicken is golden brown and its juices run clear.

2. Remove chicken to a serving platter, sprinkle with pepper and lemon juice, and serve with toothpicks.

> **DEFINITION**
>
> A **masala** is an Indian spice blend. **Garam masala** is available in many large grocery stores; tandoori masala is available often in specialty food shops. Both include coriander, cinnamon, nutmeg, and ginger, as well as other delicious spices.

Spicy Mint Chutney

Warm seasonings and cool mint serve as delicious counterpoints in this simple dish.

10	Serves: 4

½ cup fresh mint leaves

½ (4.5-oz.) can green chiles, drained and chopped

2 tsp. chopped garlic

½ tsp. sugar

¼ tsp. red chili powder

Salt

2 tsp. fresh lemon juice

1. In a food processor fitted with a metal blade, process mint leaves, green chiles, garlic, sugar, red chili powder, and salt until you get the consistency of a coarse paste.

2. Scrape chutney into a small serving bowl, add lemon juice, and mix to combine.

3. Serve with Tandoori Chicken Bites (recipe earlier in this chapter) or as a savory spread for pieces of tomato, cucumber, or bread.

Pita Crisps with Warm Mango Salsa

 Serves:
4 to 6

2 pita breads, sliced into 8 wedges
each

½ cup fresh chevre (goat's milk
cheese)

¾ (6-oz.) jar mango salsa

¼ tsp. black pepper

1. Preheat the broiler.

2. Arrange pita wedges in a single layer on a baking sheet, and broil for 1 minute
   per side. Remove from broiler.

3. Spread about 1½ teaspoons chevre in a thin layer on each pita wedge, and broil
   for about 30 seconds or until cheese begins to melt. Remove from broiler.

4. Spread about 2 teaspoons mango salsa on each pita wedge, arrange wedges on a
   serving platter, sprinkle with pepper, and serve.

 ON THE CLOCK

The speed at which something broils is directly related to how close the food is
to the heating element. On the lower rack, a piece of pita will take about 1 week
to toast (just kidding, but it *is* slow). On the high rack, about 1 minute. Corollary:
the closer to the heating element, the closer the attention you must give to what
you're broiling.

Cumin-Mint Dip

How can a dip be fiery and cool at the same time? Try this combination and find out!

 Serves:
4 to 6

1 cup plain yogurt

½ cup cream cheese, softened

¾ cup fresh mint leaves

1 TB. fresh lemon juice

2 tsp. ground cumin

½ tsp. salt

Dash hot pepper sauce

Pita bread wedges

1. In a food processor fitted with a metal blade, process yogurt, cream cheese, mint leaves, lemon juice, cumin, salt, and hot pepper sauce until completely mixed.

2. Scrape dip into a mixing bowl, and serve with pita bread wedges.

Fattoush

This traditional "bread salad" makes for an interesting sit-down-meal appetizer. It's best eaten from a plate with a fork.

10	**Serves:**
	4

3 pieces wheat bread, sliced into $\frac{1}{2}$-in. cubes	4 scallions, dark green leaves removed, and cut into $\frac{1}{4}$-in. pieces
1 cucumber, striped and cut into $\frac{1}{2}$-in. cubes	$\frac{1}{4}$ cup chopped fresh mint leaves
1 red bell pepper, ribs and seeds removed, and cut into $\frac{1}{2}$-in. pieces	$\frac{1}{4}$ cup chopped fresh parsley
	2 tsp. chopped garlic
2 cups shredded romaine or iceberg lettuce	Juice of 1 lemon
	$\frac{1}{2}$ cup olive oil
15 to 18 grape tomatoes, halved lengthwise	Salt

1. Preheat the broiler.

2. Arrange bread in a single layer on a baking sheet, and broil for 2 minutes or until bread cubes are crisp.

3. In a medium bowl, combine cucumber, red bell pepper, romaine lettuce, tomatoes, scallions, mint leaves, parsley, and garlic. Pour lemon juice and olive oil over salad, and toss again to mix.

4. Season with salt, and serve on individual plates for each guest.

Variation: To save even more time, use unseasoned (or lightly seasoned) croutons or melba toasts in place of the bread.

Scallops al Pil Pil

This quick and savory dish of scallops seared at high heat with garlic and hot peppers is popular in South America. For an appealing presentation, serve each guest several scallops on a small plate with parsley and lemon wedges.

 Serves:
4

3 TB. olive oil	½ lb. sea scallops
2 tsp. chopped garlic	Lemon wedges
2 TB. white wine	4 sprigs fresh parsley
½ tsp. crushed red pepper flakes	

1. In a wok or 10-inch skillet over high heat, heat olive oil. Add garlic, white wine, and crushed red pepper flakes, and cook for 30 seconds.

2. Add sea scallops, and cook, stirring, for 2 or 3 minutes or until scallops are firm and opaque.

3. Distribute equal portions of scallops to small plates, garnish each with lemon edges and 1 sprig parsley, and invite your guests to drizzle their scallops with lemon juice.

Variation: You can use cooked shrimp in place of scallops, but only heat the shrimp for about 1 minute.

Tutti-Fruity Bites

In This Chapter

- Unique fruit appetizers
- Sweet fruit and cream combinations
- Spicy-sweet spreads
- Nutty noshes

Fruit brings a sweet yet dramatic quality to appetizers. The inherent sweetness in most fruits carries through all the associated ingredients, making some new combinations possible. Many fruits, especially cut fruits, are also very delicate—they beg to be consumed immediately after preparation.

Because of their unique characteristics, fruit appetizers also require thought regarding when to serve them. For example, should you serve a sweet appetizer before a savory meal, or would such an appetizer be better on its own at a summer afternoon cocktail party? Ah, the weighty questions we must face ….

And let's not forget about nuts. Rich and buttery pecans are a terrific addition to appetizers. Almonds bring a milder, sweeter flavor and combine nicely with creamy and sweet food items. Walnuts bring a similarly rich, slightly woody flavor. At the end of this chapter, I've shared some of my favorite nutty appetizers.

Sautéed Balsamic Pears

These pears are meltingly soft and flavorful.

 Serves:
4 to 6

2 TB. butter

2 pears, seeds removed, and cut
lengthwise into 10 to 12 slices
each

2 tsp. balsamic vinegar

1. In a 12-inch skillet over medium heat, melt butter. Arrange pear slices in a single layer in the skillet, and cook for 1 minute. Turn and cook for 1 more minute.

2. Transfer pears to a serving tray, drizzle with balsamic vinegar, and serve with toothpicks and plenty of napkins.

Variation: In place of balsamic vinegar, drizzle pear slices with the equivalent amount of *amaretto* or similar liqueur.

 DEFINITION

Amaretto is a popular almond liqueur. A small drizzle of it works flavor-enhancing magic on fruit.

Dizzy Tropical Fruit

Because this simple yet very tasty appetizer is served in small bowls, it might be best as a sit-down dinner starter. Lemon juice not only provides a nice zing, but also helps ward off *oxidation*.

---

(10)   **Serves:**
              6 to 8

½ ripe cantaloupe, carved into balls with a melon baller

¼ ripe muskmelon, carved into balls with a melon baller

1 banana, peeled and cut into ¼-in. rounds

1 (8-oz.) can pineapple chunks, juice reserved

2 TB. fresh lemon juice

2 TB. amaretto liqueur

1. In a large serving bowl, gently combine cantaloupe, muskmelon, banana, and pineapple chunks.

2. Drizzle reserved pineapple juice, lemon juice, and amaretto liqueur over top, and serve in small bowls with a spoon.

DEFINITION

Oxidation is the browning of cut fruit that happens over time and with exposure to air. You can delay this browning by rubbing or drizzling the cut pieces with a little fresh lemon juice. While we're having fun with terms, using the acid in lemon juice in this way is called *acidulation*. Class is dismissed.

Fruit Chaat

This fresh fruit dish is inspired by Indian cuisine.

10	**Serves:** 6 to 8

1 banana, peeled and cut into ½-in. rounds	2 cups watermelon, seeds removed, cut into ½-in. pieces
1 papaya, cut into ½-in. pieces	2 cups cantaloupe, cut into ½-in. pieces
1 apple, cut into ½-in. pieces	Juice from 1 lime (about 2 TB.)
1 orange, peeled and separated into slices, each slice cut in thirds	Pinch red chili powder
	Salt
	Black pepper

1. In a large bowl, combine banana, papaya, apple, orange, watermelon, and cantaloupe.

2. Drizzle with lime juice, and sprinkle with red chili powder, salt, and pepper. Toss lightly, and serve in small bowls with spoons.

Avocado and Grapefruit Bites

These bites are pure fruit in a rich, creamy-tart mouthful. The combination is just irresistible!

10	**Serves:** 4 to 6

1 ripe avocado	2 TB. fresh lemon juice
1 ripe grapefruit, peeled, sectioned, pith removed, and each section cut in half	

1. Carefully cut avocado in half and remove the pit by embedding the blade (not the tip) of a sharp knife into it. Turn the knife slowly to release the pit. Remove peel and cut avocado into 1-inch pieces.

2. Spear 1 grapefruit piece and 1 avocado piece on a toothpick. Repeat with remaining grapefruit and avocado, and arrange on a serving plate. (A half-grapefruit, cut side up, on the center of the platter might be a nice touch.)

3. Drizzle bites with lemon juice, and serve.

Fall Orchard Fruits with Brie

 10

Serves:
6 to 8

1 (13-oz.) block baby Brie, at room temperature	2 ripe apples, seeds removed, and cut into $\frac{1}{4}$-in.-thick slices
2 ripe pears, seeds removed, and cut into $\frac{1}{4}$-in.-thick slices	$\frac{1}{2}$ lb. red seedless grapes, cut into small bunches

1. Place Brie in the center of a large platter, and surround with pear slices, apple slices, and small bunches of grapes.

2. Serve with a sharp knife for cutting and spreading Brie on slices of crisp fruit. Guests can also spread Brie on grapes, but grapes are often simply eaten separately.

Variation: Use another soft cheese such as St. Andre or Port Salut—or use all three!

 ON THE CLOCK

Take the Brie out of the refrigerator an hour or 2 before you plan to serve it, and let it come to room temperature. This will make the Brie a bit more flavorful and give it a wonderful spreadable consistency. If sliced fruits will be out for long, delay browning by rubbing the slices with the cut half of a lemon.

Cream Cheese Spread with Mediterranean Fruits

The flavors in this rich, satisfying spread derive from the concentrated essence of dried fruits.

 Serves:
4 to 6

1 cup light cream cheese, softened

4 pitted dates, cut into $\frac{1}{2}$-in. pieces

4 dried figs, cut into $\frac{1}{2}$-in. pieces

2 TB. honey

Crusty bread, toast points, fresh fig slices, or apple slices

1. In a food processor fitted with a metal blade, process cream cheese, dates, figs, and honey until thoroughly combined but still chunky.

2. Scrape spread into a serving bowl, and serve with pieces of crusty bread, toast points, and fig or apple slices.

Variation: Use dried apricot pieces in place of, or in addition to, the dates and/or figs.

 ON THE CLOCK

If the honey is too thick to mix at room temperature, 10 seconds in the microwave will loosen it up.

Blueberry-Cream Dream

10	Serves: 4

½ cup light sour cream

3 TB. sugar

1½ cups fresh blueberries

1. In a serving bowl, combine sour cream and sugar.

2. Gently stir in blueberries, and serve with coffee on the veranda as the sun sets.

Variation: Raspberries, blackberries, cherries, or seedless grapes are also lovely here.

Cream Cheese with Sweet and Sugared Fruits

Bright, sweet fruit flavors make this type of spread a favorite for kids and adults.

10	Serves: 4 to 6

1 cup light cream cheese, softened

½ cup orange marmalade

Party rye slices or celery sticks

1. In a serving bowl, combine cream cheese and orange marmalade.

2. Serve with pieces of savory cocktail bread such as "party rye" bread or celery sticks.

Variation: The potential list of sweet fruits and mixtures to pair with cream cheese is limited only by your imagination. Try cherry preserves, blueberry preserves, diced ripe peaches, or crushed pineapple (drained) and honey.

Toasted Walnut Spread with Apples

This simple yet flavorful appetizer seems to carry with it the comfort of a warm fire on a cool rainy night.

10	**Serves:** 4 to 6

1 cup plus 1 TB. chopped walnuts	1 TB. honey
1 (15-oz.) can chickpeas, drained	½ tsp. salt
¼ cup olive oil plus more if needed	Sliced apples

1. Preheat the broiler.

2. Spread walnuts in a single layer on a baking sheet, and broil on the high rack for 2 minutes, watching closely to prevent any blackening. Stir and broil for 1 more minute.

3. In a food processor fitted with a metal blade, process chickpeas, 1 cup toasted walnuts, olive oil, honey, and salt until the consistency of a thick paste. If necessary, add a little more olive oil to achieve the right consistency.

4. Scrape spread into a serving bowl, garnish with remaining toasted walnuts, and serve on a platter surrounded by freshly sliced apples as dippers.

Variation: Add cinnamon or apple pie spice for a little more warmth. If apple slices will be out for long, rub them with a cut lemon half to delay browning.

Toasted Almond-Apricot Spread

This rich and sweet spread is another firmly in the "comfort appetizer" category.

 10 **Serves:**
4 to 6

1 cup slivered almonds	¼ cup apricot preserves
1 cup cream cheese or light cream cheese, softened	Crusty bread or wheat crackers

1. Preheat the broiler.

2. Spread almonds in a single layer on a baking sheet, and broil on the high rack for 2 minutes, watching closely to prevent any blackening. Stir nuts and broil for 1 more minute.

3. In a serving bowl, combine cream cheese, all but 1 tablespoon toasted almonds, and apricot preserves.

4. Sprinkle spread with remaining 1 tablespoon toasted almonds, and serve surrounded by crusty bread pieces or wheat crackers.

Pecan and Chickpea Spread

This savory, rich spread disappears fast. Toast the nuts before preparing the spread for even better flavor.

 10 **Serves:**
4 to 6

1 (15-oz.) can chickpeas, drained	¼ cup olive oil, plus more as needed
½ cup chopped pecans or almonds	Baby carrots or pita wedges
1 TB. chopped garlic	
½ tsp. salt	

1. In a food processor fitted with a chopping blade, place chickpeas, pecans, garlic, and salt. Turn on the processor, and add olive oil in a thin stream, processing until spread achieves the consistency of a thick chunky paste. If necessary, add a little more olive oil to achieve the right consistency.

2. Scrape spread into a bowl, and serve with baby carrots or pita wedges.

Pecan and Water Chestnut Relish

The crisp freshness of *water chestnuts* paired with the toasted crunch of pecans is a compelling combination.

10	**Serves:** 4

1 cup water chestnuts	1 tsp. sugar
1 cup chopped pecans, toasted	¼ tsp. salt
¼ cup chopped fresh parsley	Belgian endive leaves
1 TB. fresh lemon juice	

1. In a food processor fitted with a shredding blade, process water chestnuts until chunky.

2. In a medium bowl, combine pecans, water chestnuts, parsley, lemon juice, sugar, and salt.

3. Scrape relish into a serving bowl, and let guests spread it on Belgian endive leaves.

> **DEFINITION**
>
> **Water chestnuts,** which are actually a tuber and not a chestnut, are a popular element in many types of Asian-style cooking. The flesh is white, crunchy, and juicy, and it holds its texture whether cool or hot.

Walnut and Roasted Red Pepper Dip

This recipe, based on *muhammara*, or Turkish hot pepper dip, is served with flat bread or on toast.

	Serves:
10	6 to 8

¼ cup olive oil, plus more as needed

½ cup ½-in.-pieces onion

½ cup roasted red peppers

½ cup breadcrumbs

½ cup walnuts, toasted

1 TB. fresh lemon juice

1 TB. chopped garlic

1 tsp. hot pepper sauce

1 tsp. ground cumin

1 tsp. salt

Pita wedges

1. In a small skillet over medium-high heat, cook olive oil and onion for 3 minutes or until onions begin to soften.

2. Meanwhile, in a food processor fitted with a metal blade, pulse roasted red peppers, breadcrumbs, walnuts, lemon juice, garlic, hot pepper sauce, cumin, and salt a few times to chop coarsely.

3. Add cooked onions and oil, and process until the consistency of a thick paste. If necessary, add a little more olive oil to achieve the right consistency.

4. Scrape dip into a serving bowl, and serve with pita wedges.

DEFINITION

Muhammara is a Turkish dip or spread that varies in ingredients, although most contain walnuts, onion, garlic, breadcrumbs, and hot peppers in some form.

Spiced Almonds

10	**Serves:** 4 to 6

2 cups lightly salted almonds
Canola oil cooking spray

1 TB. garam masala or curry
powder

1. Preheat the broiler.

2. Spread almonds in a single layer on a baking sheet, and spray with cooking spray. Evenly sprinkle garam masala over nuts, and broil for 5 to 8 minutes on the next-to-highest rack, stirring frequently, until nuts are toasted.

3. Store in the container or a bag.

Variation: This is also terrific with cashews, peanuts, walnuts, or other nuts.

Delightful Dinners

"What's for dinner?!" I wish I had a dollar for every time I heard that question! Dinner can be the most challenging meal of the day, time-wise, but with the 30-minute-or-less recipes in Part 5, getting dinner prepared and on the table will be a breeze.

Whether you're in the mood for seafood, poultry, meat, or vegetarian entrées, I've got you covered. If you're craving hearty and filling beans, there's a chapter for you. If pasta or pizza is more to your liking, turn to that chapter.

I've also included in this part a kid-friendly chapter. More than just kid-approved dinner dishes, I've also included breakfasts, lunches, snacks, and desserts your kids will love. Get the little ones in the kitchen to help you with these recipes, and you'll save even more time. Maybe ....

Seafood Suppers

In This Chapter

- The ideal 30-minute food
- Great grilled fish
- Surefire shrimp recipes
- Mussels, scallops, crabs, and more

Fresh fish is a delight for the busy cook. Fish and shellfish bring delicate flavors and textures that can be preserved by quick-cooking methods such as sautéing, grilling, and steaming. Even baking, a normally time-consuming method, works well with delicate and quick-cooking fish fillets. Frying and sautéing, among the quickest possible cooking methods, appeal to the cook in a hurry, and the rapid heating preserves flavor and moisture. Anyone who has enjoyed fish and chips, with that irresistible combination of crispy coating and moist, flaky interior, knows the appeal of fried fish.

To help ensure seafood success, always buy the freshest fish and shellfish possible from a vendor you trust. And be sure to wash it and pat it dry with paper towels before final preparation and cooking.

I've included some of my favorite seafood recipes in this chapter. Let's go fishing!

Brewpub Fried Fish

Serves:
4

4 TB. canola oil
½ cup beer
1 egg
1 cup breadcrumbs
1 tsp. dried rosemary

½ tsp. dried sage
1 tsp. salt
½ tsp. black pepper
1½ lb. haddock, cod, flounder, or
   other whitefish fillets

1. In a large skillet over medium-high heat, heat canola oil.

2. In a small bowl, whisk together beer and egg.

3. In a wide bowl or tray, mix breadcrumbs, rosemary, sage, salt, and pepper.

4. Dip haddock in beer-egg mixture, dredge through seasoned breadcrumbs, and
   add to the hot skillet. Fry for about 6 minutes or until done, turning once. Serve
   with rice and salad for a quick, tasty, and healthy meal.

 TIME WASTER

Choose your seafood meal's side dishes carefully. A heavy dressing on a salad can
overwhelm the fish's delicate flavors.

Broiled Soy Salmon

Serves:
4

2 TB. olive oil
3 TB. soy sauce
1½ lb. salmon fillets

3 scallions, roots and dark green
   parts removed, sliced into very
   thin rings

1. Preheat the broiler.

2. In a small bowl, combine olive oil and soy sauce.

3. Place salmon in an oven-proof baking dish.

4. Pour oil–soy sauce mixture over fillets, turning salmon to coat. Broil for 4 minutes. Turn over salmon, sprinkle with scallion slices, and broil for 4 more minutes or until flesh just turns opaque.

5. Distribute to plates, and serve.

Variation: You can also prepare this salmon dish on a grill, although you'll need to take care not to lose your scallion slices.

Grilled Salmon Steaks

This family favorite often appears on our table during grill season. The rich salmon meat holds up well to the spicy-crispy coating.

20	Serves: 4

3 TB. olive oil	$\frac{1}{2}$ tsp. black pepper
Juice of $\frac{1}{2}$ lime	$\frac{1}{2}$ tsp. chili powder
$1\frac{1}{2}$ lb. salmon steaks	$\frac{1}{2}$ tsp. salt
$\frac{1}{2}$ tsp. cumin	

1. Preheat the grill.

2. In a small bowl, combine olive oil and lime juice.

3. Place salmon in a large bowl, pour olive oil–lime juice mixture over salmon, and turn to coat.

4. In a cup, combine cumin, pepper, chili powder, and salt, and sprinkle mixture on all sides of salmon steaks.

5. Move steaks to the grill, placing them over the coals, and cook for 12 minutes or until done, turning once.

6. Drizzle with additional olive oil if necessary, and serve with fresh sweet corn and bread for a summer feast. (Even if it's March, this meal will make you *feel* like it's summer.)

Sizzling Salmon

 20   **Serves:**
4

1½ lb. salmon fillets

1 TB. soy sauce

½ tsp. ginger

1 onion, chopped

½ cup olive oil

Fresh cilantro leaves, coarsely chopped

1. Preheat the broiler.

2. Place salmon in a baking dish, drizzle with soy sauce, and sprinkle with ginger and onion. Broil for 4 minutes per side or until cooked.

3. In a small saucepan over high heat, heat olive oil.

4. Remove salmon from the oven, and sprinkle with cilantro. Pour heated olive oil over salmon, taking care not to get too close to hot oil. Distribute to plates, and serve.

Salmon Burgers with Lemon-Caper Mayonnaise

30   **Serves:**
4

4 (6-oz.) cans pink salmon meat, drained, skin and bones discarded, and chopped

3 scallions, roots and dark green tops removed, minced

2 tsp. olive oil

½ tsp. plus ⅛ tsp. dried dill

½ tsp. salt

¼ tsp. plus pinch black pepper

3 TB. whole-wheat flour

3 TB. *unprocessed bran*

¼ cup mayonnaise

1 TB. small capers, drained and rinsed

1½ tsp. lemon juice

1. In a large bowl, combine salmon, scallions, olive oil, $\frac{1}{2}$ teaspoon dill, salt, and $\frac{1}{4}$ teaspoon pepper. Form mixture into 4 patties.

2. Spread whole-wheat flour and unprocessed bran on a plate, and roll salmon burgers in mixture to coat.

3. In a nonstick skillet over medium heat, add salmon burgers, and cook for 3 minutes per side or until cooked and coating is crisp.

4. Meanwhile, in a small bowl, combine mayonnaise, capers, lemon juice, remaining $\frac{1}{8}$ teaspoon dill, and remaining pinch pepper. Serve alongside salmon burgers.

Variation: Fresh dill is even better than dried dill. Use 1 teaspoon if you're going with fresh. You can substitute breadcrumbs for the unprocessed bran. Also, this is the world's best use for leftover salmon (be sure to remove skin and bones and break fish into small pieces). If you've got fresh skinless salmon, so much the better than canned (prep and cooking will take a bit longer, though).

DEFINITION

Unprocessed bran is a wheat product known for its crunchy texture, similar in usage in this recipe to breadcrumbs. It brings lots of vitamins and fiber but not a lot of calories. Find it near the hot cereals in most grocery stores.

Easy Microwave Wine-Poached Salmon

 10   **Serves:**
4

1$\frac{1}{2}$ lb. salmon fillets

2 TB. olive oil

2 TB. white wine

1 TB. lemon juice

1$\frac{1}{2}$ tsp. chopped fresh oregano or
$\frac{1}{2}$ tsp. dried

Salt

Black pepper

Lemon wedges

1. Place salmon in a microwave-safe casserole dish with a lid.

2. Pour olive oil, white wine, and lemon juice over salmon, and turn to coat. Sprinkle oregano, salt, and pepper over salmon, cover, and cook on high for 4 to 6 minutes or until done, turning once or twice if your microwave does not have a turntable (times vary depending on microwave power).

3. Serve with lemon wedges.

Variation: Replace white wine, lemon juice, oregano, and pepper with 2 tablespoons teriyaki sauce. Or if you're a sauce fan like me, make a quick sauce out of wine cooking liquid (after removing the cooked salmon) by stirring in 2 or 3 tablespoons light sour cream. Drizzle that nectar over the salmon.

 TIME WASTER

Fish "leather" might be a new idea for shoes, but that appeal doesn't apply to dinner. Watch fish carefully while cooking in the microwave to avoid tough, overcooked fish. Remove fish from the microwave when the flesh is just barely white (or light salmon, in the case of salmon).

Rosemary-Lemon Halibut

 20   **Serves:**
4

1½ lb. halibut steaks (about 2 steaks)

Juice of ½ lemon

2 TB. olive oil

1 TB. fresh chopped rosemary or 1 tsp. dried

½ tsp. Italian seasoning

½ tsp. salt

½ tsp. black pepper

Fresh parsley (optional)

1. Preheat the broiler.

2. Place halibut in a baking dish. Drizzle with lemon juice, followed by olive oil, turning to coat.

3. Sprinkle rosemary, Italian seasoning, salt, pepper, and parsley (if using) over all sides of steaks.

4. Broil on the second-from-the-top rack for 4 or 5 minutes per side or until flesh has just barely turned opaque. Serve with a glass of your favorite dry white wine.

Variation: Halibut steaks can also be grilled. Other whitefish fillets, such as cod, haddock, and even sole, will also work with this method under the broiler, although thinner cuts will cook much more quickly.

TIME WASTER

Watch these broiling steaks carefully, and remove them quickly so they don't dry out.

Grilled Southwest Tuna Steaks

20	**Serves:** 4

1½ lb. tuna steaks
Juice of ½ lime
3 TB. olive oil
½ tsp. ground cumin

½ tsp. black pepper
½ tsp. chili powder
½ tsp. salt

1. Preheat the grill.

2. Place tuna steaks in a dish. Drizzle with lime juice followed by olive oil, turning to coat.

3. In a cup, combine cumin, pepper, chili powder, and salt, and sprinkle over tuna, turning to coat.

4. Grill for 4 minutes per side or until barely done. (Fish will continue to cook after you remove it from heat.)

Variation: For a less-intense seasoning, omit the cumin. Other fish steaks, such as halibut, salmon, or shark, will work well with this method, too.

MINUTE MORSEL

Some people prefer to cook tuna for a much shorter period of time, say 2 minutes per side, resulting in a rare red interior. The flavor of tuna prepared this way is delicious; however, you'll need to be comfortable with the increased risk of consuming uncooked fish.

Poached Black Pepper Cod

This simple dish brings a hint of pepper and the zing of lemon to cod's delicate flavor.

20 | **Serves:**
| 4

1 cup white wine	2 TB. butter
Juice of ½ lemon	¼ tsp. black pepper
1 cup water	½ tsp. salt
1½ lb. cod or other whitefish fillets	¾ cup sour cream

1. In a large saucepan or skillet over medium heat, mix white wine, lemon juice, and water, and bring to a low boil.

2. Add cod to the saucepan, and simmer for about 8 minutes or until done.

3. Meanwhile, heat a small skillet over medium heat. Add butter, and stir until melted. Add pepper and salt, and heat, stirring, until bubbles appear. Turn off heat.

4. Stir in sour cream, remove from heat, and set aside.

5. Remove and distribute cod to serving plates, pour pepper cream over each piece, and serve. Try it with baked potatoes and buttered green beans.

Pan-Seared Cod with Toasted Almond Sauce

	Serves:
20	4

3 TB. butter or olive oil	$\frac{1}{3}$ cup light sour cream
1$\frac{1}{2}$ lb. cod fillets	2 TB. light cream
$\frac{1}{2}$ tsp. black pepper	1 TB. cognac or brandy (optional)
$\frac{3}{4}$ cup sliced almonds	Pinch salt

1. In a large skillet over medium heat, heat butter.

2. Sprinkle both sides of each cod fillet with pepper. Place in the skillet, and cook for 3 minutes per side or until done. (A spatter screen is a good idea here.) Remove fish to a warm plate, and cover with foil to keep warm.

3. Increase heat to high, and add almonds to remaining butter in the skillet. If necessary, add a little more butter to prevent burning. Cook, stirring rapidly, for 1 minute or until nuts begin to brown lightly. Turn off heat.

4. Add sour cream, light cream, cognac (if using), and salt, and stir. Distribute cod to serving plates, and distribute toasted almond sauce along with each plate.

Variation: Other whitefish fillets, such as halibut, tilapia, or haddock, also work well.

Whisker-Licking-Good Catfish

	Serves:
20	4

$\frac{1}{3}$ cup olive oil	1 tsp. coriander
$\frac{1}{2}$ cup cornmeal	$\frac{2}{3}$ cup milk
$\frac{1}{2}$ cup whole-wheat flour	3 catfish fillets, about 1$\frac{1}{2}$ lb. total
1 tsp. kosher salt	Lemon wedges
1 tsp. dried basil	

1. In a large skillet over medium-high heat, heat olive oil.

2. On a plate or wide, shallow tray, combine cornmeal, whole-wheat flour, kosher salt, basil, and coriander.

3. Pour milk in another wide, shallow bowl.

4. Dip first catfish fillet in milk, coating both sides. Dredge catfish through cornmeal mixture, and place it in hot oil in the skillet. Repeat with remaining fillets, being sure not to let the skillet get too crowded.

5. Cook for about 6 minutes, turning once, or until done. Serve with lemon wedges.

Baked Sole

This simple and delicious sole dish balances the flavors of fish and Parmesan.

20	Serves: 4

4 TB. butter, sliced thin	$\frac{1}{2}$ cup shredded Parmesan cheese
12 saltine crackers, crumbled	$\frac{1}{2}$ tsp. black pepper
$1\frac{1}{2}$ lb. sole or other thin whitefish fillets	Lemon wedges

1. Preheat the oven to 400°F.

2. Arrange 2 tablespoons butter and 6 crumbled saltine crackers across the bottom of a metal baking pan.

3. Arrange sole in a single layer over crumbled crackers. Spread remaining crackers over sole, top with remaining butter, and sprinkle Parmesan cheese and pepper on top.

4. Bake for 17 minutes or until done. Serve with lemon wedges, sautéed snap beans, and fresh bread.

Sole Amandine

20 | **Serves:** 4

1½ lb. sole, cod, haddock, or other whitefish fillets
2 TB. lemon juice
Pinch salt

Pinch black pepper
¼ cup heavy or whipping cream
¼ cup sliced almonds

1. Preheat the oven to 350°F.
2. Place sole in a baking dish. Drizzle with lemon juice, and sprinkle with salt and pepper. Spread whipping cream over sole, followed by almonds.
3. Bake for 10 minutes or until sole is cooked. Divide among serving plates, and serve.

DEFINITION

Amandine is French for "with almonds."

Sole Meuniere

The slight brown crispness of the flour, the zing of lemon, and the delicate flavor of the sole all combine to make this dish a delight.

10 | **Serves:** 4

2 TB. butter
Juice of ½ lemon
1 TB. flour

1½ lb. sole fillets
Lemon wedges for serving

1. In a skillet over medium heat, melt butter. Stir in lemon juice.
2. Sprinkle flour on a clean countertop.

3. Lightly press each side of each sole fillet in flour, and place in the heated skillet. Cook for about 6 minutes or until done, turning once.

4. Serve with lemon wedges, rice, steamed vegetables, and a glass of dry white wine. Ah.

 ON THE CLOCK

Don't feel the need to add lots of seasonings to seafood. Simple fish and shellfish dishes succeed specifically because the minimal seasoning allows fresh seafood flavors to shine through.

Crisp Fried Haddock

 20   **Serves:**
4

$\frac{1}{3}$ cup unprocessed bran	$\frac{1}{4}$ cup canola oil
$\frac{1}{3}$ cup whole-wheat flour	$1\frac{1}{2}$ lb. haddock or other whitefish fillets
$\frac{1}{2}$ tsp. salt	Lemon wedges
1 tsp. Italian seasoning	
$\frac{1}{2}$ cup milk	

1. In a wide bowl or tray, mix unprocessed bran, whole-wheat flour, salt, and Italian seasoning.

2. Pour milk into a shallow bowl.

3. In a large skillet over medium heat, heat canola oil.

4. Dip haddock in milk, and dredge in flour mixture, turning to coat all sides.

5. Place haddock in the skillet, and cook for 3 minutes per side or until cooked through. Serve with lemon wedges.

 MINUTE MORSEL

Few recipes in this chapter include breading for fried fish. When I have called for a light breading, I've tried to keep it light and creative, hence the unprocessed bran in this recipe.

Broiled Haddock with Mozzarella

20 | **Serves:**
4

1½ lb. haddock or other whitefish fillets	½ tsp. ground cumin
2 TB. lemon juice	½ tsp. black pepper
2 TB. olive oil	Pinch salt
1½ tsp. chopped fresh oregano or ½ tsp. dried	1 cup shredded part-skim milk mozzarella cheese
	Lemon wedges

1. Preheat the broiler.

2. Place haddock fillets in an oven-proof baking dish, skin side down, in a single layer.

3. In a small bowl, combine lemon juice, olive oil, and oregano, and drizzle over haddock, turning to coat both sides, but return to skin side down. Sprinkle haddock with cumin, pepper, and salt.

4. Broil on the next-to-highest rack for 5 minutes or until flesh has just barely turned opaque.

5. Drizzle any remaining liquid from the dish over haddock, sprinkle with mozzarella cheese, and broil on the next-to-highest rack for 1 minute more or until cheese is melted. Serve with lemon wedges.

Variation: Other whitefish fillets, such as cod, halibut, or tilapia, also do well in this recipe.

Grilled Shrimp Scampi

20　**Serves:**
　　　4

1 TB. garlic, minced

¼ cup olive oil

1 lb. (31 to 40 count) fresh shrimp, peeled, and thawed, if frozen

¼ cup chopped fresh parsley

Salt

Black pepper

Lemon wedges

1. Preheat the grill.

2. In a medium bowl, mix garlic and olive oil. Add shrimp, and toss to coat. Sprinkle shrimp with parsley.

3. Slide 4 or 5 shrimp onto a skewer, sprinkle with salt and pepper, and grill for 2 or 3 minutes per side. Serve with lemon wedges.

 DEFINITION

Scampi, originally from the Italian word for shrimp, is commonly used to refer to shrimp that's been cooked in olive oil and garlic.

 # Sautéed Shrimp and Artichokes

10　**Serves:**
　　　4

3 TB. olive oil

1 (9-oz.) pkg. frozen artichoke hearts, thawed

1 tsp. Italian seasoning

1 TB. chopped garlic

1 lb. (31 to 40 count) cooked shrimp, tail off

½ tsp. kosher salt

2 TB. shredded Parmesan cheese

1. In a large skillet over medium heat, heat olive oil. Add artichoke hearts, Italian seasoning, and garlic, and cook for 3 minutes, stirring.

2. Add shrimp, and cook, stirring, for 1 or 2 more minutes.

3. Distribute shrimp and artichoke hearts to serving plates, sprinkle with kosher salt and Parmesan cheese, and serve.

Variation: For a hearty meal, stir 1 (15-ounce) can drained and rinsed chickpeas in with the shrimp.

 ON THE CLOCK

Shrimp-based dishes fit into the "fast" category thanks to time-saving options available at the grocery store. Buy shrimp that's already cleaned, or to really get moving in a hurry, purchase precooked "tail-off" shrimp.

Mussels in Wine

 20   **Serves:** 4

1 cup dry white wine
½ cup water
1 TB. chopped garlic
1 tsp. Italian seasoning
Pinch salt

Pinch black pepper
3 lb. mussels, cleaned
Freshly squeezed lemon juice
Parsley

1. In a large saucepan over medium-high heat, bring white wine, water, garlic, Italian seasoning, salt, and pepper to a boil.

2. Add mussels, cover, and cook for 5 minutes or until mussels have opened. Discard any mussels that have not opened.

3. Scoop mussels into large serving bowls, and drizzle with broth from the pan. Drizzle with fresh lemon juice, and garnish with parsley. A chilled glass of Sauvignon Blanc alongside makes this picture complete.

Variation: It's decadent but sometimes irresistible to drizzle cooked mussels with melted butter (or to dip them, like lobster meat).

ON THE CLOCK

Mussels and other mollusks live on the ocean bottom, so cleaning is important. Scrub them with a stiff brush under cold, running water. Remove any fibers (the "beard") coming from the concave side. And discard any mussels that are open before you cook them. They're dead already—not a good thing.

Ginger Scallops

 20 **Serves:** 4

3 TB. butter or olive oil

1½ lb. fresh bay scallops or 1½ lb. fresh sea scallops, quartered

1 TB. freshly grated ginger

½ cup white wine

2 TB. lemon juice

2 TB. heavy cream

Pinch nutmeg

Salt

Black pepper

1. In a large skillet over medium heat, melt butter.

2. Thoroughly rinse scallops in cold water, and pat dry with paper towels. Add to the skillet along with ginger, and cook, stirring, for 3 minutes. Remove to a warm plate, and cover with foil.

3. Increase heat to high, and add white wine and lemon juice to the skillet. Boil for 2 minutes or until liquid is reduced by half. Remove from heat, and stir in heavy cream, nutmeg, salt, and pepper.

4. Distribute scallops to serving plates, pour sauce over each plate, and serve.

Pan-Broiled Scallops, Bacon, and Rice

Use an oven-safe skillet (such as cast iron) for this flavorful dish.

 20   **Serves:**
4

½ lb. bacon
2 TB. sherry
½ tsp. dried thyme
¼ tsp. ground sage
1 *bunch* scallions, dark green parts
   removed, white and light green
   parts thinly cross-sliced

1 lb. sea scallops
3 cups cooked rice
½ cup shredded Swiss cheese
Salt
Black pepper

1. Preheat the broiler.

2. In a large skillet over medium-high heat, cook bacon for 5 minutes or until done. Remove bacon to paper towels, and set aside.

3. Add sherry, thyme, sage, and scallions to the skillet, and cook for 3 minutes. Using a slotted spoon, remove about half of scallions to a small bowl. Add sea scallops to the skillet, and cook, stirring, for 2 minutes per side or until done.

4. While sea scallops are cooking, crumble bacon. Add crumbled bacon and cooked rice to the skillet, and stir to thoroughly combine. Sprinkle with Swiss cheese and reserved scallions.

5. Place the skillet under the broiler for 3 minutes or until cheese melts. Season with salt and pepper, and serve.

 DEFINITION

A **bunch** is a generic term for a group of long, slender vegetables. In the case of scallions, it usually means 5 to 10 scallions.

Quick Crab Cakes

30   **Serves:**
           4

3 (5-oz.) cans or 1 (15-oz.) can crabmeat, drained, and picked over

²/₃ cup unprocessed bran

3 scallions, roots and dark green
   parts removed, minced

1 egg

2 TB. mayonnaise

1 tsp. Worcestershire sauce

1 tsp. Dijon-style mustard

Dash hot pepper sauce (optional)

4 TB. butter or canola oil

Lemon wedges

1. In a large bowl, combine crabmeat, unprocessed bran, scallions, egg, mayonnaise, Worcestershire sauce, Dijon-style mustard, and hot pepper sauce (if
   using). Mixture should be moist enough to stick together. If not, add a little
   more bran.

2. Shape mixture into 8 cakes, each about 2 inches across and ¾ inch thick.

3. In a large skillet over medium heat, heat butter. Add crab cakes, and cook for
   3 minutes per side or until crisp and golden. If necessary, cook cakes in batches,
   keeping the cooked ones on a plate tented with aluminum foil to keep them
   warm. Serve 2 per person with lemon wedges.

Variation: Fresh crabmeat is delicious in place of the canned crab. You can also use
finely chopped salmon or lobster meat in place of the crabmeat.

Lightning Seafood Stir-Fry

20 **Serves:**
4

2 TB. canola oil

1 large onion, chopped

1 TB. chopped garlic

1 (1-lb.) pkg. seafood mix

1 (1-lb.) pkg. frozen pea pods

1 (6-oz.) can water chestnuts

3 TB. soy sauce

1. In a wok or large skillet over medium-high heat, heat canola oil. Add onion and garlic, and cook for 2 minutes.

2. Add seafood mix, increase heat to high, and cook for 5 to 8 minutes or until seafood is cooked.

3. Add frozen pea pods, water chestnuts, and soy sauce, and cook, stirring, for 4 minutes or until just done (slightly crispy pea pods are the goal). Serve over rice.

Variation: For added zing, add a few drops of hot oil to the canola oil.

Gorgeous Seafood Stew

 30

Serves:
4 to 6

6 TB. extra-virgin olive oil

2 tsp. chopped garlic

5 cups 20-Minute Tomato Sauce
(recipe in Chapter 24)

2 TB. tomato paste

$\frac{1}{2}$ tsp. rosemary

1 tsp. dried parsley

1 tsp. dried basil

$\frac{1}{2}$ tsp. crushed red pepper flakes

$\frac{3}{4}$ cup red wine

$1\frac{1}{2}$ lb. assorted calamari (optional),
scallops, shrimp, and fish chunks

1. In a large skillet over medium heat, heat extra-virgin olive oil. Add garlic, and sauté for 1 minute.

2. Add 20-Minute Tomato Sauce, tomato paste, rosemary, parsley, basil, and crushed red pepper flakes, and simmer for 5 minutes.

3. Add red wine, and return to a simmer. Add calamari (if using), and cook for 5 minutes. Add scallops, shrimp, and fish, and cook for 7 to 9 minutes or until cooked through. Serve with fresh Italian bread, a garden salad, and a white or light-bodied red wine.

Pleasing Poultry Entrées

In This Chapter

- Perfect poultry, every time
- Quick chicken stir-fries
- Spicy chicken dishes
- Chicken curries, stews, and more

Many busy cooks rely on poultry as the base for their meals. And why not? Chicken is quick and easy to prepare, affordable, and mild enough to let the added seasonings shine through.

With 30-minute cuisine in mind, the cut of meat is very important. Opt for thin cuts—boneless breasts, legs, wings, thighs, and drumsticks (both components of a chicken leg)—for quick cooking.

Grilling and broiling bring appealing smoky grill flavors to chicken dishes. There's something appealing and satisfying about chicken prepared this way! And of course, there's frying. Frying is a time-honored cooking tradition across the country. From north to south, east to west, everybody has favorite methods and seasonings. The recipes in this chapter pick up on several of these tasty regional themes.

Buffalo Wings

 Serves:
4 to 6

4 lb. chicken wings (about 40 wings)	4 cups canola oil
Salt	¼ cup butter
Black pepper	2 to 5 TB. Tabasco sauce
	1 TB. white wine vinegar

1. Remove and discard tips from wings. Cut each wing into 2 pieces, and trim away fat. Rinse wings, and pat dry. Sprinkle with salt and pepper.

2. In deep fryer, heat canola oil. Add about half of wings, and deep-fry for 10 minutes, stirring occasionally, or until golden brown. Drain and place wings on a warm platter.

3. In a small, microwave-safe bowl, melt butter. Add Tabasco sauce and white wine vinegar, and mix well. Drizzle over wings, and serve.

Variation: Keep the tips if you want. It's essential to remove them, but many restaurant wing dishes are prepared this way.

MINUTE MORSEL

The Tabasco serves as the heat throttle. The more you add, the hotter it gets. If you are hesitant about spicy foods, start with 2 tablespoons and go from there.

Drumroll Chicken

This crispy and fun chicken is for kids and adults alike. For an adult table, ramp up the red pepper. For a kid table, tone it down.

 20   **Serves:**
4

¾ cup canola oil

1 egg

½ cup milk

½ cup cornmeal

1 tsp. dried sage

¼ tsp. ground red pepper

¼ tsp. black pepper

2 lb. chicken drumsticks

1. In a medium saucepan over high heat, heat canola oil.

2. In a glass measuring cup, whisk egg and milk.

3. In a small bowl, combine cornmeal, sage, red pepper, and pepper in a bowl.

4. Dip each drumstick in egg-milk mixture, roll meat end in cornmeal mixture, and carefully place in hot oil. A splatter screen and tongs are good tools to use. Cook for 9 minutes or until done, and serve.

Derek's Nutty Chicken Stir-Fry

20   **Serves:**
4

2 TB. vegetable oil

1½ TB. crushed garlic

1½ tsp. fresh ginger, grated

1 tsp. Chinese chili paste

4 TB. soy sauce

2 TB. peanut butter

1½ lb. boneless, skinless chicken breasts, rinsed, dried, and cut into ¾-in. cubes

3 cups green beans, cut in half

1. In a wok or large skillet over medium heat, heat vegetable oil. Add garlic, ginger, Chinese chili paste, soy sauce, and peanut butter, and stir. Increase heat to medium-high, and stir until peanut butter melts into sauce.

2. Stirring constantly, add chicken. Cook for about 5 minutes or until chicken is browned all over.

3. Add green beans, and cook for about 5 minutes or until slightly crisp. Serve over rice.

Sesame-Scallion Chicken Stir-Fry

 20 **Serves:**
4

1½ lb. skinless, boneless chicken breasts, rinsed, dried, and cut into 1-in. chunks	½ tsp. crushed red pepper flakes
¼ cup canola oil	1 (6-oz.) can sliced water chestnuts, drained
3 TB. sesame seeds	2 cups snow peas, stemmed and rinsed
4 scallions, roots and dark green leaves removed, chopped into ¼-in. pieces	⅓ cup fresh chives, cut into ¼-in. pieces
	3 TB. soy sauce

1. In a large bowl, place chicken. Pour canola oil over top, and turn to coat. Sprinkle chicken with sesame seeds.

2. Heat a wok or a large skillet over medium-high heat. Add chicken, scallions, and crushed red pepper flakes, and cook, stirring, for 2 minutes.

3. Add water chestnuts, snow peas, and chives, and continue to cook, stirring, for 3 more minutes or until chicken is cooked.

4. Pour soy sauce over, stir, and serve over brown rice.

Stir-Fried Peanut Chicken

20

Serves:
4

2 TB. vegetable oil

1 TB. chopped garlic

1½ tsp. fresh ginger, peeled and grated

Dash hot pepper sauce

4 TB. soy sauce

2 TB. natural peanut butter

1½ lb. boneless, skinless chicken breasts, rinsed, dried, and cut into ¾-in. cubes

3 cups green beans, stemmed and cut in half crosswise

1. In a wok or large skillet over medium heat, heat vegetable oil. Add garlic, ginger, hot pepper sauce, soy sauce, and peanut butter, and cook, stirring, for about 3 minutes or until peanut butter blends smoothly with other ingredients.

2. Add chicken, and cook, stirring, for 5 minutes or until just done.

3. Add green beans, and cook for about 3 minutes or until slightly crisp.

4. Serve as is or over ½ cup brown rice.

TIME WASTER

Look carefully at peanut butter ingredients. The ingredients in "natural" peanut butter, found in your grocery store, are "Peanuts and salt." That's it. Others contain sweeteners, hydrogenated oils, and other not-so-good stuff. In my opinion, natural-style peanut butter is both better for you, and *tastes* better.

🍎 Orange Chicken

	Serves:
20	4

2 TB. olive oil

1 TB. chopped garlic

1½ lb. boneless, skinless chicken breasts, rinsed, dried, and cut into strips about ½-in. thick

½ tsp. salt

Pinch black pepper

¼ cup orange juice

4 thin (¼-in.), circular orange slices (optional)

1. In a large skillet over medium heat, heat olive oil. Add garlic, and cook, stirring, for 1 minute.

2. Add chicken in a single layer, and sprinkle with salt and pepper. Cook for 3 minutes, turn over strips, and cook for 1 more minute. Pour orange juice over chicken in the skillet, and continue to cook until chicken is done.

3. Remove chicken to serving plates, and continue cooking orange juice for 1 more minute. Drizzle juice from the skillet over chicken, garnish each serving with 1 orange slice (if using), and serve.

Quick Home-Style Barbecued Chicken

Microwave precooking accelerates this meal. Sweet-spicy homemade barbecue sauce makes it a real treat.

	Serves:
30	4 to 6

3 lb. chicken legs, cut into parts

1 cup ketchup

2 TB. cider vinegar

3 TB. molasses

1 TB. ground mustard

½ tsp. cumin

½ tsp. ginger

¼ tsp. dried sage

¼ tsp. ground red pepper

¼ tsp. black pepper

1. Preheat the grill.

2. In a large, microwave-safe bowl, place chicken legs. Microwave for 10 minutes, turning to assure even cooking.

3. Meanwhile, in a small bowl, combine ketchup, cider vinegar, molasses, mustard, cumin, ginger, sage, red pepper, and pepper.

4. Carefully move hot, partially cooked chicken to the grill, and brush generously with barbecue sauce. Grill for about 5 minutes or until chicken is done and skin is crispy. Serve with bread, salad, and a glass of rich red wine for a quick, flavorful summer-theme meal.

TIME WASTER

If you like to use barbecue sauce for dipping, be sure to keep it separate from the sauce used for brushing the chicken to avoid contamination from raw meat.

U. B.'s Salsa Chicken

 20   **Serves:**
4

2 TB. olive oil

¹⁄₄ cup flour

4 skinless, boneless chicken breast halves

Salt

Black pepper

1 cup salsa

1 can chopped tomatoes, drained, or 2 small tomatoes, chopped

¹⁄₄ cup sliced kalamata or other black olives

¹⁄₄ cup white wine

1. In a large skillet over medium heat, heat olive oil.

2. Place flour on a plate or in a shallow bowl.

3. Season chicken breasts with salt and pepper, dredge through flour, and add to the skillet. Cook for 6 to 8 minutes or until done, turning once. Remove to warm plate, and cover with aluminum foil.

4. In a medium bowl, combine salsa, tomatoes, and kalamata olives.

5. Add white wine to the skillet, and stir in salsa mixture. Heat for about 3 minutes. Distribute chicken pieces to 4 plates, pour salsa mixture in even portions over each piece of chicken, and serve. *Olé!*

Aunt Jean's Dijon Chicken

20 **Serves:**
4

⅓ cup breadcrumbs

1 TB. grated Parmesan cheese

½ tsp. dried basil

½ tsp. dried oregano

½ tsp. dried thyme

¼ tsp. salt

¼ tsp. pepper

2 TB. olive oil

2 TB. Dijon-style mustard

4 skinless, boneless chicken breast halves

1. In a shallow bowl, combine breadcrumbs, Parmesan cheese, basil, oregano, thyme, salt, and pepper.

2. In large skillet over medium heat, heat olive oil.

3. Brush Dijon-style mustard on both sides of chicken, dredge chicken pieces through breadcrumb mixture, and add chicken to the skillet. Cook for 12 minutes or until done, turning once. Serve with rice and snow peas.

"Tarragarlic" Chicken

 20

Serves:
4

2 TB. olive oil

2 tsp. chopped garlic

4 skinless, boneless chicken breast
  halves

Salt

Black pepper

¼ cup white wine

¼ cup sour cream

Juice of ½ lemon

1 tsp. dried tarragon

½ tsp. salt

1. In a large skillet over medium heat, heat olive oil. Add garlic, and cook for 3 minutes.

2. Season chicken breasts with salt and pepper, add to the skillet, and cook for 7 or 8 minutes or until done, turning once.

3. Meanwhile, in a small bowl, combine white wine, sour cream, lemon juice, tarragon, and salt.

4. Distribute chicken pieces to 4 plates.

5. Pour sauce into the skillet, heat for 2 minutes, pour even portions over each piece of chicken, and serve.

Chicken Marsala

20 | **Serves:** 4

2 TB. butter

¼ cup unprocessed bran

½ tsp. salt

½ tsp. black pepper

1½ lb. boneless, skinless chicken breasts, rinsed, dried, and cut in half lengthwise

2 TB. olive oil

1 cup chicken broth

½ cup marsala wine

¼ lb. fresh white mushrooms, wiped with a damp paper towel and sliced

Juice of ½ lemon

1. In a large skillet over medium heat, melt butter.

2. In a small bowl, mix unprocessed bran, salt, and pepper.

3. Dredge chicken in bran mixture, arrange in the skillet, and cook for 6 minutes or until done, turning once. Remove chicken to a warm plate, and cover with aluminum foil to keep warm.

4. Increase heat under the skillet to medium-high, and add olive oil, chicken broth, marsala wine, white mushrooms, and lemon juice. Cook, stirring, for 5 minutes or until reduced by half.

5. Distribute chicken breasts to serving plates, spoon sauce over top, and serve.

Lightning Chicken Curry

This is a brief glimpse into Indian cooking, a rich and diverse cuisine that one could spend a lifetime exploring.

⏲ 20   **Serves:**
4 to 6

2 TB. olive oil

1 lb. boneless, skinless chicken breasts, cut into 1-in. cubes

3 TB. butter

1 onion, finely chopped

1½ tsp. curry powder

3 TB. flour

¾ tsp. salt

¾ tsp. sugar

⅛ tsp. ground ginger

1 cup chicken broth, or 1 chicken bouillon cube dissolved in 1 cup hot water

1 cup milk

1 tsp. lemon juice

4 cups cooked rice

1. In a medium skillet over medium heat, heat olive oil. Add chicken, and cook, stirring, for 8 minutes or until cooked through. Turn off heat.

2. Meanwhile, in a large skillet over low heat, melt butter. Add onion and curry powder, and sauté for 3 minutes. Stir in flour, salt, sugar, and ginger, and cook until bubbling and smooth.

3. Add chicken broth and milk, and bring to a boil, stirring. Boil for 1 minute, add cooked chicken and lemon juice, and cook for 3 more minutes.

4. Distribute rice to serving plates, pour curry mixture over, and serve.

Chicken-Crab Curry

20	**Serves:** 4

2 TB. olive oil

1 lb. boneless, skinless chicken, rinsed, dried, and cut into 1-in. cubes

3 TB. butter

1 medium onion, finely chopped

2 large bell peppers, ribs and seeds removed, and chopped into $\frac{1}{2}$-in. pieces

$1\frac{1}{2}$ tsp. curry powder

3 TB. whole-wheat flour

$\frac{1}{4}$ tsp. ground ginger

1 cup chicken broth, or 1 chicken bouillon cube dissolved in 1 cup hot water

1 cup milk

1 (6-oz.) can crabmeat, drained and picked over

1 tsp. lemon juice

Salt

1. In a medium skillet over medium heat, heat olive oil. Add chicken, and cook, stirring, for 6 minutes or until cooked through. Turn off heat.

2. Meanwhile, in a large skillet over medium heat, melt butter. Add onion, bell peppers, and curry powder, and sauté for 5 minutes.

3. Stir in whole-wheat flour and ginger, and cook, stirring, until bubbling and smooth. Add chicken broth and milk, and bring to a boil, stirring. Boil for 1 minute.

4. Add cooked chicken, crabmeat, and lemon juice, and cook for 2 or 3 minutes. Serve in bowls, either as is or over $\frac{1}{2}$ cup brown rice, seasoned with salt.

Variation: Curry powder is the flavor throttle in this dish. Some mixes are more intense than others. If you're new to spicy foods, start with less. Also, using 2 skillets accelerates this recipe.

 TIME WASTER

Overcooked poultry becomes dry and unappetizing. Watch your meal closely to prevent overcooking.

Chive Chicken

This piquant recipe makes the most of the onion family for a dish just bursting with flavor.

 20

Serves:
4

2 TB. olive oil

¼ cup flour

4 boneless, skinless chicken breast halves, rinsed and dried

Salt

Black pepper

1 onion, chopped

2 tsp. chopped garlic

1 cup chicken broth

½ tsp. salt

1 tsp. dried thyme

⅓ cup sour cream

⅓ cup fresh chives, chopped

1. In a large skillet over medium heat, heat olive oil.

2. Place flour in a shallow bowl.

3. Season chicken breasts with salt and pepper, dredge through flour, and add to the skillet. Cook for 8 minutes or until done, turning once. Remove to a warm plate, and cover with aluminum foil.

4. Add onion and garlic to the skillet, and sauté for 2 minutes or until onion is translucent and tender.

5. Increase heat to high, add chicken broth, remaining ½ teaspoon salt, and thyme, and cook, stirring, for 5 minutes.

6. Add sour cream, and cook for 1 more minute. Distribute chicken to serving plates, pour sauce over each piece, sprinkle with chives, and serve with rice and steamed broccoli.

Brigitte's Speedy Chicken

 Serves:
4

2 TB. canola oil

4 boneless, skinless chicken breasts, rinsed, dried, and cut lengthwise into ¼-in. strips

2 onions, sliced

1 tsp. salt

1. In a large skillet over high heat, combine canola oil, chicken, onions, and salt. Cook for 2 minutes.

2. Turn over breasts, cover, and cook for 8 more minutes or until done. Serve with peas and couscous or rice.

Variation: Sprinkle in 1 teaspoon Indian spice such as curry powder or garam masala at the beginning.

Broiled Lemon-Rosemary Chicken

 Serves:
4

1½ lb. boneless, skinless chicken breasts, rinsed and dried

Juice of 1 lemon

2 TB. olive oil

2 tsp. chopped garlic

½ tsp. dried rosemary

Salt

Black pepper

1. Preheat the broiler.

2. In a large bowl, place chicken. Drizzle with lemon juice.

3. In a measuring cup, combine olive oil and garlic. Pour over chicken, and turn to coat. (If you're not a garlic fan, omit it.) Sprinkle rosemary, salt, and pepper over chicken.

4. Place chicken in a single layer in a baking dish, and broil for 8 minutes or until done, turning once.

Variation: Cooking this chicken in an oiled skillet results in a slightly crispier exterior.

ON THE CLOCK

Black pepper is one of the world's best all-purpose seasonings, but it loses much of its flavor soon after it's been ground. To get the best pepper flavor, freshly grind your own pepper in a mill.

Chicken with Garlicky Wine Sauce

 20   **Serves:**
4

2 TB. olive oil

1 TB. chopped garlic

1½ lb. skinless, boneless chicken breasts, rinsed, dried, and cut into 1-in.-thick strips

Salt

Black pepper

¼ cup dry white wine

1 TB. freshly squeezed lemon juice

¼ cup light sour cream

1. In a large skillet over medium heat, heat olive oil. Add garlic, and cook, stirring, for 2 minutes.

2. Season chicken with salt and pepper, add to the skillet, and cook for 6 minutes or until done, turning once. Remove chicken to a plate, and cover with aluminum foil to keep warm.

3. Increase heat under the skillet to high, and add white wine and lemon juice. Boil for 1 minute, stirring. Turn off heat, and stir in sour cream.

4. Arrange chicken strips on serving plates, and spoon garlicky wine sauce over chicken.

TIME WASTER

Sour cream is versatile in cooking, but don't let it boil. It curdles, and that's not pretty.

Mustard-Glazed Chicken Breasts

20 **Serves:** 4

3 TB. olive oil

2 TB. Dijon-style mustard

1 TB. balsamic vinegar

1½ lb. skinless, boneless chicken breasts, rinsed and dried

Salt

Black pepper

1. In a large skillet over medium heat, heat 2 tablespoons olive oil.

2. In a small bowl, combine Dijon-style mustard, remaining 1 tablespoon olive oil, and balsamic vinegar. Brush glaze over chicken.

3. Add chicken to the skillet, and cook for 6 minutes or until done, turning once. Serve, seasoning with salt and pepper.

Variation: Red wine or cider vinegar also works in place of the balsamic vinegar.

Tuscan Chicken Breasts

20 **Serves:** 8

⅓ cup plus 2 TB. olive oil

Juice of ½ lime

2 or 3 lb. boneless, skinless chicken breasts, rinsed and dried

1½ tsp. dried oregano

1 tsp. dried rosemary

Salt

Black pepper

1. In a large frying pan over medium heat, heat ⅓ cup olive oil.

2. In a small bowl, combine remaining 2 tablespoons olive oil and lime juice.

3. Place chicken breasts in a large bowl, pour lime juice and olive oil mixture over, and turn to coat. Sprinkle with oregano, rosemary, salt, and pepper.

4. Add chicken to the frying pan, and cook for about 5 minutes per side or until a cut through the thickest breast shows complete cooking. Serve with rice and fresh vegetables such as steamed carrots.

MINUTE MORSEL

Is it done? To be sure your meat is cooked, make a cut with a sharp knife into the thickest part. If the juices run clear, it's done.

Chili-Crusted Chicken Breasts

20	**Serves:** 4

1 egg
2 TB. olive oil
3 TB. unprocessed bran
3 TB. whole-wheat flour

1 TB. chili powder
$\frac{1}{2}$ tsp. salt
$1\frac{1}{2}$ lb. skinless, boneless chicken breasts, rinsed and dried

1. Preheat the oven to 400°F. Lightly coat a baking tray with cooking oil spray.

2. In a small bowl, crack egg. Add olive oil, and mix well.

3. On a plate, combine unprocessed bran, whole-wheat flour, chili powder, and salt.

4. Dip each piece of chicken into egg mixture, dredge in chili-flour mix, and set on the baking tray. Bake for 15 minutes or until done.

Variation: Feel free to adjust the amount of chili powder to suit your taste.

Right-Brain Chicken and Apples

 Serves:
4

2 TB. olive oil

1 onion, chopped

2 cloves garlic, chopped

1 lb. chicken breast, rinsed, dried, and cut into $\frac{1}{2}$-in. pieces

$\frac{1}{2}$ tsp. ground ginger

1 tsp. dried oregano

$\frac{1}{2}$ tsp. dried rosemary

1 bunch kale

$\frac{1}{4}$ cup raisins

1 Granny Smith apple, cut into $\frac{1}{2}$-in. pieces

1. In a large skillet over medium heat, heat olive oil. Add onion and garlic, and cook for 5 minutes.

2. Add chicken, ginger, oregano, and rosemary, and cook, stirring and turning chicken, for 6 to 8 minutes or until cooked through.

3. Add kale and raisins, and cook for 3 minutes or until greens are wilted.

4. Add apple, and cook for 1 minute. Serve immediately with salt and pepper.

Variation: Cabbage, chard, and frozen or fresh spinach are great substitutes for the kale. If using frozen spinach, microwave-thaw it, and squeeze dry before using.

Chicken Sautéed with Olives, Lemon, and Capers

20   **Serves:**
4

2 TB. olive oil

1 TB. chopped garlic

2 tsp. Italian seasoning

1½ lb. boneless, skinless chicken breasts, rinsed, dried, and cut into 1-in.-thick strips

Salt

Black pepper

3 TB. capers, drained and rinsed

½ cup pitted kalamata olives

Juice of ½ lemon

3 TB. toasted pine nuts

1. In a large skillet over medium heat, heat olive oil. Add garlic and Italian seasoning, and cook, stirring, for 2 minutes.

2. Add chicken, and cook for 4 minutes, turning once. Sprinkle chicken with salt and pepper as it cooks.

3. Add capers and kalamata olives, and cook, stirring, for 3 minutes or until chicken is done. Scoop to serving plates, drizzling each serving with lemon juice and sprinkling with pine nuts.

ON THE CLOCK

The capers used in this recipe bring a lot of salty flavor, so taste the dish before adding any additional.

Chicken Paprika

20	Serves: 4

2 TB. olive oil

1½ lb. boneless, skinless chicken breasts, rinsed, dried, and cut into 1-in.-thick strips

1 TB. paprika

¼ tsp. salt

Pinch black pepper

1 cup fat-free chicken broth

⅔ cup light sour cream

1. In a large skillet over medium heat, heat olive oil.

2. Sprinkle chicken with ½ tablespoon paprika, salt, and pepper, add to the skillet, and cook for 5 minutes or until done, turning once. Remove to a serving plate and cover with aluminum foil to keep warm.

3. Increase heat under the skillet to high, add chicken broth and remaining ½ tablespoon paprika, and bring to a boil. Cook for 5 minutes until broth is reduced by half or more. Remove the skillet from heat, and stir in sour cream, allowing it to warm from the skillet.

4. Distribute chicken to serving plates, spoon creamy paprika sauce over chicken, and serve.

ON THE CLOCK

To accelerate dishes that call for chicken pieces, use that good pantry standby: canned chunk white chicken meat (drained).

Grilled Chicken with Spiced Chickpea Purée

20	**Serves:**
	4

2 TB. olive oil

1 lb. boneless, skinless chicken breasts, rinsed, dried, and cut into 1-in. chunks

½ medium onion, chopped into ¼-in. pieces

1 tsp. ground cumin

½ (15-oz.) can (1 cup) *chickpeas, drained and rinsed*

1 TB. chopped garlic

3 TB. diced prosciutto

½ cup light sour cream

¼ cup milk

½ tsp. salt

¼ tsp. black pepper

¼ cup sliced almonds, toasted if possible

1. In a large skillet over medium heat, heat olive oil. Add chicken and onion, and cook, stirring, for 5 minutes or until chicken is cooked. Sprinkle chicken with cumin as it cooks.

2. Meanwhile, in a food processor fitted with a steel blade, blend chickpeas, garlic, prosciutto, sour cream, milk, salt, and pepper to an almost creamy consistency.

3. Remove chicken to serving plates.

4. Scrape chickpea purée into the skillet, and cook, stirring, for 2 minutes. Distribute equal amounts of chickpea purée over chicken, sprinkle with sliced almonds, and serve.

Variation: This purée is also delicious over grilled pork.

> **DEFINITION**
>
> **Chickpeas** (also known as garbanzo beans) are the base ingredients in hummus and many other dishes. Chickpeas are high in fiber and low in carbohydrates and fat, making them a delicious and healthful component of many appetizers and main dishes.

Chicken and Shrimp Paella

This quick version brings to life some of that magic *paella* taste.

 Serves:
4 to 6

8 cups cooked white or brown rice, or 2 bags boil-in-bag rice

3 TB. olive oil

2 tsp. paprika

$\frac{3}{4}$ lb. boneless, skinless chicken breasts, rinsed, dried, and sliced crosswise into $\frac{1}{4}$-in.-thick pieces

Salt

Black pepper

3 TB. butter

1 onion, chopped

1 TB. crushed garlic

1 (16-oz.) can chopped tomatoes, with juice

1 cup baby peas

$\frac{1}{8}$ tsp. saffron

3 TB. sherry or cooking wine

$\frac{1}{2}$ tsp. crushed red pepper flakes

$\frac{3}{4}$ lb. cooked jumbo shrimp

Juice of $\frac{1}{2}$ lemon

1. Cook rice according to the package instructions, and set aside.

2. Meanwhile, in a large skillet over medium-high heat, heat olive oil.

3. Sprinkle paprika over all sides of chicken, season with salt and pepper, and add to the skillet. Cook, turning, for 5 minutes or until done. Remove chicken to a plate.

4. Add butter to the skillet to melt. Add onion, and cook for 5 minutes.

5. Add garlic, and cook for 1 minute. Add chopped tomatoes, peas, saffron, sherry, and crushed red pepper flakes, and cook for 4 minutes.

6. Stir in shrimp and cooked rice, and heat for 3 minutes.

7. Serve from the skillet or from a serving platter, drizzling first with lemon juice and seasoning with more salt and pepper.

 DEFINITION

Paella, a feast for the eyes as well as the stomach, is a grand Spanish mélange of rice, shellfish, onion, meats, rich broth, and herbs.

Chicken and Paprika Cream

This spicy-creamy variation on the classic Hungarian Chicken Paprika is fun for dinner and suitable for guests. Serve with steamed vegetables and rice.

 20

	Serves:
	4

2 TB. olive oil

1½ lb. boneless, skinless chicken breasts, rinsed, dried, and each breast cut into 3 strips lengthwise (about ¾-in. thick)

2 tsp. paprika

¾ tsp. plus ½ tsp. salt

Pinch black pepper

1 cup fat-free chicken broth

⅔ cup fat-free or low-fat sour cream

1. In a large skillet over medium-high heat, heat olive oil.

2. Sprinkle chicken breasts with 1 teaspoon paprika, ¼ teaspoon salt, and pepper, and add to the skillet. Cook for 8 minutes or until done, turning once. Remove to a serving plate, and cover with aluminum foil to keep warm.

3. Increase heat under the skillet to high. Add chicken broth, remaining 1 teaspoon paprika, remaining ½ teaspoon salt, and more pepper, and bring to a boil. Cook for 7 minutes or until broth reduces by about ¾. Turn off heat, and stir in sour cream.

4. Arrange chicken slices on serving plates, pour paprika cream over top, and serve.

Chicken, Vegetable, and White Bean Stew

20	Serves: 8

4 TB. olive oil

1 medium onion, chopped into ¼-in. pieces

1 TB. chopped garlic

2 large carrots, peeled and sliced into ¼-in. rounds

4 large celery stalks, cut into ¼-in. pieces

1½ lb. boneless, skinless chicken breasts, rinsed, dried, and cut into ½-in. pieces

½ tsp. salt

Black pepper

1 tsp. Italian seasoning

2 (15-oz.) cans fat-free chicken broth

1 (15-oz.) can cannellini beans, drained and rinsed

1 cup tomato sauce or 1 cup crushed tomatoes with liquid

Shredded Parmesan cheese

1. In a large saucepan over medium heat, heat 2 tablespoons olive oil. Add onion, and cook for 2 minutes, stirring. Add garlic, carrots, and celery, and cook for 3 minutes.

2. Meanwhile, in a large skillet over medium-high heat, heat remaining 2 tablespoons oil. Add chicken, sprinkle with salt and pepper, and cook, stirring, for 5 minutes or until done.

3. When chicken is cooked, add it to the saucepan along with Italian seasoning, chicken broth, cannellini beans, and tomato sauce. Cook, stirring occasionally, for 5 minutes.

4. Serve in bowls topped with Parmesan cheese.

MINUTE MORSEL

This farmhouse-style stew tastes great now and will be even better tomorrow. To accelerate the dish, cook the chicken in a separate skillet before adding it to the rest of the stew. If you have another few minutes, you can prepare the whole stew in one pot.

Pork Main Dishes

In This Chapter

- Quick grilled pork
- Fun pork kebabs
- Hearty ham dishes

Pork—the other white meat—is a healthful, low-fat, nutritious meat. Like poultry, pork can be extremely versatile, lending itself to a range of flavors, cooking styles, and cuisines. Plus, pork can be very affordable compared to other meats and seafoods.

Pork tenderloin is one of the most delicious cuts of pork available. It's generally a 2- or 3-pound piece (not to be confused with a pork *loin*, which is also delicious, but much bigger). For quick cooking, I like to slice it into medallions about 1 inch thick.

But that's just one option when it comes to pork. Turn the page for more!

Grilled Rosemary and Garlic Pork Tenderloin

20	Serves: 4

3 TB. olive oil

1 TB. chopped garlic

1½ lb. pork tenderloin, rinsed, dried, and cut into medallions

Juice of ½ lime

1 TB. fresh rosemary or 1 tsp. dried

1 tsp. salt

½ tsp. black pepper

1. Preheat the grill.

2. In a small bowl, mix olive oil and garlic.

3. In a large bowl, place pork tenderloin medallions. Pour lime juice and then garlic–olive oil mixture over pork, turning to coat. Sprinkle rosemary, salt, and pepper over pork, turning to coat.

4. Grill pork for 8 minutes, turning once, or until cooked through. Serve with a fruity red wine, such as pinot noir.

ON THE CLOCK

How do you know when it's done? To check for doneness, pierce the center of the piece of pork with a sharp knife. When liquid runs slightly pink (for rare) or clear (well done), the meat is cooked. If liquid is red, keep cooking!

Grilled Cumin-Ginger Pork Chops

Spicy and juicy grilled pork chops are just the right thing for a summer night with friends or family.

20   **Serves:**
4

1½ lb. center-cut pork chops,
　　rinsed and dried

Juice of ½ lime

2 TB. olive oil

1 tsp. ground cumin

1 tsp. ground ginger

1 tsp. salt

1. Preheat the grill.

2. In a large bowl, place pork chops. Drizzle lime juice over chops, followed by olive oil, turning to coat. Sprinkle cumin, ginger, and salt over pork, turning to coat.

3. Grill pork for 8 minutes, turning once, or until cooked through. Serve with an earthy red wine, like a côtes du rhône.

MINUTE MORSEL

Many "white meats" are also "light"; in other words, low in fat. Because of this, it's often important to add moisture (oil, butter, and so on) and also watch these meats closely as they cook to prevent drying.

Grilled Apple Chops

20 | **Serves:**
4

2 TB. olive oil

1½ lb. center-cut pork chops, rinsed and dried

Salt

Black pepper

½ cup unsweetened applesauce

½ cup light sour cream

2 TB. Dijon-style mustard

1. In a large skillet over medium heat, heat olive oil.

2. Sprinkle pork chops with salt and pepper on both sides, add to the skillet, and cook for 8 minutes or until cooked through, turning once. Transfer sizzling chops to serving plates.

3. Add applesauce, sour cream, and Dijon-style mustard to the skillet, and cook for 1 minute or until hot. Distribute sauce over chops, and serve.

Spiced Pork Loin Chops

20 | **Serves:**
4

2 TB. canola oil

1 tsp. cumin

1 tsp. paprika

2 TB. honey

1 lb. center cut pork loin chops, rinsed, dried, and sliced thin

Salt and pepper

1. Preheat the broiler.

2. In a small bowl, combine canola oil, cumin, paprika, and honey.

3. Place pork slices in a single layer on a baking sheet. Drizzle marinade over pork, turn to coat, and season with salt and pepper. Broil for 4 minutes, turn, and broil for 4 more minutes or until cooked through.

4. Serve over rice with buttered green beans and your favorite chilled white wine.

Variation: For **Grilled Sweet and Spicy Pork,** place marinated chops on the grill and cook 10 minutes or until done, turning once.

Curried Pork

20	**Serves:** 4

3 TB. olive oil

1½ lb. boneless center-cut pork chops, rinsed, dried, and cut into ½-in. pieces

1 medium onion, chopped into ½-in. pieces

2 tsp. curry powder

1 (15-oz.) can fat-free chicken broth

½ cup dried apricots, cut into ¼-in. pieces

1 crisp Granny Smith apple, cut into ½-in. pieces

1 tsp. salt

¼ tsp. black pepper

1. In a large skillet over medium heat, heat olive oil. Add pork, onion, and curry powder, and sauté, stirring, for 5 minutes.

2. Add chicken broth, apricots, and apple, and cook for 3 more minutes or until pork is cooked through. Sprinkle with salt and pepper, and stir.

3. Serve over brown rice for a hearty meal.

MINUTE MORSEL

To peel, or not to peel? That is the question when it comes to using some vegetables and fruits in cooking. Before you reach for that peeler, though, consider keeping the peel on some fruits and veggies like apples and new potatoes, especially if they're organic. Those peels (appropriately scrubbed, of course) add color, texture, flavor, and, perhaps most important, nutrition. You also save time—a good thing in my book.

Pork Kebabs

20	Serves:
	4

1½ lb. center-cut pork chops, rinsed, dried, and cut into 1-in. chunks

1 (8-oz.) pkg. small white mushrooms, wiped with a damp paper towel and cut in half lengthwise

1 large Vidalia or other sweet onion, cut into 1-in.-square pieces

2 large bell peppers, ribs and seeds removed, and cut into 1-in.-square pieces

⅓ cup Italian dressing

1. Preheat the grill.

2. On skewers, alternate pieces of pork, mushroom, Vidalia onion, and bell pepper.

3. Lay kebabs in a baking dish or platter, and drizzle with Italian dressing.

4. Grill for 8 minutes, turning once, or until pork is fully cooked.

Variation: You can use a wide range of marinades, or even simple olive oil, in place of Italian dressing. (Be sure to read the marinade and dressing ingredient lists. Many are loaded with sugar.)

 ON THE CLOCK

Wooden (often bamboo) skewers are inexpensive but flammable. To solve that problem, soak them in water for a few minutes before assembling your kebabs. Another option is to purchase reusable metal skewers. You can find both in grocery stores.

Pork and Broccoli Stir-Fry

 20 **Serves:**
4

1 lb. boneless center-cut pork
   chops, rinsed, dried, and cut into
   1-in. pieces

3 TB. soy sauce

1 TB. olive oil

1 medium onion, chopped into
  $\frac{1}{2}$-in. pieces

2 cups broccoli florets, about 1 in.
  in size

1 TB. freshly peeled and grated
  ginger (optional)

1 TB. sesame seeds

1. In a large bowl, combine pork and soy sauce.

2. In a wok or large skillet over medium heat, heat olive oil. Add onion and pork, and cook, stirring, for 5 minutes.

3. Add broccoli and ginger (if using), and cook for 5 more minutes or until pork is cooked through and broccoli is tender-crisp.

4. Serve, sprinkling with sesame seeds.

Ham Steaks with Sweet Mustard Sauce

 10 **Serves:**
4

2 TB. canola oil

2 TB. spoon-for-spoon sweetener

3 TB. Dijon-style mustard

2 (.75-lb.) ham steaks

1. In a small bowl, combine canola oil, spoon-for-spoon sweetener, and Dijon-style mustard.

2. Place ham steaks in a flat dish such as a pie plate, and pour sauce over, turning ham to coat both sides.

3. In a skillet over medium heat, place steak. Scrape remaining sauce into the skillet, and cook for 4 minutes, turning once.

4. Cut steak into quarters, and move to serving plates. Spoon sauce over each serving.

Choucroute Garni

 20   **Serves:**
4

2 TB. cooking oil

1 medium onion, cut into $\frac{1}{2}$-in. pieces

2 carrots, peeled and cut into $\frac{1}{2}$-in. sections

1 crisp Granny Smith apple, cored and chopped into $\frac{1}{2}$-in. pieces

1 lb. cooked knockwurst, kielbasa, or pork sausage, cut into $\frac{1}{2}$-in. slices

1 (14.5-oz.) can sauerkraut, drained and rinsed

1 bay leaf

1 cup dry white wine

1 tsp. caraway seeds

Mustard

1. In a large skillet over medium heat, heat oil. Add onion and carrots, and cook, stirring, for 5 minutes.

2. Add apple, knockwurst, sauerkraut, bay leaf, white wine, and caraway seeds, and cook, stirring, for 10 more minutes.

3. Remove bay leaf, distribute to *choucroute garni* serving bowls, spread with mustard, and serve.

Variation: Canned sauerkraut can have an unpleasantly sharp flavor. To soften this assault on your palate, rinse the sauerkraut in a colander under cold running water, drain, and use.

 DEFINITION

Choucroute garni is an Alsatian dish that comes in many forms but commonly includes sauerkraut (*choucroute* is French for "sauerkraut"), caraway, white wine, potatoes, vegetables, and cooked meats.

Hearty Red Meat Meals

In This Chapter

- Surefire beef recipes
- Meaty favorites from around the globe
- Quick and easy beefy stir-fries
- Lamb chops and kebabs

While some cooks turn to pork and poultry for speed, others prefer beef and lamb for terrific flavor. These richer meats offer flavors that stand out in recipes, flavors that feature more prominently than in a similar recipe made with lighter meats.

Some have a misperception that richer meats somehow require longer to cook. Allow me to change your mind about that. This chapter is packed with examples of 30-minute beef and lamb cuisine to prove that many richer meat cuts and methods of preparation are well suited to quick cooking.

When it comes to beef, stick with thin cuts such as tips, fillets, steaks, chops, and strips—and of course, ground beef. Within these limits, you'll find a world of opportunity. I've included some of my favorites in this chapter.

And then there's lamb. Lamb is an incredibly flavorful, rich meat that deserves more attention. Give one of the recipes in this chapter a try, and you'll see what I mean.

My favorite wines to enjoy with rich meats like beef and lamb include correspondingly rich red wines made from cabernet sauvignon, malbec, and Syrah or Shiraz grapes.

Quick Cajun Kebabs

 20

Serves:
4 to 6

1 lb. steak tips, cut into 1-in. pieces

1 Vidalia onion, cut into 1-in. pieces

1 large green pepper, ribs and seeds removed, and cut into 1-in. pieces

1 pt. button mushrooms

2 TB. olive oil

2 tsp. Cajun seasoning

1. Preheat the grill.

2. On a skewer, slide alternating pieces of steak, Vidalia onion, green pepper, and mushroom. Repeat until the skewer is full to within 2 inches of the end. Place skewer on a large plate, and repeat with more skewers until ingredients are used up.

3. In a small bowl, combine olive oil and Cajun seasoning. Drizzle generously over each skewer.

4. Place skewers, parallel to each other, on the grill over the flame, and cook for 10 minutes or until meat is cooked, turning frequently. If the grill has a "hot spot," when turning kebabs, rotate the less done ones to the hot spot and the more done ones out to cooler areas of the grill so all kebabs will be done at about the same time.

Variation: If you don't have Cajun seasoning, use 1 teaspoon salt, $\frac{1}{2}$ teaspoon crushed red pepper flakes, $\frac{1}{4}$ teaspoon black pepper, $\frac{1}{2}$ teaspoon garlic powder, and $\frac{1}{4}$ teaspoon cumin instead. You could also use firm cherry tomatoes, hot peppers, and zucchini or summer squash in these kebabs.

Mediterranean Beef Skewers

 Serves:
6

1 lb. steak tips, cut into 1-in. pieces

1 medium sweet onion, cut into 1-in. pieces

1 cup large pimiento-stuffed olives

1 pt. grape tomatoes

1 (8-oz.) pkg. button mushrooms, stems removed and wiped with a damp paper towel

2 TB. olive oil

2 tsp. Italian seasoning

Salt

Black pepper

Lemon juice

1. Preheat the grill.

2. On a skewer, slide alternating pieces of steak, sweet onion, olive, tomato, and mushroom. Repeat with more skewers until ingredients are used up.

3. Stack loaded skewers on a large plate, drizzle with olive oil, and sprinkle with Italian seasoning, salt, and pepper.

4. Grill kebabs for 6 minutes or until meat is cooked, turning once. Drizzle with lemon juice, and serve.

Variation: Use hot peppers, squash, or bell peppers (green, yellow, or red) on your skewers.

 TIME WASTER

Onions don't cook completely in these kebabs, so you'll get a blast of unwelcome sharp flavor with sharp onions. Stick with the sweet, mild varieties, like Vidalia, Bermuda, or Maui. Sweet onions don't completely cook either, but the mild flavor and pleasingly crisp texture is a welcome addition.

Quick-Grilled Beef Satay

20 | **Serves:** 4

½ cup natural-style "crunchy" peanut butter

2 TB. soy sauce

2 TB. canola oil

Double dash hot pepper sauce

1½ lb. sirloin steak tips, cut into ¾-in. pieces

2 TB. hot pepper oil, or 2 TB. canola oil mixed with ¼ tsp. hot pepper sauce

2 TB. teriyaki sauce

3 TB. sesame seeds

1. Preheat the grill.

2. In a small serving bowl, combine peanut butter, soy sauce, canola oil, and hot pepper sauce.

3. In a large bowl, place steak. Pour hot pepper oil and teriyaki sauce over, and turn to coat.

4. Spear 2 beef morsels on the tip of a skewer, and repeat with more skewers until ingredients are used up. Arrange beef on the grill with skewer extending off the grill to minimize burning and facilitate turning. Grill for 5 minutes or until done, turning once.

5. Arrange skewers on a serving platter in a circle with meat in the center, surrounding the bowl of dipping sauce. Sprinkle sesame seeds over beef, and serve so diners can lift a skewer, dip, and devour.

DEFINITION

A **satay** is a popular Southeast Asian dish of broiled skewers of fish or meat, often served with peanut sauce.

Steak and Onions

20	Serves: 4

2 TB. butter

2 TB. olive oil

1 medium onion, sliced thin into $\frac{1}{4}$-in. pieces

$1\frac{1}{2}$ lb. steak, such as sirloin

1 tsp. salt

$\frac{1}{2}$ tsp. black pepper

1. In a large skillet over medium heat, heat butter and olive oil. Add onion, and cook, stirring, for 4 minutes.

2. Meanwhile, sprinkle steak with salt and pepper.

3. Increase heat under the skillet to high, move onions to the edge of the skillet, and place steak in the middle. Cook steak for 8 minutes or to your desired doneness, turning once.

4. Top each serving of steak with onions, and serve with a rich red wine like a California cabernet sauvignon.

TIME WASTER

Heat varies from stovetop to stovetop. If your skillet gets hot enough to burn the onions (in spite of the butter and oil in the skillet), take them out before you cook the steak.

Tenderloin Strips with Pepper Cream

20   **Serves:**
4

2 TB. butter or olive oil

1½ lb. tenderloin steak, sliced into ½-in. strips

1½ tsp. ground cumin

½ tsp. salt

¼ tsp. black pepper

½ cup light sour cream

1. In a large skillet over medium heat, melt butter.

2. Dust steak with cumin, salt, and pepper, add to the skillet, and cook for 3 minutes per side or to your preferred doneness. Distribute strips to serving plates, and turn off the heat.

3. Scrape sour cream into the skillet, and mix thoroughly with any butter and spices remaining. Spoon cream mixture over strips, and serve.

ON THE CLOCK

Is it done? With steak, red in the middle is rare, pink is medium, and gray all the way is well done. For me, between rare and medium is perfect. I find that a well-done steak loses its flavor and isn't as tender.

Turkish Beef Pockets

	Serves:
20	4

1 TB. olive oil

1 lb. sirloin steak, cut into ¼-in. strips

1 tsp. ground cumin

Salt

Black pepper

½ cup plain yogurt

2 tsp. lemon juice

2 tsp. chopped garlic

½ cup peeled and finely chopped cucumber

¼ tsp. black pepper

2 small whole-wheat pita bread loaves

1 cup (¼-in. strips) purple or green cabbage

1. In a large skillet over medium heat, heat olive oil.

2. Sprinkle sirloin steak with cumin, salt, and pepper. Add to the skillet, and cook for 6 minutes or until done, turning once.

3. Meanwhile, in a small bowl, combine yogurt, lemon juice, garlic, cucumber, and ¼ teaspoon pepper.

4. Cut each pita in half. Distribute steak among pita halves, arranging them lengthwise. Top with cabbage and yogurt mixture, and serve.

Citrus Stir-Fry

20 **Serves:** 4

2 TB. sesame or olive oil

1 lb. steak tips, cut into ¾-in. pieces

½ tsp. salt

1 large onion, chopped into ¼-in. pieces

1 TB. chopped garlic

2 cups fresh sugar snap peas, stemmed and rinsed, or 1 (9-oz.) pkg. frozen sugar snap peas, thawed

1 (6-oz.) can sliced water chestnuts, drained

2 TB. lime juice

2 TB. soy sauce

2 TB. orange zest

¼ tsp. black pepper

Lime slices (optional)

1. In a wok or a large skillet over medium-high heat, heat sesame oil.

2. Sprinkle steak tips with salt, add to the skillet, and cook 4 minutes or until done, turning once. Remove beef to a separate plate.

3. Reduce heat under the wok to medium, add onion, and cook, stirring, for 2 minutes. Add garlic, and cook for 1 more minute.

4. Add snap peas and water chestnuts, and cook for 3 more minutes, stirring, or until pods are tender-crisp. Return beef to wok, and add lime juice, soy sauce, orange zest, and pepper. Cook, stirring, for 1 minute. Serve, garnished with lime slices (if using).

Variation: Serve over ½ cup brown rice.

ON THE CLOCK

Stir-frying, with its high heat, is one of the best methods for quick preparation of one-pot (or is that one-wok?) meals.

Beef and Broccoli Stir-Fry

This flavorful, crunchy dish makes quick use of traditional Chinese ingredients and methods.

 20   **Serves:**
4

1 TB. canola oil

1 lb. flank steak, cut into thin strips

½ tsp. salt

¼ tsp. pepper

1½ tsp. fresh ginger, grated

2 cups chopped Chinese cabbage or bok choy, thick stem pieces separated from leaves

2 cups broccoli *florets*

2 TB. soy sauce

2 TB. sesame oil

4 cups cooked rice

1. In a wok or a large skillet over high heat, heat canola oil.

2. Sprinkle flank steak with salt and pepper, add to the skillet with ginger, and cook, stirring constantly, for 3 minutes or until almost done.

3. Add thick stem pieces of Chinese cabbage and broccoli florets, and cook for 2 minutes. Add cabbage leaves, and cook for 2 more minutes or until leaves wilt and soften.

4. Add soy sauce and sesame oil, toss to coat, and serve over rice.

 DEFINITION

A **floret** is the part of broccoli or cauliflower that holds all the flower or bud ends. It's the nonstem part.

Garlic Beef and Asparagus Stir-Fry

20 | **Serves:**
4

2 TB. sesame or olive oil

1 lb. steak tips, cut into ¾-in. pieces

1 lb. fresh asparagus, rinsed, tough bottoms removed, cut into 1-in. sections

2 TB. chopped garlic

3 TB. teriyaki sauce

2 TB. sesame seeds

1. In a wok or a large skillet over medium-high heat, heat sesame oil. Add steak tips, and cook for 2 minutes.

2. Add asparagus and garlic, and cook for 4 minutes, stirring, or until beef is done.

3. Drizzle with teriyaki sauce, sprinkle each serving with sesame seeds, and serve.

Variation: Serve over ½ cup brown rice.

Fast Stuffed Peppers

20   **Serves:**
4

1 lb. lean ground beef

1 medium onion, chopped into
    $\frac{1}{2}$-in. pieces

2 tsp. chopped garlic

1 (14.5-oz.) can diced tomatoes,
    drained with juice reserved

$\frac{1}{4}$ cup unprocessed bran

1 TB. Worcestershire sauce

2 tsp. Italian seasoning

$\frac{1}{2}$ tsp. salt

$\frac{1}{4}$ tsp. black pepper

2 large green bell peppers, sliced in
    half lengthwise, ribs and seeds
    removed

$\frac{1}{2}$ cup shredded cheddar cheese

1. Preheat the broiler.

2. In a large skillet over medium heat, add ground beef, onion, and garlic, and
   cook, stirring, for 5 minutes or until done. Drain fat from the skillet.

3. Add tomatoes, unprocessed bran, Worcestershire sauce, Italian seasoning,
   salt, and pepper. Cook, stirring, for 4 minutes. If mixture is too dry to cling
   together, add some reserved tomato juice.

4. Meanwhile, in a microwave- and oven-safe (Pyrex type) baking dish, place green
   bell pepper halves, cut side up, with $\frac{1}{4}$ inch water in the bottom of the dish.
   Microwave on high for 3 or 4 minutes or until softened.

5. Stuff bell peppers with cooked ground beef mixture, and return to the baking
   dish. (Keep a little water in the bottom of the baking dish.) Top each bell pepper with some cheddar cheese, and slide under the broiler for 3 minutes or until
   cheese has melted.

Variation: Use ground pork, turkey, or sausage in place of the ground beef.

Fleisch Kuchle (Austrian Meat Cakes)

Hearty and quick, this carries all the comfort food attributes of meatloaf or a good burger.

 Serves:
4

4 TB. canola oil	2 eggs
1 cup dry whole-wheat or white breadcrumbs	1 onion, finely chopped
1 lb. ground beef	$\frac{1}{2}$ cup milk
2 slices bread, crusts removed, torn into pieces	$\frac{1}{2}$ cup sour cream
	1 tsp. salt

1. In a skillet over medium heat, heat canola oil.

2. Place breadcrumbs in a shallow bowl.

3. In a large bowl, combine ground beef, bread, eggs, and onion. Form mixture into patties, roll in breadcrumbs, and add to the skillet. Fry for 10 minutes or until done, turning once. Remove cakes from the skillet to serving plates.

4. Add milk, sour cream, and salt to the skillet, and mix thoroughly, scraping up any bits attached to the bottom of the pan. Reduce heat to low, cook for 4 minutes, and pour over cakes. Serve with boiled new potatoes seasoned with dill and salt.

Fast Start Chili

30	**Serves:** 8

2 TB. olive oil	2 TB. chili powder
1 lb. lean ground beef	1 TB. ground cumin
1 (16-oz.) can refried beans	1 tsp. salt
1 (15-oz.) can red kidney beans, drained and rinsed	$\frac{1}{2}$ tsp. black pepper
1 (14-oz.) can diced tomatoes with juice	$\frac{1}{2}$ cup light sour cream

1. In a large skillet over medium heat, heat olive oil. Add ground beef, and cook for 5 minutes, stirring, or until browned.

2. Stir in refried beans, red kidney beans, tomatoes, chili powder, cumin, salt, and pepper, and cook for 10 minutes, stirring.

3. Serve, topping with a dollop of sour cream.

Variation: Use ground chicken, pork, or turkey in place of ground beef. You could also add sliced mushrooms or canned corn. And few will object to shredded cheese on top.

ON THE CLOCK

Many beef- and lamb-based mixtures, including chili and stews, are not only delicious immediately but also improve as the seasonings have time to meld. Talk about a reason to look forward to leftovers!

Burgers with a Twist

20   **Serves:**
4

1 lb. ground lamb	1 egg
1 small onion, finely chopped	¼ cup dry breadcrumbs (optional)
1 tsp. dried rosemary	2 tsp. olive oil

1. In a bowl, thoroughly combine lamb, onion, rosemary, and egg. (If you're not squeamish, the best way to do this is with your hands!) Shape into round, flat patties approximately $2\frac{1}{2}$ inches in diameter. If mixture is too moist, add breadcrumbs.

2. In a large skillet over medium heat, heat olive oil. Add burgers to the skillet (as many as can easily fit without touching each other), and cook for 10 minutes or until done, turning once.

3. Serve on a bun with cheese, sliced sweet onion, fresh tomato slices, crispy lettuce, and ketchup. Or just top with ketchup and serve with bread and salad for a quick and flavorful meal.

Variation: I usually make these burgers with ground lamb, but the basic concept is the same with ground poultry, pork, or beef. The lamb burgers take a little longer to cook than some of the other alternatives.

Lamb Chops on Wilted Greens with Balsamic Drizzle

20	Serves: 4

3 TB. canola oil

1½ lb. lamb loin chops

Salt

Black pepper

1 (8-oz.) pkg. fresh baby spinach, stemmed, rinsed, and dried

1 TB. crushed garlic

3 TB. balsamic vinegar

1. In a large skillet over medium-high heat, heat 1 tablespoon canola oil.

2. Rub lamb chops with salt and pepper, add to the skillet, and brown for 1 minute on each side. Reduce heat to medium, and cook for 6 more minutes or until done, turning once. Remove chops to a plate, and cover with aluminum foil.

3. Add 1 tablespoon canola oil to the skillet. Add spinach, cover, and cook for 1 minute or until spinach is wilted. Distribute spinach to serving plates, and top with a lamb chop.

4. Add remaining 1 tablespoon canola oil to the skillet along with garlic and balsamic vinegar, and cook for 1 minute. Drizzle vinegar mixture over lamb chops and spinach on each plate, and serve with a salad, and maybe a glass of red Bordeaux, and all is right with the world.

Moroccan Lamb Kebabs

20	**Serves:**
	4

1½ lb. lamb steak, cut into 1-in. chunks

1 large red bell pepper, ribs and seeds removed, and cut into 1-in.-square pieces

1 large green bell pepper, ribs and seeds removed, and cut into 1-in.-square pieces

1 (8-oz.) pkg. small white mushrooms, stems trimmed, wiped with a damp paper towel, and cut in half lengthwise

1 large Vidalia or other sweet onion, peeled and cut into 1-in.-square pieces

3 TB. olive oil

1 tsp. salt

1 tsp. cumin

½ tsp. black pepper

¼ tsp. ground cardamom

¼ tsp. ground cinnamon

1. Preheat the grill.

2. On a skewer, slide alternating pieces of lamb, red bell pepper, green bell pepper, mushroom, and Vidalia onion. Repeat with more skewers until ingredients are used up. Stack loaded skewers on a large plate, and drizzle with olive oil.

3. In a small bowl, combine salt, cumin, pepper, cardamom, and cinnamon, and sprinkle over kebabs.

4. Grill kebabs for 8 minutes or until meat is cooked, turning once.

Variation: You could also use cubes of steak, chicken, or pork instead of the lamb. Experiment with grape tomatoes and vegetables, too.

Versatile Vegetarian Dinners

In This Chapter

- Naturally fast vegetarian cuisine
- Hearty veg casseroles
- Sizzling veggie stir-fries
- Savory tofu delicacies

If the term *vegetarian* makes you think of lentils, brown rice, and other "weird" ingredients, you're in for a pleasant surprise. The main course dishes in this chapter are savory and hearty and include everything from stuffed vegetables to casseroles.

When it comes to vegetarian meals, time is on your side. Many of this chapter's recipes rely on bright flavors from fresh ingredients—flavors that would be dulled or destroyed by long cooking. Flavorful and packed with nutrition, these vegetarian main dishes are a must-have part of a good diet.

Tofu is an important part of the vegetarian diet. The versatile, cheeselike soy product made from soybeans and soy milk has a mild flavor that makes it easy to flavor. Tofu is a good source of fiber and protein. For added interest, use a marinated and flavored tofu, available at your grocery store. Firm tofu will hold its shape in your recipe.

Rice Medley

20   **Serves:**
4

3 TB. olive oil	3 cups cooked rice
1 medium onion, chopped	½ cup sliced black olives
1 tsp. crushed red pepper flakes	2 cups feta cheese, crumbled
2 cups oil-packed sun-dried tomatoes, drained and chopped	Salt
	Black pepper

1. In a large skillet over medium heat, heat olive oil. Add onion, crushed red pepper flakes, and sun-dried tomatoes, and sauté for 6 minutes.

2. Add cooked rice and black olives, and cook, stirring, for 4 minutes.

3. Stir in feta cheese and serve, passing with salt and pepper.

Rice Palao

20   **Serves:**
4

1 TB. butter	1 tsp. salt
1 TB. canola oil	2 TB. golden raisins
2 cups quick-cooking white rice	8 cashews, sliced lengthwise
1 tsp. ground cardamom	10 almonds, sliced lengthwise
1 bay leaf	¼ tsp. ground cloves
3½ cups water	½ tsp. coriander

1. In a large skillet over medium heat, heat butter and canola oil. Add white rice, cardamom, and bay leaf, and cook, stirring, for about 5 minutes, or until rice starts to stick.

2. Add water and salt, and bring to a boil.

3. Add raisins, cashews, almonds, cloves, and coriander. Cover and cook 10 minutes or until rice is cooked. Remove bay leaf, and serve.

MINUTE MORSEL

Bay leaves bring a wonderful flavor to soups, stews, and savory dishes. The dried leaf is added at the beginning of cooking and then removed before serving because they don't soften and can be bitter if bitten into.

Rosemary's Quick Enchiladas

Colorful and tasty, this recipe can be doubled easily.

20	**Serves:** 4 to 6

1 (16-oz.) can black beans (drained)

1 cup corn kernels (fresh, frozen, or canned)

4 oz. light cream cheese

2 cups Monterey Jack or cheddar cheese, shredded

$\frac{1}{2}$ tsp. cumin

1 cup salsa

4 large flour tortillas

1. Preheat the oven to 400°F.

2. In a large saucepan over medium-low heat, combine black beans, corn, cream cheese, $\frac{1}{2}$ of Monterey Jack cheese, cumin, and $\frac{2}{3}$ cup salsa, and cook, stirring, for 5 minutes or until cheese is melted and ingredients are combined.

3. Place $\frac{1}{4}$ heated mixture in 1 tortilla, and roll it up. Repeat until remaining mixture and tortillas used up. (Should make 3 medium or 3 large filled enchiladas.)

4. Place enchiladas close together in a baking pan. Spoon remaining $\frac{1}{3}$ cup salsa over tightly spaced enchiladas, and sprinkle with remaining $\frac{1}{2}$ of Monterey Jack cheese. Bake for 10 minutes, or until top is golden brown and bubbly.

Sautéed Mushroom Enchiladas

10 **Serves:**
2

3 TB. olive oil

1 TB. chopped garlic

1 tsp. Italian seasoning

2 cups sliced white mushrooms

2 large whole-wheat or low-carb
soft tortillas

Pinch salt

Pinch black pepper

1 cup shredded low-fat cheddar
cheese

1. In a large skillet over medium heat, heat olive oil. Add garlic and Italian season-ing, and cook, stirring, for 1 minute.

2. Add mushrooms, and cook, stirring, for 3 minutes or until mushrooms are soft.

3. Lay each tortilla on a microwave-safe serving plate, and place $\frac{1}{2}$ of mushrooms in a line along one side. Sprinkle mushrooms with salt and pepper, and top mushrooms with about $\frac{1}{4}$ cup cheddar cheese per tortilla.

4. Roll tortilla over its filling, top with another $\frac{1}{4}$ cup cheese per tortilla, and microwave for 1 minute or until cheese on top is melted.

Variation: Serve topped with sour cream.

Tostadas

10 **Serves:**
4

4 small whole-wheat or low-carb
tortillas

1 cup salsa, drained

2 cups shredded Mexican-style or
Monterey Jack cheese

1 (4-oz.) can sliced black olives,
drained

$\frac{1}{2}$ cup light sour cream

1. Preheat the broiler.

2. Arrange tortillas on a large baking tray or 2, and broil on the top rack for 1 minute to crisp a bit.

3. Divide salsa among heated tortillas, and top salsa with shredded Mexican-style cheese and sliced black olives. Broil for 3 minutes or until cheese melts.

4. Slice pizza-style, and serve each with a *dollop* of sour cream.

> **DEFINITION**
>
> A **dollop** is a spoonful of something creamy and thick, like sour cream or whipped cream.

South-of-the-Border Eggs

20	Serves: 2

2 TB. canola or olive oil	2 tsp. fresh chopped cilantro
4 large eggs	1 tsp. chili powder
¼ cup skim milk	Salt
1 tomato, cored, seeded, and diced	Black pepper
1 TB. fresh chopped basil or 1 tsp. dried	

1. In a small skillet over medium-low heat, heat canola oil.

2. In a medium bowl, combine eggs, skim milk, tomato, basil, cilantro, and chili powder. Pour egg mixture into the skillet, and cook, stirring slowly to bring uncooked eggs in contact with the skillet, for 4 minutes, or to your desired consistency.

3. Distribute to serving plates, season with salt and pepper, and serve.

Variation: If you don't have fresh cilantro, you can omit it.

Ratatouille

30 **Serves:** 8

3 TB. olive oil

1 medium onion, chopped into ½-in. pieces

1 TB. chopped garlic

1 large bell pepper, ribs and seeds removed, and chopped into ½-in. pieces

2 small zucchini, ends removed, cut into ½-in. pieces

1 eggplant, peeled, stem removed, cut into ½-in. chunks

3 large tomatoes, cored and roughly chopped, or 1 (28-oz.) can whole tomatoes, roughly chopped, with juice

2 tsp. Italian seasoning

1 tsp. salt

½ tsp. black pepper

½ cup shredded Parmesan cheese

1. In a large skillet over medium heat, heat olive oil. Add onion, and cook, stirring, for 4 minutes.

2. Add garlic, and cook for 1 minute. Add bell pepper, zucchini, eggplant, tomatoes, Italian seasoning, salt, and pepper, and cook, stirring constantly, for 15 minutes.

3. Serve in bowls topped with Parmesan cheese.

ON THE CLOCK

If you've got fresh herbs, you've got a chance to make something great even better. In place of the Italian seasoning, use ¼ cup chopped fresh basil leaves and 1 teaspoon fresh oregano. Adding ½ teaspoon each fresh thyme and fresh rosemary would be good, too.

Minestrone Pasta

Hearty and flavorful, this large pasta dish inspires visions of hillsides in Tuscany.

 Serves:
8

1 lb. gemelli or other small pasta

3 TB. olive oil

2 onions, chopped

1 tsp. chopped garlic

1 (14.5-oz.) can vegetable broth

2 carrots, peeled and chopped

2 zucchini, striped and chopped

1 TB. dried basil

1 (15.5-oz.) can cannellini beans, drained

2 cups 20-Minute Tomato Sauce (recipe in Chapter 24)

Salt

Black pepper

Parmesan cheese

1. Cook pasta according to package directions.

2. Meanwhile, in a large skillet over medium heat, heat olive oil. Add onions and garlic, and sauté for 5 minutes.

3. Add vegetable broth and carrots. Bring to a boil, and cook for 3 minutes.

4. Add zucchini, basil, cannellini beans, and 20-Minute Tomato Sauce. Bring back to a boil, and cook for 5 minutes.

5. When pasta is done, drain, and return to cooking pot. Add vegetable mixture, toss to thoroughly mix, and serve seasoned with salt, pepper, and Parmesan cheese.

 MINUTE MORSEL

Vegetable broth adds body and flavor to many dishes and serves as a good alternative to chicken or beef broth.

Family-Style Arugula Pasta

Sour and spicy arugula, sweet tomatoes, and rich Parmesan make this pasta something special. If you use pasta left over from last night, this can be a 5-minute meal!

	Serves:
	4 to 6

1 lb. box penne or other tube-shape or ridged pasta

1 large bunch (about 3 cups) fresh arugula

2 or 3 TB. olive oil

1 clove garlic, or to taste, chopped

8 or 9 plum tomatoes, chopped into eighths

Salt

Black pepper

2 cups shredded mozzarella cheese

Parmesan cheese

1. Cook pasta according to directions. Drain when finished and return to the cooking pot. Turn off the heat.

2. Meanwhile, wash and drain arugula. Chop roughly, and set aside.

3. In a large bowl, combine olive oil and garlic. Add tomatoes, season with salt and pepper, and stir to coat.

4. Add tomato mixture to drained pasta, and toss. Add mozzarella cheese, and mix. Add arugula, toss, and serve immediately, topped with grated Parmesan cheese.

Ricotta-Spinach Casserole

 20

Serves:
6

3 TB. olive oil

1 medium onion, chopped into ½-in. chunks

1 TB. chopped garlic

1 (10-oz.) pkg. frozen chopped spinach, thawed and squeezed dry

1 tsp. paprika

¼ tsp. nutmeg

½ cup light sour cream

1 (15-oz.) can cannellini beans, drained and rinsed

1 cup part-skim ricotta cheese

½ cup chopped walnuts

½ tsp. freshly black pepper

½ cup shredded part skim mozzarella cheese

1. In a large skillet, heat olive oil. Add onion and garlic, and cook, stirring, for 5 minutes.

2. Meanwhile, spread spinach on the bottom of a 9×9-inch casserole pan.

3. In a small bowl, combine paprika, nutmeg, and sour cream, and spread sour cream mixture over spinach.

4. Add cannellini beans, and spread in an even layer.

5. In the small bowl, combine ricotta cheese, walnuts, and pepper, and spread over cannellini beans.

6. Scrape sautéed onions on top of ricotta cheese, and top with mozzarella cheese. Microwave for 5 minutes or until cheese is melted and casserole is bubbling.

Variation: If you have a few extra minutes, you can cook this in a preheated 350°F oven for 25 minutes.

Stuffed Tomatoes

20	Serves: 4

4 medium ripe tomatoes

2 TB. olive oil

1 medium onion, chopped into ½-in. pieces

2 tsp. chopped garlic

1 (15-oz.) can chickpeas, drained and rinsed

1 cup diced tomatoes

¼ cup unprocessed bran

¼ cup chopped walnuts

¼ cup fresh basil, chopped

1 tsp. fresh oregano leaves

½ tsp. fresh thyme

½ tsp. fresh rosemary

½ tsp. ground cumin

½ tsp. salt

¼ tsp. black pepper

¼ cup plus 2 TB. shredded Parmesan cheese

1. Preheat the oven to 375°F.

2. Slice off top ⅓ of each tomato, scoop out insides, and reserve insides. Place tomatoes, cut side up, in an oven-safe baking dish with ¼ inch water in the bottom, and slide tomatoes into the oven. Cook for 7 to 10 minutes.

3. Meanwhile, in a large skillet over medium heat, heat olive oil. Add onion and garlic, and cook, stirring, for 3 minutes.

4. Mix in chickpeas, tomatoes, reserved tomato flesh, unprocessed bran, walnuts, basil, oregano, thyme, rosemary, cumin, salt, and pepper. Cook for 4 minutes, stirring.

5. Stir in ¼ cup Parmesan cheese.

6. Remove tomatoes from the oven, and stuff with skillet mixture. (Keep a little water in the bottom of the baking dish.) Top with remaining 2 tablespoons Parmesan cheese. Slide tomatoes in the baking dish back into the oven, and heat for 4 minutes or until cheese begins to melt.

Variation: Fresh flavors from fresh herbs are delicious, but to save time, use 2 teaspoons Italian seasoning in place of fresh basil, oregano, thyme, and rosemary.

Cheesy Stuffed Peppers

 20   **Serves:**
4

3 TB. olive oil

1 medium onion, chopped into
    ½-in. pieces

2 tsp. chopped garlic

1 cup diced tomatoes, juice
    reserved

¼ cup unprocessed bran

¾ tsp. salt

½ tsp. black pepper

⅛ tsp. ground nutmeg

1 cup part-skim ricotta cheese

4 medium red bell peppers, top
    1 in. cut off, ribs and seeds
    removed

½ cup shredded cheddar cheese

1. Preheat the broiler.

2. In a large skillet over medium heat, heat olive oil. Add onion and garlic, and cook, stirring, for 4 minutes.

3. Add tomatoes, unprocessed bran, salt, pepper, and nutmeg, and cook, stirring, for 4 minutes. Turn off heat, and stir in ricotta cheese.

4. Meanwhile, place red bell peppers, cut side up, in a microwave- and oven-safe baking dish with ½ inch water in the bottom. Microwave on high for 4 or 5 minutes or until softened.

5. Remove and stuff peppers with tomato-ricotta mixture. (Keep a little water in the bottom of the baking dish.) Top each pepper with some shredded cheddar cheese, and broil on the second rack for 3 minutes or until cheese has melted.

 TIME WASTER

Closely watch broiling and grilling dishes. The difference between "done" and "burnt sacrifice" is only a minute or two with these quick-cooking methods.

Sautéed Vegetable Medley

 Serves:
4

3 TB. olive oil

1 medium onion, chopped into
   $\frac{1}{2}$-in. pieces

1 large green bell pepper, ribs and
   seeds removed, and chopped
   into $\frac{1}{2}$-in. pieces

1 TB. chopped garlic

$\frac{1}{2}$ tsp. crushed red pepper flakes

$\frac{1}{2}$ tsp. ground cumin

1 (15-oz.) can chickpeas, drained
   and rinsed

1 (14.5-oz.) can diced tomatoes,
   with juice

$\frac{1}{2}$ cup pitted kalamata olives

2 TB. fresh chopped basil or 2 tsp.
   dried

$\frac{1}{2}$ tsp. salt

$\frac{1}{2}$ cup crumbled feta cheese

1. In a large skillet over medium heat, heat olive oil. Add onion and green bell
   pepper, and cook, stirring, for 4 minutes.

2. Add garlic, crushed red pepper flakes, and cumin, and cook for 1 minute.

3. Add chickpeas, tomatoes, kalamata olives, basil, and salt, and cook, stirring once
   or twice, for 5 minutes. Serve, topped with feta cheese.

ON THE CLOCK

Sautéed Vegetable Medley can take many forms, all of them tasty, fast, and
flexible. You don't have chickpeas? White or black beans will work. No feta?
Parmesan will do the trick. No kalamata olives? Use another olive—but go for the
pitted ones. Like less heat? Omit the crushed red pepper flakes. The journey is
half the fun.

Grilled Vegetable Kebabs

20 | **Serves:** 8

1 medium sweet onion, cut into 1-in. pieces

1 (16-oz.) pkg. extra-firm tofu, drained and cut into 1-in. cubes

1 large bell pepper, ribs and seeds removed, cut into 1-in. pieces

1 pt. grape tomatoes, stemmed and rinsed

2 TB. olive oil

Lemon juice

2 tsp. Italian seasoning

Salt

Black pepper

1. Preheat the grill.

2. On a skewer, slide alternating pieces of sweet onion, tofu, bell pepper, and tomato. Repeat with more skewers until ingredients are used up.

3. Stack skewers on a large plate, drizzle with olive oil and lemon juice, and sprinkle with Italian seasoning, salt, and pepper.

4. Grill for 6 minutes, turning and circulating kebabs around those inevitable hot spots.

Variation: For **Spiced Vegetable Kebabs,** instead of the Italian seasoning, season with 2 teaspoons spice seasoning blend featuring crushed red pepper flakes, pepper, paprika, and salt, such as Cajun, Italian, or even curry.

 ON THE CLOCK

Tofu producers are pretty good these days about making their "extra-firm" product solid enough to survive a skewer and a grill. But just to be on the safe side, I like to bracket each piece of tofu between onion and pepper. The naturally curved shape of these two pieces of vegetable hold that tofu chunk in place.

Vegetable Stir-Fry

20	Serves: 4

2 TB. sesame or olive oil

1 large onion, chopped into $\frac{1}{4}$-in. pieces

2 cups fresh broccoli, cut into 1-in. florets

1 TB. chopped garlic

$\frac{1}{2}$ (14-oz.) pkg. seasoned extra-firm tofu, drained and cut into $\frac{1}{2}$-in. cubes

1 (6-oz.) can sliced water chestnuts, drained

1 egg

2 TB. soy sauce

1. In a wok or a large skillet over medium heat, heat sesame oil. Add onion, and cook, stirring, for 2 minutes.

2. Add broccoli and garlic, and cook, stirring, for 3 minutes.

3. Add tofu and water chestnuts, and cook, stirring, for 3 more minutes.

4. In a small bowl, whisk egg and soy sauce. Pour over vegetables in the wok, and cook for 1 minute or until egg is cooked and broccoli florets are tender-crisp.

Variation: Serve over $\frac{1}{2}$ cup brown rice.

Sizzling Tofu and Asparagus Stir-Fry

 Serves:
4

2 TB. sesame or olive oil

1 lb. fresh asparagus, rinsed, tough bottoms removed, cut into 1-in. sections

1 (14-oz.) pkg. extra-firm plain tofu, drained and cut into ¾-in. pieces

3 scallions, roots and dark green leaves removed, cut into ¼-in. segments

1 TB. chopped garlic

3 TB. teriyaki sauce

2 TB. sesame seeds

1. In a wok or a large skillet over medium-high heat, heat sesame oil. Add asparagus, and cook, stirring, for 4 minutes.

2. Add tofu, scallions, and garlic, and cook, stirring occasionally, for 3 minutes or until asparagus is *tender-crisp*.

3. Drizzle with teriyaki sauce, and serve, sprinkling each serving with sesame seeds.

Variation: Serve over ½ cup brown rice.

 DEFINITION

Tender-crisp is a magic point in the cooking of vegetables where they're no longer raw, but still keep a slight appetizing crunch. Different vegetables will reach this point at different times. For example, broccoli takes longer than pea pods.

Sautéed Artichoke Hearts and Tofu

20   **Serves:**
4

2 TB. olive oil

1 (9-oz.) pkg. frozen artichoke
hearts, thawed

1 TB. chopped garlic

2 tsp. Italian seasoning

1 (14-oz.) pkg. extra-firm plain
tofu, drained and cut into ¾-in.
pieces

½ cup pitted kalamata olives

¼ cup chopped walnuts, toasted
if possible

2 TB. shredded Parmesan cheese

Salt

Black pepper

1. In a wok or a large skillet over medium heat, heat olive oil. Add artichoke
   hearts, garlic, and Italian seasoning, and cook, stirring, for 2 minutes.

2. Add tofu, and cook, stirring, for 4 minutes.

3. Add kalamata olives and walnuts, and cook, stirring, for 1 more minute.

4. Serve, sprinkling with Parmesan cheese and seasoning with salt and pepper.

Skillet Tofu Scramble

Serves:
2

2 TB. canola or olive oil

1 tsp. Italian seasoning

1 (15-oz.) pkg. firm tofu

½ cup shredded low-fat cheddar
cheese

Dash hot pepper sauce

Salt

Black pepper

1. In a small skillet over medium heat, heat canola oil and Italian seasoning.

2. In a medium bowl, combine tofu, cheddar cheese, and hot pepper sauce. Scrape tofu mixture into the skillet, and cook, stirring, for 3 or 4 minutes.

3. Distribute to serving plates, season with salt and pepper, and serve.

Variation: Add fresh herbs such as oregano, basil, and dill in place of the Italian seasoning. You could also sauté ½ onion in the skillet before adding tofu. Adding ½ cup of your favorite cooked vegetables, such as bell peppers, is also a tasty option.

Portobello Pizza

20 **Serves:**
2

2 large, flat portobello mushroom caps, stems and gills removed and wiped with a damp paper towel

3 TB. olive oil

$\frac{1}{2}$ tsp. dried tarragon

$\frac{1}{2}$ cup pizza sauce

$\frac{2}{3}$ cup shredded part-skim mozzarella cheese

Salt

Black pepper

1. Preheat the broiler. If your broiler has multiple settings, select the medium setting.

2. Place portobello mushroom caps on a baking tray, top side up. Brush each with some olive oil, and broil on the next-to-highest rack for 3 minutes.

3. Flip over caps, drizzle each with $\frac{1}{2}$ of remaining olive oil, sprinkle with tarragon, and broil for 3 more minutes.

4. Slide sizzling mushrooms out of the oven, and divide pizza sauce and then mozzarella cheese between mushrooms, spreading each layer smooth. Broil for 3 more minutes or until cheese is melted.

5. Place each pizza on a plate, and serve with a knife and fork, seasoning with salt and pepper.

 ON THE CLOCK

This recipe is for a basic cheese Portobello Pizza. Feel free to add your favorite toppings. Even a vegetarian pasta sauce can be used in place of the pizza sauce.

Bountiful Bean Dishes

In This Chapter

- Bean recipes from around the world
- Nutritious bean-filled main dishes
- New and delicious uses for familiar beans
- Hearty bean stews

Beans form the foundation of many healthy meals across the globe. They bring a hearty consistency and a nutrition profile that's nearly unmatched.

In the recipes in this chapter, I've specified shell beans most commonly found canned in grocery stores, such as white beans (a.k.a. cannellini beans), chickpeas (also called garbanzo beans), black beans, and red beans (or kidney beans). Shell beans are high in protein and fiber and low in net carbohydrates. As an added bonus, many of the dishes in this chapter are quick, one-pot meals.

In these pages, we have some fun exploring different ways to prepare beans, from bean-based salads to "pancakes" to pure comfort food: ham and beans! After trying some of the bean-based dishes in this chapter, you'll learn how flexible—and delicious—bean cuisine can be.

White Bean Salad

10 **Serves:**
4

1 (15-oz.) can cannellini beans, drained

1 medium tomato, seeded and chopped into ¼-in. pieces, or about 10 grape tomatoes, quartered

1 cup fresh basil leaves, chopped into ¼-in. pieces

⅓ cup chopped sweet onion

¼ cup shredded Parmesan cheese

1 TB. balsamic vinegar

1 TB. olive oil, plus more as needed

½ tsp. salt, plus more as needed

⅛ tsp. black pepper, plus more as needed

4 Belgian endive heads, broken into leaves

3 pieces cooked bacon (optional)

1. In a large bowl, combine cannellini beans, tomato, basil, sweet onion, Parmesan cheese, balsamic vinegar, olive oil, salt, and pepper, being sure to preserve the shape of most beans.

2. Arrange Belgian endive leaves on 4 serving plates, ends touching at the center and tips pointing out flower style.

3. Distribute bean salad among plates, crumbling bacon (if using) over each serving and seasoning, if desired, with additional salt, pepper, and olive oil as dressing.

Variation: Substitute red wine vinegar for the balsamic vinegar. For a more hearty salad, add 1 (6-ounce) can chunk white tuna in water (drained).

MINUTE MORSEL

If you're careful how you scoop the salad onto the Belgian endive leaves, the tips will rise slightly from the weight of the salad in the center, creating a "flower" effect. It's always fun to play with your food.

Red Beans and Rice

 30   **Serves:**
4

3 TB. butter or olive oil	$\frac{1}{2}$ tsp. crushed red pepper flakes (optional)
1 medium onion, chopped into $\frac{1}{2}$-in. pieces	$\frac{1}{2}$ tsp. black pepper
2 tsp. Cajun seasoning	2 or 3 cups cooked rice (your favorite)
2 TB. chopped garlic	1 TB. lime juice
1 cup chicken broth	Salt
1 (15-oz.) can red kidney beans, drained and rinsed	

1. In a large skillet over medium heat, melt butter. Add onion and Cajun seasoning, and cook, stirring, for 5 minutes.

2. Add garlic, and cook for 1 more minute.

3. Add chicken broth, red kidney beans, crushed red pepper flakes (if using), and pepper. Cook, stirring, for 8 minutes.

4. Serve hot beans over cooked rice, drizzling with lime juice and seasoning with salt, if desired. (There's salt in chicken broth, so it might not be necessary.)

 TIME WASTER

Beans and other high-fiber foods such as cabbage, broccoli, onions, and many fruits often result in gas in the lower intestine—the gas is the result of normal bacteria doing its work. If you eat beans regularly, this might not be as much of a problem for you. Rinsing beans before cooking them also removes much of the problem. Finally, there's that little container of Beano.

Minestra

	Serves:
20	4

1 bunch (about 1 lb.) greens such as chard, kale, or escarole, rinsed

4 TB. olive oil

1½ TB. crushed garlic

1 (15-oz.) can cannellini beans, drained and rinsed

Salt

Black pepper

Freshly shredded Parmesan cheese

1. Chop greens and separate the stems from the leaves.

2. In a large skillet over medium heat, heat olive oil. Add garlic, and cook, stirring, for 2 minutes or until garlic begins to turn golden.

3. Add stems, and cook, stirring, for 4 minutes. Add greens, and cook, stirring, for another 5 minutes.

4. Add cannellini beans, and heat for 2 more minutes.

5. Distribute to serving plates, seasoning with salt and pepper and sprinkling with Parmesan cheese.

Mediterranean Skillet Meal

Serves:
4

3 TB. olive oil

1 medium onion, chopped into
½-in. pieces

2 TB. chopped garlic

1 tsp. Italian seasoning

1 (14-oz.) can chickpeas, drained
and rinsed

1 (14-oz.) can chopped tomatoes,
drained

½ cup pitted kalamata olives

½ cup chopped fresh parsley

½ cup crumbled feta cheese

Salt

Black pepper

1. In a large skillet over medium heat, heat olive oil. Add onion, and cook, stirring, for 4 minutes.

2. Add garlic and Italian seasoning, and cook for 1 more minute.

3. Add chickpeas, tomatoes, and kalamata olives, and cook, stirring, for 5 more minutes.

4. Stir in parsley, and serve, topping with crumbled feta cheese and seasoning with salt and pepper.

Quick Wok Chickpeas and Chicken

 Serves:
4

3 TB. sesame or olive oil

1 lb. boneless, skinless chicken breasts, rinsed and dried, and cut into ¾-in. pieces

½ (10-oz.) head broccoli, broken into 1-in. florets, stems reserved for another use

2 TB. chopped garlic

Dash hot pepper sauce

1 (15-oz.) can chickpeas, drained and rinsed

2 TB. lemon juice

1 TB. grated fresh peeled ginger

2 TB. sesame seeds

Salt

1. In a wok or a large skillet over medium-high heat, heat sesame oil. Add chicken, broccoli, garlic, and hot pepper sauce, and cook, stirring, for 4 minutes or until chicken is just done.

2. Add chickpeas, and cook, stirring, for 1 minute.

3. Turn off heat, drizzle with lemon juice, and sprinkle with ginger. Toss to coat, and serve, sprinkling each serving with sesame seeds and seasoning with salt.

Herbed White Beans with Baby Spinach

20	Serves: 4

3 TB. olive oil

1 medium onion, chopped into $\frac{1}{2}$-in. pieces

2 TB. chopped garlic

1 TB. chopped fresh rosemary or 1 tsp. dried

2 (15-oz.) cans white beans, drained and rinsed

1 (7-oz.) pkg. fresh baby spinach, rinsed

2 TB. balsamic vinegar

$\frac{1}{3}$ cup shredded Parmesan cheese

$\frac{1}{2}$ tsp. black pepper

Salt

1. In a large skillet over medium heat, heat olive oil. Add onion, and cook, stirring, for 4 minutes.

2. Add garlic and rosemary, and cook, stirring, for 1 minute.

3. Add white beans, and cook, stirring, for 3 minutes.

4. Add spinach, cover, and cook for 2 minutes or until spinach is wilted. Turn off heat.

5. Drizzle with balsamic vinegar, stir to coat, and serve, sprinkling each serving with Parmesan cheese and seasoning with pepper and salt.

Variation: Substitute 1 pound boneless, skinless chicken breasts, cut into $\frac{3}{4}$-inch pieces, for 1 can white beans. Add chicken after onions have cooked for 4 minutes and add about 5 minutes to the cooking time before adding beans and spinach to give chicken time to cook. Substitute frozen spinach, thawed, drained, and pressed dry, for fresh spinach. Substitute lemon juice for balsamic vinegar. (This will change the dish, but it's delicious.)

White Beans with Olive Oil, Gorgonzola, and Sage

| 20 | Serves: 4 |

4 cups water

2 (15-oz.) cans white beans, drained and rinsed

3 TB. extra-virgin olive oil

1 TB. minced fresh sage leaves or ½ tsp. dried

½ cup crumbled *Gorgonzola dolce* cheese

Salt

Black pepper

1. In a large saucepan over medium-high heat, bring water to a boil. Add white beans, and return to a boil. Drain beans.

2. Add extra-virgin olive oil, sage, and Gorgonzola dolce cheese, and toss with beans. Serve warm, seasoning with salt and pepper.

Variation: Crumbled blue cheese will work in place of the Gorgonzola dolce cheese. The taste won't be the same, but it'll be in the same ballpark.

DEFINITION

Gorgonzola dolce is a creamy and rich Italian blue cheese. *Dolce* means "sweet," and that's the kind you want.

Pan-Broiled White Bean, Bacon, and Scallop Dinner

20 | **Serves:**
6

½ lb. bacon

1 bunch scallions, roots and dark green parts removed, minced

2 TB. sherry

1½ tsp. fresh thyme or ½ tsp. dried

1 tsp. fresh sage, minced, or ¼ tsp. ground

½ lb. bay scallops

1 (15-oz.) can white beans, drained and rinsed

½ cup shredded Swiss cheese

Black pepper

Salt (optional)

1. Preheat the broiler.

2. In a large skillet over medium heat, cook bacon for 2 minutes per side or until crisp. Remove bacon to a paper towel–lined plate. Pour most fat from skillet, leaving enough to coat the bottom of the skillet.

3. Add scallions, sherry, thyme, and sage, and cook, stirring, for 3 minutes.

4. Add bay scallops, and cook, stirring, for 3 minutes or until done.

5. Crumble bacon, and add, with white beans, to the skillet, and stir to thoroughly combine. Heat for 1 minute, turn off heat, and sprinkle Swiss cheese over top of bean mixture.

6. Broil for 2 minutes or until cheese melts. Remove from the oven, and serve, seasoning with pepper. You might not need salt because bacon will already have introduced salt to the dish.

 MINUTE MORSEL

A cast-iron skillet will survive the trip this recipe calls for, from the stovetop to the broiler.

White Bean Vegetable Pancakes

20	Serves: 4

1 (15-oz.) can cannellini beans, drained and rinsed

1 TB. chopped garlic

½ tsp. salt

¼ tsp. black pepper

¼ tsp. ground cumin

¼ tsp. dried thyme

1 small zucchini squash, rinsed and trimmed

1 portobello mushroom, stemmed and wiped with a damp paper towel

2 large eggs, whisked

4 TB. olive oil

½ cup light sour cream

1. In a food processor fitted with a steel blade, process cannellini beans, garlic, salt, pepper, cumin, and thyme just enough to break up beans but leave plenty of texture. Scrape beans into a large bowl.

2. Switch out the steel blade with the shredder wheel. (Don't bother cleaning the bowl.) Cut zucchini squash into pieces to fit into the feed tube, and shred zucchini squash. Do the same with mushroom. Pour shredded mushroom and zucchini squash on top of beans.

3. Add eggs to the large bowl with beans, mushroom, and zucchini squash, and stir thoroughly.

4. In a large skillet over medium heat, heat olive oil. Using a ¼-cup measure, spoon lumpy batter into the skillet, and cook for about 3 minutes on one side, flip pancake over, and cook for 1 more minute. (Watch for the point when pancakes are solid enough to flip: too early and they tend to break apart.)

5. Serve hot, with a spoonful of sour cream on top.

MINUTE MORSEL

I first made these pancakes because a friend challenged me to make what he called an "edible" pancake based on beans. I can never resist a challenge, so I came up with these savory, crisp-creamy burgers. The consistency is somewhat like crab cakes. These, apparently, are more than "edible": my challenging friend had thirds.

Black Bean Stew

20	**Serves:**
	6

2 TB. olive oil

1 large onion, chopped

1 TB. chili powder

1 tsp. ground cumin

2 (15-oz.) cans chicken broth

2 (15-oz.) cans black beans, drained

1 (14-oz.) can chopped tomatoes, with juice

½ cup fresh cilantro, chopped

2 TB. lime juice

⅔ cup light sour cream

½ tsp. freshly black pepper

Salt

1. In a large stockpot over medium heat, heat olive oil. Add onion, and cook, stirring, for 3 minutes.

2. Add chili powder and cumin, and cook, stirring, 2 minutes.

3. Add 1 can chicken broth, 1 can black beans, and tomatoes to the saucepan, and cook for 10 minutes.

4. Meanwhile, pour remaining can chicken broth and remaining can black beans into a blender, and purée to a smooth consistency. Add puréed beans to soup in the stockpot for the remainder of the cooking time.

5. Stir in cilantro and lime juice, and serve in bowls with a dollop of sour cream, seasoning with pepper and salt, if necessary. (There's salt in chicken broth, so it might not be necessary.)

ON THE CLOCK

Soups and stews traditionally use flour or cornstarch for thickening. A quick purée of cooked beans can serve this same delicious purpose while adding fiber and nutrition.

North African Bean Stew

30	Serves: 6

3 (15-oz.) cans chicken stock

3 TB. olive oil

1 medium onion, chopped into $\frac{1}{2}$-in. pieces

2 celery stalks, chopped into $\frac{1}{2}$-in. pieces

2 TB. chopped garlic

$\frac{1}{2}$ cup dried apricots, quartered

2 tsp. ground cinnamon

2 tsp. ground paprika

1 tsp. ground cumin

1 tsp. ground coriander

1 tsp. salt

Dash hot pepper sauce

1 (15-oz.) can black beans, drained and rinsed

1 (15-oz.) can chickpeas, drained and rinsed

1 (14-oz.) can diced tomatoes with juice

$\frac{1}{2}$ cup fat-free plain yogurt

1. In a large pot over high heat, heat chicken stock until near boiling.

2. Meanwhile, in a large frying pan over medium heat, heat olive oil. Add onion, celery, and garlic, and cook, stirring, for 4 minutes.

3. Add apricots, cinnamon, paprika, cumin, coriander, salt, and hot pepper sauce, and cook, stirring constantly, for 2 or 3 more minutes.

4. Reduce heat under the large pot to medium, and add black beans, chickpeas, tomatoes with juice, and contents of the large frying pan to the heated broth. Cook for 5 minutes, stirring occasionally.

5. Serve in bowls topped with dollop of yogurt.

Italian Farmhouse Stew

30   **Serves:**
4

4 TB. olive oil

1½ lb. boneless, skinless chicken breasts, rinsed, dried, and chopped into ½-in. cubes

1 medium onion, chopped

2 large celery stalks, cut into ¼-in. slices

2 large carrots, peeled and cut into ¼-in. rounds

1 TB. crushed garlic

1 (16-oz.) can cannellini beans, drained and rinsed

2 (15-oz.) cans chicken broth

1 (14-oz.) can crushed tomatoes with juice

1 TB. fresh basil, chopped

1 tsp. fresh oregano

1 tsp. fresh sage, chopped

1 tsp. fresh rosemary leaves

Crushed red pepper flakes

1 TB. balsamic vinegar

Parmesan cheese

Salt (optional)

Black pepper

1. In a large skillet over medium heat, heat 2 tablespoons olive oil. Add chicken, and cook, stirring, for 5 minutes or until done.

2. Meanwhile, in a large stockpot over medium heat, heat remaining 2 tablespoons olive oil. Add onion, celery, and carrots, and cook for 4 minutes.

3. Add garlic, and cook for 1 more minute.

4. When chicken is done, add it to the stockpot with vegetables. Add cannellini beans, chicken broth, tomatoes with juice, basil, oregano, sage, rosemary, and crushed red pepper flakes, and cook, stirring, for 10 minutes.

5. Turn off heat, stir in balsamic vinegar, and serve in big bowls, sprinkling with Parmesan cheese and seasoning with additional salt (if desired; there's salt in chicken broth, so it might not be necessary) and pepper.

 ON THE CLOCK

As with many stews of this type, leftovers will taste even better the next night.

Two-Bean Ham Stew

20	Serves: 8

3 TB. olive oil

2 tsp. mustard seed

1 medium onion, chopped into
½-in. pieces

3 celery stalks, including leafy tops,
cut into ½-in. pieces

1 bay leaf

2 (15-oz.) cans chicken broth

1 (15-oz.) can white navy beans or
cannellini beans, drained and
rinsed

1 (15-oz.) can black beans, drained
and rinsed

1 (14-oz.) can diced tomatoes with
juice

1 (.75-lb.) ham steak, cut into ½-in.
cubes

Dash hot pepper sauce

Salt

Black pepper

1. In a large stockpot over medium heat, heat olive oil. Add mustard seed, onion, celery, and bay leaf, and cook, stirring, for 5 minutes.

2. Add chicken broth, white navy beans, black beans, tomatoes with juice, ham steak, and hot pepper sauce, and cook for 10 minutes.

3. Remove bay leaf, and serve, seasoning with salt (if desired; there's salt in broth and ham, so it might not be necessary) and pepper.

Cassoulet

30 **Serves:**
6

1 lb. pork sausage links, cut into
   1-in. pieces

3 TB. olive oil

1 medium onion, chopped into
   $\frac{1}{2}$-in. pieces

2 large carrots, peeled and cut into
   $\frac{1}{2}$-in. pieces

1 TB. chopped garlic

2 (15-oz.) cans white beans, drained
   and rinsed

2 (15-oz.) cans chicken broth

$\frac{1}{4}$ cup dry white wine

1 TB. fresh basil, chopped

1 tsp. fresh oregano

1 tsp. fresh sage, chopped

1 tsp. fresh rosemary leaves

2 tsp. ground mustard

1 bay leaf (optional)

$\frac{1}{2}$ tsp. black pepper

Salt

1. In a large skillet over medium heat, add sausage, and cook, stirring, for 5 minutes or until done.

2. Meanwhile, in a large stockpot over medium heat, heat olive oil. Add onion and carrots, and cook for 4 minutes.

3. Add garlic, and cook for 1 more minute.

4. Using a slotted spoon, add sausage to the stockpot with onion and carrots. Add white beans, chicken broth, white wine, basil, oregano, sage, rosemary, ground mustard, bay leaf (if using), and pepper, and cook, stirring, for 10 minutes.

5. Remove bay leaf, and serve cassoulet in big bowls with additional salt (if desired; there's salt in chicken broth, so it might not be necessary) and pepper.

Variation: Substitute 2 teaspoons Italian seasoning for the fresh herbs. If you've got the time, use half pork and half sausage in the skillet, and put everything in a slow cooker and cook on low for 6 to 8 hours.

ON THE CLOCK

To accelerate rich meat and bean dishes, cook the meat in a separate skillet while cooking the vegetables in a stockpot. If you've got a few extra minutes, you can save cleaning by cooking the chicken in the stockpot, adding the vegetables, and cooking everything in one pot.

Chickpea Bisque

20	Serves: 4

2 TB. butter or olive oil

1 medium onion, chopped into ½-in. pieces

1 TB. curry powder

1 (15-oz.) can chicken broth

1 (15-oz.) can chickpeas, drained and rinsed

1 TB. marsala cooking wine (optional)

1 tsp. salt

¼ tsp. black pepper

Double dash hot pepper sauce

1 cup heavy cream or plain yogurt

2 TB. fresh chives, minced

1. In a large saucepan over medium heat, heat butter. Add onion, and cook, stirring, for 5 minutes.

2. Add curry powder, and cook, stirring, for 2 minutes.

3. Add chicken broth, chickpeas, marsala, salt, pepper, and hot pepper sauce, and cook, stirring, for 5 minutes.

4. Working in batches, put *bisque* in a blender and purée to a smooth consistency. Return bisque to the saucepan.

5. Stir in heavy cream, and heat for 1 more minute or until soup is hot. (If using yogurt, be careful not to bring it to a boil.) Serve bisque in bowls, sprinkled with chives.

Variation: Use garam masala in place of the curry powder. The result will be slightly less spicy but just as rich.

DEFINITION

A **bisque** is a thick, creamy soup made with puréed vegetables, meats, and usually seafood.

Pasta and Pizza

In This Chapter

- Quick and delicious pasta dishes
- Sensational seafood pasta combinations
- Perfect pizza recipes

Pizza and pasta often hold a place of honor at the dinner table. Quick cooking and easy, these dishes are an important part of the busy cook's repertoire. In this chapter, we explore some of my favorites.

Pasta is magic. The appeal of pasta is not only its simplicity but its variety. Pasta usually takes from 6 to 15 minutes to cook, depending on the type (fresh pasta cooks much more quickly than dried), so when you're in a hurry, pick one of the quicker-cooking types! Pasta can be served with tomatoes and many other kinds of vegetables. Pasta can be divine with seafood, from shrimp and scallops to fish. Lighter meats, richer meats, cheeses, and cream—they're all welcome to the pasta party.

If pasta is convenient, pizza is a dream food. All the same basics are there—flour, tomato sauce, and cheese. And when it comes to topping, there's no limit.

20-Minute Tomato Sauce

With this quick sauce as a base, delicious pizza, pasta, chili, and many other dishes are within quick reach. I like to make a big batch and freeze a container for later when I don't have the time to prepare it from scratch.

	Serves: 4

3 TB. olive oil	2 TB. tomato paste
1 large onion, chopped	1 tsp. dried oregano
2 cloves garlic, crushed	1 tsp. dried basil
1 (28-oz.) can plum tomatoes, chopped, juice reserved	1 tsp. salt
	½ tsp. sugar

1. In a large sauté pan over medium heat, heat olive oil. Add onion, and sauté for 3 minutes.

2. Add garlic, and cook for 4 or 5 more minutes. Add tomatoes, tomato juice, tomato paste, oregano, basil, salt, and sugar, and cook, stirring, for 8 to 10 minutes.

Variation: Use a blender or food processor to turn this chunky sauce into a smooth, creamy sauce.

ON THE CLOCK

You may be tempted to add other ingredients, from new herbs (rosemary, sage) to cooked hamburger or a number of other hearty ingredients. Go for it! Serve plates of pasta topped with sauce and Parmesan cheese, accompanied by a garden salad and fresh bread, and the stage is set for a great little meal.

10-Minute Chicken and Herb Pasta

Serves:
4

2 TB. olive oil

1 onion, chopped

1 clove garlic, chopped

¾ lb. cooked chicken, cut into 1-in. pieces

¾ lb. cooked small-shape pasta or spaghetti

1 TB. fresh basil, minced, or 1 tsp. dried basil

½ tsp. crushed red pepper flakes

3 TB. fresh parsley, minced, or 1 TB. dried parsley

Salt

Black pepper

Parmesan cheese

1. In a large frying pan over medium heat, heat olive oil. Add onion and garlic, and cook for 5 minutes.

2. Add chicken, pasta, basil, crushed red pepper flakes, and parsley, and cook, stirring, for 5 more minutes.

3. Season with salt and pepper, top with Parmesan cheese, and serve with steamed vegetables and a glass of dry white wine for a simple, tasty meal.

Fettuccini Alfredo

Sour cream gives this recipe a creamy, tangy richness.

⏱ 20	**Serves:** 4 to 6

1 lb. spaghetti	¾ cup shredded Parmesan cheese
1 cup sour cream	Salt
3 TB. butter	Black pepper

1. Cook spaghetti according to package directions. Drain.

2. In a large bowl, combine spaghetti, sour cream, butter, and Parmesan cheese. Season with salt and pepper, and serve.

Linguini with Hot Pepper and Oil

⏱ 20	**Serves:** 4 to 6

1 lb. linguini	1 tsp. crushed red pepper flakes
¼ cup olive oil	Parmesan cheese
1 onion, chopped	Salt
3 tsp. chopped garlic	Black pepper

1. Cook linguini according to package directions. Drain.

2. Meanwhile, in a large skillet over medium-low heat, heat olive oil. Add onion, garlic, and crushed red pepper flakes, and sauté for 5 minutes.

3. Increase heat to medium-high. Add pasta to oil-onion mixture, and cook, stirring, for 1 or 2 minutes. Serve from the skillet, topping with Parmesan cheese, salt, and pepper.

Penne with Asparagus and Ham

 20

Serves:
4 to 6

1 lb. penne pasta
¼ cup olive oil
1 TB. chopped garlic
1 lb. (about 2 or 3 cups) fresh
   asparagus, stem ends removed,
   cut into 1-in. pieces

1 tsp. dried oregano
½ tsp. dried sage
1½ to 2 cups ham, finely chopped
Parmesan cheese
Salt
Black pepper

1. Cook penne according to package directions. Drain.

2. Meanwhile, in a large skillet over medium-low heat, heat olive oil. Add garlic, and sauté for 3 minutes.

3. Add asparagus, oregano, and sage, and cook, stirring, for 7 to 9 minutes or until asparagus reaches the desired level of softness. (The more you cook it, the softer it gets.)

4. Stir in ham.

5. Place cooked penne in a serving bowl, add asparagus mixture, and stir to mix thoroughly. Serve immediately, topping with Parmesan cheese, salt, and pepper.

Penne à la Vodka

 20

Serves:
6 to 8

¼ cup olive oil
1 TB. chopped garlic
1 (28- or 35-oz.) can Italian peeled
   plum tomatoes, broken up
   within the can with a knife
1 tsp. dried parsley
½ tsp. crushed hot pepper

1 lb. penne pasta
⅓ cup vodka
½ cup heavy cream
Parmesan cheese, freshly grated
Salt
Black pepper

1. In a large saucepan over medium-high heat, put water on for pasta and bring to a boil.

2. In a large pot over medium heat, heat olive oil. Add garlic, and cook for 1 minute.

3. Add tomatoes, parsley, and crushed hot pepper, and cook for about 10 minutes.

4. Meanwhile, cook penne for 5 minutes. Drain.

5. Add vodka and heavy cream to tomato mixture, followed by adding partially cooked pasta. Cook for 5 more minutes or until pasta is cooked.

6. Serve with Parmesan cheese, salt, and pepper.

Baby Spinach and Feta Penne

The dark green spinach adds color, flavor, and texture to this simple but delicious dish.

20	**Serves:** 4 to 6

1 lb. penne	6 cups fresh baby spinach
¼ cup olive oil	Parmesan cheese
1 large onion, chopped	Salt
1 (8-oz.) pkg. feta cheese, crumbled	Black pepper

1. Cook penne according to package directions. Drain and return to the pot.

2. Meanwhile, in a large skillet over medium-low heat, heat olive oil. Add onion, and sauté for 5 minutes.

3. Add cooked onion and olive oil, feta cheese, and baby spinach to the pot, and toss.

4. Serve with Parmesan cheese, salt, and pepper.

Rotelle with Mushrooms and Spinach

The spinach in this recipe is cooked and simmered with the mushrooms and chicken broth for extra flavor.

20	**Serves:** 4 to 6

1 lb. rotelle or other small pasta	1 tsp. dried basil
¼ cup olive oil	1 tsp. dried oregano
1 large onion, chopped	6 cups fresh baby spinach
1 pt. fresh mushrooms, sliced (or baby button mushrooms, whole)	Parmesan cheese
	Salt
1 cup chicken broth	Black pepper

1. Cook rotelle according to package directions. Drain and return to the pot.

2. Meanwhile, in a large skillet over medium-low heat, heat olive oil. Add onion, and sauté for 5 minutes.

3. Add mushrooms, and sauté for 3 minutes.

4. Add chicken broth, basil, and oregano. Increase heat to high, and cook for 7 minutes. (Broth will reduce in volume by about half.)

5. Add spinach, cook for 1 minute, cover, and remove from heat.

6. Add onion-mushroom-spinach mixture to the pot with pasta, and toss.

7. Serve with Parmesan cheese, salt, and pepper.

Chicken Chunk Pasta

 Serves:
4 to 6

1 lb. small pasta (your favorite shape)

1 batch 20-Minute Tomato Sauce (recipe earlier in this chapter)

1 tsp. dried thyme

2 cups cooked chicken pieces, chopped

Parmesan cheese

Salt

Black pepper

1. Cook pasta according to package directions. Drain.

2. Meanwhile, in a saucepan over medium heat, heat 20-Minute Tomato Sauce. Add thyme and chicken, and cook, stirring, for about 5 minutes or until heated through and beginning to bubble.

3. Distribute pasta to serving plates, and top with sauce. Serve with Parmesan cheese, salt, and pepper.

Variation: Cubed boneless chicken breasts could also be cooked at the same time to fit within the time frame.

Shrimp Shells

The rich taste of shrimp and garlic just might make this dish your favorite.

 Serves:
4 to 6

1 lb. small-shell pasta

¼ cup olive oil

1 large onion, chopped

1½ TB. chopped garlic

1 lb. cooked small (50 to 60 count, or more) shrimp

2 cups feta cheese, crumbled

Parmesan cheese

Salt

Black pepper

1. Cook shells according to package directions. Drain.

2. Meanwhile, in a large skillet over medium-low heat, heat olive oil. Add onion and garlic, and sauté for 5 minutes.

3. Add cooked shrimp, and heat, stirring, for 2 or 3 minutes. (Shelled raw shrimp can be used, but add 3 to 5 more minutes, or enough time to cook them thoroughly.)

4. Add cooked pasta to onion-garlic-shrimp mixture in the skillet. Add feta cheese, and mix thoroughly.

5. Serve with Parmesan cheese, salt, and pepper. Along with a salad, Italian bread, and a crisp white wine, this is a summer meal for the scrapbook.

Angel Hair Pasta with Shrimp and Feta

This recipe, from my wife's cousin Anya (a super cook), is a real crowd-pleaser.

 20

Serves:
4 to 6

2 or 3 TB. olive oil	2 TB. capers
1 tsp. minced garlic	1 lb. raw medium (41 to 50 count) shrimp, shelled and deveined
1 tsp. crushed red pepper flakes (optional)	Salt
1 tsp. dried oregano	Black pepper
¼ cup clam juice (optional)	¼ to ⅓ lb. feta cheese, crumbled into good-size chunks
1 (28-oz.) can chopped plum tomatoes, drained, juice reserved	16 oz. angel hair pasta
2 TB. tomato paste (optional if using clam juice)	

1. In large pot, bring salted water to boil for pasta. Lower heat to low and simmer until ready to cook pasta 5 minutes before serving.

2. In a large skillet over medium heat, heat olive oil. Add garlic, and sauté for 3 or 4 minutes or until translucent and sizzling.

3. Add crushed red pepper flakes (if using), oregano, clam juice (if using), and reserved tomato juice. Increase heat to high, and cook until liquid is reduced by half.

4. Add tomatoes, tomato paste (if using), and capers. Reduce heat to medium-low and simmer for 5 minutes.

5. Add shrimp, and simmer for 5 more minutes.

6. Add salt, pepper, and feta cheese, and gently mix. (Stir feta gently. The goal is not to dissolve cheese in sauce but to have chunks of warm, soft feta floating.)

7. When shrimp is added to tomato sauce, turn up pasta water to high and cook angel hair for 7 minutes or until *al dente*. Drain.

8. Serve angel hair with shrimp feta tomato sauce. Garnish with additional crumbled feta, or serve finely crumbled feta alongside for garnish. With bread and salad, this is an elegant meal.

Variation: If you like saucier pasta for this recipe, double the chopped tomatoes, garlic, and capers. (Easy on the oregano and crushed red pepper flakes; they're potent, so don't necessarily double them.) Clam juice is optional but adds a nice depth to the sauce. No salt needed as the feta cheese, clam juice, and capers are salty.

DEFINITION

Al dente is Italian for "against the teeth." It refers to pasta that's neither soft nor hard, but just slightly firm against the teeth. This, according to many pasta aficionados, is the perfect way to cook pasta.

Pasta with Herbs

Light and flavorful, this pasta is perfect with a glass of white wine.

20	**Serves:** 4 to 6

1 lb. gemelli pasta (or your favorite)	1 tsp. dried oregano
¼ cup olive oil	2 TB. dried parsley (or several sprigs fresh, chopped)
1 bunch scallions, dark green parts removed, white and light green parts chopped	Parmesan cheese
	Salt
2 tsp. dried basil	Black pepper

1. Cook gemelli according to package directions. Drain and return to the pot.

2. Meanwhile, in a large skillet over medium-low heat, heat olive oil. Add scallions, basil, and oregano, and sauté for 5 minutes.

3. Add scallion mixture to cooked gemelli. Add parsley, and toss to coat.

4. Serve with Parmesan cheese, salt, and pepper.

Pasta with Chicken, Mozzarella, and Sweet Red Peppers

 20 **Serves:**
4 to 6

3 TB. olive oil	1 tsp. dried basil
1 large onion, coarsely chopped	$\frac{1}{2}$ tsp. ground cumin seed
1 lb. boneless, skinless chicken breasts, sliced thin	1 lb. rotelle or other shaped pasta, cooked
2 sweet red peppers, ribs and seeds removed, and diced	*Parmesan cheese*
2 cups mozzarella cheese, shredded	Salt
1 tsp. dried oregano	Black pepper

1. In a large sauté pan over medium-high heat, heat olive oil. Add onion, and sauté for 5 minutes.

2. Add chicken, and sauté for about 5 minutes or until browned on all sides.

3. Add red peppers, and sprinkle with mozzarella cheese, oregano, basil, and cumin seed. Stir and sauté for 5 minutes.

4. Toss with cooked rotelle, and season with Parmesan cheese, salt, and pepper.

5. Serve with tossed salad and Italian bread.

 DEFINITION

Parmesan cheese is an aged, hard, flavorful Italian cheese served grated or shredded on a multitude of dishes starting with pasta, its soul mate on the table. Grated Parmesan cheese has been around for a long time on grocers' shelves. Now shredded Parmesan, usually sold in reclosable bags, is available in most grocery stores.

20-Minute Homemade Pizza

Serves:
3 or 4

1 (16-oz.) ball store-bought white
  or whole-wheat pizza dough, at
  room temperature

Cornmeal

1 TB. olive oil

$^2/_3$ cup 20-Minute Tomato Sauce
  (recipe earlier in this chapter)

$1^1/_2$ to 2 cups shredded mozzarella
  cheese

1. Preheat the oven to 450°F. If you have a pizza stone or pizza brick, preheat it in the oven on the middle rack.

2. Separate pizza dough into 2 halves, each about 8 ounces. Sprinkle cornmeal on a counter, and using a rolling pin, roll each dough ball to the desired size.

3. Sprinkle cornmeal generously on a pizza paddle or flat baking sheet with no edge over an area the size of your crust. (This keeps your pizza from sticking.)

4. Lay out pizza doughs on the paddle, pulling them from the edge to remove any folds. (You might have to do this in batches if both doughs won't fit on the paddle at once.)

5. Using a tablespoon measure, drizzle olive oil in a swirl over doughs, and spread so oil coats most of doughs.

6. Spoon 20-Minute Tomato Sauce on doughs, and spread so it evenly coats doughs to within about $^1/_2$ inch of edges. Spread mozzarella cheese over sauce.

7. If you're using a pizza stone, open the oven and slide out the baking rack with baking stone. Lift the pizza paddle or baking tray, and slide your pizzas onto the stone. If the pizzas don't want to slide, encourage them with a spatula around the edges. If you're not using a pizza stone, place the baking tray straight in the oven.

8. Bake for 12 to 15 minutes or until crusts are crispy when you tap them with your finger and cheese is bubbly.

Variation: Although 2 slightly smaller ones are easier to work with, you can also make 1 large pizza with this recipe. If you don't have a rolling pin, you can use the side of a wine bottle you've washed and dried.

MINUTE MORSEL

A fun way to prepare dough is to toss it, twirling, in the air, like you see in pizza parlors. Some people prefer to roll the dough on a floured surface, using a rolling pin. If the dough resists spreading, the words of my friend and pizza guru Lisa Cooper come to mind: "Treat stubborn pizza dough a lot like you would an uncooperative kid: Give it a five-minute time-out and then try again."

Fresh Herb Pizza

 Serves:
3 or 4

1 baked 20-Minute Homemade Pizza	1 small handful (perhaps 12), young edible flowers, such as nasturtium
1 handful small arugula leaves	
1 handful small basil leaves	

1. Upon removing 20-Minute Homemade Pizza from the oven, arrange arugula, basil, and edible flowers across top of pizza.

TIME WASTER

Don't end up with dried, flavorless greens on your pizza. The key to fresh herbs on pizza is to add them as the pizza comes out of the oven, so they soften but still retain their color and flavor.

Feta and Black Olive Pizza

The creaminess of feta and the tang of olives make this a perennial favorite.

 Serves:
3 or 4

1 unbaked 20-Minute Homemade
 Pizza

1 cup crumbled feta cheese

1 cup sliced black olives

1. Before baking prepared 20-Minute Homemade Pizza, spread feta cheese and then black olives across pizza.

2. Bake as directed. Check at 12 minutes, but with the extra toppings, this pie might take a few minutes longer.

Shrimp and Basil Pizza

 Serves:
3 or 4

1 unbaked 20-Minute Homemade
 Pizza

20 small precooked shrimp (5 oz.)

1 tsp. dried basil

Pinch garlic powder

1. Before baking 20-Minute Homemade Pizza, spread shrimp across pizza. Sprinkle with basil, and dust with a pinch of garlic powder.

2. Bake as directed. Check at 12 minutes.

Variation: Raw shelled shrimp can also be used but require a quick (3 to 5 minutes or until done) cook in a skillet over medium heat with olive oil before topping your pizza.

Roasted Red Pepper and Artichoke Pizza

 20   **Serves:**
3 or 4

1 unbaked 20-Minute Homemade
  Pizza

½ cup drained roasted red
  peppers, cut into bite-size
  pieces

½ cup drained artichoke hearts,
  cut into bite-size pieces

Pinch garlic powder

1. Before baking 20-Minute Homemade Pizza, spread roasted red peppers and
   artichoke heart pieces across pizza. Dust with garlic powder.

2. Bake as directed. Check at 12 minutes.

 TIME WASTER

When cleaning your pizza stone, use only water and a brush. Never use soap
because the porous surface of the pizza stone will absorb soap flavors. Pepperoni
and Soap Pizza probably won't be on anyone's favorites list.

White Pizza with Olives and Fresh Mozzarella

 10   **Serves:**
4

1 (10-oz.) prepared thin pizza crust

1 cup shredded mozzarella cheese

10 fresh mozzarella balls, cut in half

10 pitted kalamata olives, sliced in
  half lengthwise

1 TB. olive oil

½ tsp. dried basil

¼ tsp. garlic salt

1. Preheat the broiler.

2. Place pizza crust on a baking sheet, and sprinkle with shredded mozzarella cheese. Scatter fresh mozzarella balls and kalamata olive halves on top, drizzle with olive oil, and sprinkle with basil and garlic salt.

3. Broil for about 3 minutes or until shredded mozzarella begins to melt. Slice into slender pieces and serve. *Voilà!* Er, I mean *presto!*

MINUTE MORSEL

Pizza is not just for the main meal, but also makes a great appetizer, thanks to prepared pizza crusts. For appetizer pizza, stick with thin crusts. Some of the same themes for larger pizzas are fine with appetizers (pepperoni, pepper, onion, sausage, and so on), but with appetizers, where the intent is focused flavors, there's also room to take chances. Think of sliced kalamata olives with fresh mozzarella, garlic, shrimp, even anchovies. Feel free to experiment to find your favorites.

Tortilla and Scallion Pizza

A touch of sour cream makes this a magical bite.

 10 | **Serves:** 4

2 large soft flour tortillas	4 scallions, washed, dark green parts and roots removed, white and light green parts thinly sliced
2 cups shredded Monterey Jack cheese	1 tsp. chili powder

1. Preheat the broiler.

2. Place tortillas on a baking sheet, and broil for 3 minutes, turning once, until tortillas begin to brown and turn crispy. Carefully remove tortillas on their baking sheets from the oven.

3. Sprinkle each tortilla with $\frac{1}{2}$ of Monterey Jack cheese. Distribute scallions over each tortilla, and sprinkle $\frac{1}{2}$ teaspoon chili powder over each.

4. Broil for 2 or 3 more minutes or until cheese is melted and starting to bubble.

Tortilla Roma

Okay, okay, so this is mixing cultural influences ... try it, you'll like it. This recipe calls for less cheese than others because of Romano's richness. Even so, you'll find this a flavor explosion.

 20

Serves:
4

2 large soft flour tortillas

1 TB. olive oil

1 tsp. chopped garlic

1½ cups Romano cheese

1½ cups roasted red pepper, chopped into ½-in. pieces

1½ cups cooked chicken, chopped into ½-in. pieces

Salt

Black pepper

1. Preheat the broiler.

2. Place tortillas on a baking sheet, and broil for 3 minutes, turning once, until tortillas begin to brown and turn crispy. Carefully remove tortillas on their baking sheets from the oven.

3. Meanwhile, in a small cup, mix olive oil and garlic. Spoon oil-garlic mixture over each tortilla, and spread with the back of a spoon.

4. Sprinkle each tortilla with Romano cheese, and broil for 2 or 3 minutes or until cheese begins to melt.

5. Arrange roasted red pepper and chicken pieces over each tortilla, and broil for 3 more minutes, watching closely to prevent burning.

6. Season with salt and pepper, slice on a cutting board, and serve pizza-style.

Kid-Approved Cuisine

In This Chapter

- Breakfast for the little ones
- Burgers your kids will love
- Chicken dishes that will have your kids clucking
- South-of-the-border kid favorites
- Sweet treats

If you're a parent, you know what a special challenge it is to feed children. You want to serve healthful food *you'll* be happy with but also delicious dishes your kids will actually eat! I've packed this chapter with recipes both kids and adults can enjoy, from quick breakfasts and filling lunches to kid-friendly burgers and delicious chicken dishes. I've also included some Mexican favorites and other fun foods your kids will request over and over again.

To help get kids on board with any meal, get them to "help" you cook, whether it's stirring things in a bowl or measuring ingredients. When they watch dinner in progress and see something they helped make, they're a lot more likely to eat it!

Light and Fluffy Pancakes

| 20 | **Serves:** 4 |

1 cup *white whole-wheat* or *white flour*

1 tsp. baking soda

Pinch salt

$\frac{1}{2}$ cup unsweetened applesauce

2 large eggs

2 TB. canola oil

1. In a medium bowl, combine white whole-wheat flour, baking soda, and salt.

2. In another medium bowl, combine applesauce and eggs.

3. Stir flour mixture into egg mixture until batter is mixed but still a little lumpy.

4. In a large skillet over medium heat, heat canola oil. Make 4 pancakes by spooning batter into the skillet, being sure pancakes stay separate. Cook until bubbles burst and stay open. Flip over, and cook for 1 more minute. Serve or put in the oven on warm.

Variation: Use soy flour in place of the white whole-wheat flour.

DEFINITION

White whole-wheat flour is now available in most grocery stores. It's whole grain, with all the health benefits, but a lighter shade and a milder flavor. It's often a kid favorite in recipes, like pancakes, where it masquerades as white flour. Parents are happy, kids are happy, and everyone wins. A **pinch** is the amount of a substance (typically a dry, granular substance such as an herb or seasoning) that can be held between finger and thumb.

Orange French Toast

The tang of citrus and the sweetness of syrup make this a breakfast kids will love.

	Serves:
20	4

2 TB. canola oil

3 eggs

$\frac{1}{3}$ cup orange juice

$\frac{2}{3}$ cup milk

2 tsp. grated orange or lemon *zest*

$\frac{1}{2}$ tsp. salt

2 TB. sugar

1 tsp. ground cinnamon or baking spice mix

8 slices white or whole-wheat bread

1. In a large skillet over medium heat, add canola oil.

2. In a medium bowl, whisk eggs, orange juice, milk, orange zest, salt, sugar, and cinnamon. Keep the bowl next to the heated skillet.

3. Dip 1 slice white bread in egg-milk mixture, coating but not completely soaking. Quickly move bread to the skillet. Cook for 2 or 3 minutes, turn over french toast, and cook for 2 or 3 more minutes or until done.

4. Serve with butter and a dusting of confectioners' sugar to accentuate the citrus flavor. Maple syrup isn't bad, either.

DEFINITION

Zest is small slivers of peel, usually from a citrus fruit like lemon, lime, or orange. Lemon zest is used in many recipes to add a tart taste of citrus. A zester is a small kitchen tool used to scrape lemon zest off a lemon. A grater also works fine.

Eggy Mess

 20

Serves:
4 to 6

3 TB. canola or olive oil

1 large onion, chopped

6 eggs

²⁄₃ cup milk

½ cup shredded cheddar (or other) cheese

1 ham steak, cubed

1 large tomato, chopped

1 tsp. dried basil

Salt

Black pepper

1. In a large skillet over medium heat, add canola oil. Add onion, and sauté for 5 minutes.

2. Meanwhile, in a large bowl, whisk eggs, milk, cheddar cheese, ham steak, tomato, basil, salt, and pepper.

3. Pour mixture into the heated skillet, and cook, stirring slowly to bring uncooked eggs in contact with the skillet, for 3 or 4 minutes or to your desired consistency.

4. Distribute to serving plates, and season with salt and pepper.

 ON THE CLOCK

The Eggy Mess is, by definition, adaptable to what's in your fridge. While the platform—the egg-milk mixture—remains the same, the cast changes frequently. I've made Eggy Mess with mushrooms, olives, and feta cheese; with hot salsa; and many other variations. Have fun experimenting!

Chunky Chicken Vegetable Soup

 Serves:
8

3 TB. olive or canola oil

1 medium onion, chopped into $\frac{1}{2}$-in. pieces

1 lb. boneless, skinless chicken, rinsed, dried, and cut into $\frac{1}{2}$-in. pieces

2 large carrots, peeled and cut into $\frac{1}{4}$-in. slices

2 large celery stalks, with leaves, cut into $\frac{1}{2}$-in. slices

3 (14.5-oz.) cans chicken broth

$\frac{1}{4}$ cup prepared pesto

$\frac{1}{2}$ tsp. black pepper, plus more as needed

Salt

1. In a stockpot or large saucepan over medium heat, heat olive oil. Add onion, and cook, stirring, for 2 minutes.

2. Add chicken, and cook for 5 minutes or until chicken is done.

3. Add carrots, celery, chicken broth, pesto, and pepper, and cook for 12 minutes or until carrots and celery are tender.

4. Distribute to bowls, and serve, seasoning with salt and additional pepper, if desired.

Variation: This rich, flavorful soup is possible even more quickly by using canned chicken (in your grocery store next to the canned tuna). Add 1 (15-ounce) can white beans (drained) to make it a one-pot meal.

⍾ Meatballs

20

Serves:
4

3 TB. canola oil

1½ lb. ground beef

1 TB. chopped garlic

1 TB. Italian seasoning

1 tsp. salt

½ tsp. black pepper

Dash hot pepper sauce

1. In a large skillet over medium heat, heat canola oil.

2. In a large bowl, thoroughly mix ground beef, garlic, Italian seasoning, salt, pepper, and hot pepper sauce. Shape into 1-inch meatballs using your hands or a melon baller.

3. Add meatballs to the skillet, and cook, rotating once or twice, for 8 minutes or until done.

Variation: You can also bake these meatballs. Preheat the oven to 400°F. Arrange meatballs on a baking tray, and bake for 15 minutes or until done. This method takes longer, but it's neater and requires no oil. Also, to tone down the spiciness, reduce or eliminate the pepper and hot pepper sauce.

To serve meatballs with **Spicy-Sweet Dipping Sauce,** combine ⅓ cup soy sauce, ⅓ cup honey, heated for 15 seconds in the microwave, and 2 tablespoons sesame oil in a bowl, and sprinkle 1 scallion, dark green leaves removed, finely sliced on top.

Secret Cheeseburgers

| 20 | Serves: 4 |

1 lb. lean ground beef

1 tsp. Worcestershire sauce

1 cup shredded cheddar cheese

3 TB. ketchup

1. In a large bowl, combine ground beef and Worcestershire sauce. Shape into 8 thin patties about $\frac{1}{4}$ inch thick and $3\frac{1}{2}$ inches across.

2. Distribute cheddar cheese among 4 patties, centering cheese in middle of patty, being sure to leave at least $\frac{1}{4}$ inch exposed meat all the way around.

3. Top cheesed patties with remaining 4 patties, and pinch edges to bind burgers together.

4. On a preheated grill over a medium flame, or in a large skillet over medium heat, cook burgers for 6 to 8 minutes or until done, turning once. (A splatter screen is a great item to use to prevent unnecessary mess on the stovetop.)

5. Distribute burgers to serving plates, and serve with ketchup. Tell the kids these burgers have a secret, and let the fun begin.

Feather Burgers

20	**Serves:** 6

1½ lb. ground turkey or chicken

¼ cup unprocessed bran

1 large egg

2 tsp. Worcestershire sauce

1 tsp. salt

Pinch black pepper

2 TB. canola or olive oil

6 TB. ketchup

1. In a large bowl, combine ground turkey, unprocessed bran, egg, and Worcestershire sauce. Shape into 6 patties about ½ inch thick and 3½ inches across. Season with salt and pepper.

2. In a large skillet over medium heat, heat canola oil. Add burgers, and cook for 8 minutes or until done, turning once.

3. Serve with ketchup.

Variation: There's ample opportunity for fun with these burgers. Substitute ground ostrich for ground chicken and still keep the feather theme. Then, of course, there are buffalo burgers, not to mention ground pork and ground beef. You can also cook these burgers on the grill and prepare as cheeseburgers. They have a lower fat content than beef and cook quicker.

ON THE CLOCK

Ground chicken, turkey, and ostrich are low-fat meats. For this reason, you'll need to use oil in the skillet while cooking to prevent burning.

Beefy Mac and Cheese

 Serves:
4

2 boxes macaroni and cheese mix

1 lb. ground beef

1 tsp. salt

1 (16-oz.) can chopped tomatoes

Pinch crushed red pepper flakes

1. Prepare macaroni and cheese according to package directions.

2. Meanwhile, in a large skillet over medium-high heat, cook ground beef with salt for 8 minutes, stirring, or until done, and drain.

3. When macaroni and cheese is ready, stir in ground beef, chopped tomatoes, and crushed red pepper flakes.

Easy Cheese Puffs

 Serves:
4

1 cup grated cheese (mixture of sharp cheddar and Swiss is recommended)

½ cup flour

2 TB. butter, softened

Water

2 TB. grated or minced fresh onion

Dash cayenne

1. Preheat the oven to 400°F. Lightly coat a cookie sheet with cooking spray.

2. In a medium bowl, and using your fingertips, mix grated cheese, flour, butter, and just enough water to make a *stiff dough*.

3. Add onion and cayenne, and mix.

4. Roll dough into 1 inch balls, place on the greased cookie sheet, and bake for 15 minutes. Serve hot.

> **DEFINITION**
>
> A **stiff dough** is a dough that's solid and holds its shape, as opposed to a dough with a lot of liquid that, if you left it on the counter, would spread out flat.

Grilled Cheese "Hamwiches"

 10

Serves:
4

8 (2½-in.) round thick-cut Canadian back bacon slices	4 slices cheddar (or your favorite) cheese, trimmed to fit bacon
	1 TB. canola oil or butter

1. Set out 4 pieces of Canadian bacon. Add 1 slice cheddar cheese on each piece of bacon, and top with remaining 4 pieces bacon.

2. In a skillet over medium heat, heat canola oil. Add hamwiches, and cook for 5 minutes or until cheese inside is melted, turning once.

3. Serve on plates. Kids will like these as is. Adults probably will like mustard.

> **ON THE CLOCK**
>
> I've yet to find a kid who doesn't like grilled cheese. This version, made with thick Canadian bacon instead of bread, has a decent chance of being even more appealing to those little cheese fanatics. If you can't find Canadian back bacon, use ⅛-inch slices of smoked ham from your deli instead.

Ham 'n' Swiss Roll-Ups

10	**Serves:** 2

6 to 8 slices thickly sliced deli ham

2 TB. Dijon-style mustard

1 cup shredded Swiss cheese

1. Spread each ham slice with Dijon-style mustard, and sprinkle with Swiss cheese. Roll ham over cheese to form a cylinder.

2. Serve immediately, or to take them with you, store in a sandwich bag or a small rectangular plastic container with a lid.

Variation: It's hard to resist heating these for 30 seconds in the microwave to melt the cheese before serving.

MINUTE MORSEL

The challenge of transport (of wraps and roll-ups) can be addressed by picking up a set of washable containers. They're reusable, convenient, and will keep your kid's lunch together beautifully. You'll also save on constantly buying and tossing baggies.

Chicken Kebabs

20	**Serves:** 4

$1\frac{1}{2}$ lb. boneless, skinless chicken breast, cut into 1-in. cubes

1 pt. grape tomatoes, halved

$\frac{1}{2}$ sweet onion, cut into 1-in. pieces

3 TB. olive oil

Juice of $\frac{1}{2}$ lemon

1 TB. chopped garlic

$\frac{1}{2}$ tsp. cumin

Salt

Black pepper

1. Preheat the grill.

2. On a skewer, alternate pieces of chicken, tomatoes, and sweet onion. Repeat with more skewers until ingredients are used up. Arrange kebabs on a plate.

3. In a small bowl, combine olive oil, lemon juice, and garlic, and drizzle over kebabs. Sprinkle kebabs with cumin, salt, and pepper.

4. Grill for 8 minutes or until done, turning to ensure even cooking. Serve with rice.

Chicken 'n' Apples

 Serves:
4

3 TB. olive oil

1 medium onion, chopped into ½-in. pieces

2 celery stalks, chopped into ½-in. pieces

2 tsp. chopped garlic

1½ lb. boneless, skinless chicken breasts (about 3 breasts), rinsed, dried, and cut into ½-in. pieces

1 crisp Granny Smith apple, cut into ½-in. pieces

10 dried apricots, quartered

½ tsp. ground ginger

½ tsp. salt, plus more as needed

Black pepper

1. In a large skillet over medium heat, heat olive oil. Add onion, celery, and garlic, and cook, stirring, for 4 minutes.

2. Add chicken, apple, apricots, ginger, and salt, and cook, stirring, for 8 minutes or until chicken is cooked through.

3. Serve, seasoning with salt and, if kids tolerate it, pepper.

Barbecued Chicken

 20   **Serves:**
4

2 lb. chicken parts, rinsed, dried, and patted dry with paper towels

1 tsp. salt

Pinch plus ¼ tsp. black pepper

1 cup light ketchup

2 TB. cider vinegar

2 TB. spoon-for-spoon sweetener

1 TB. Dijon-style mustard

½ tsp. ground cumin

½ tsp. ground ginger

1. Preheat the grill.

2. In a large, microwave-safe bowl, place chicken parts. Sprinkle with salt and pinch pepper, and microwave on high for 10 minutes.

3. Meanwhile, in a small bowl, combine ketchup, cider vinegar, spoon-for-spoon sweetener, Dijon-style mustard, cumin, ginger, and remaining ¼ teaspoon pepper.

4. Place partially cooked chicken on the grill, and brush with barbecue sauce. Grill for 5 minutes, turning once, or until chicken is done and outside is crisp.

 TIME WASTER

Some kids (and adults, too!) like to use sauce for dipping. Be sure to keep dipping sauce separate from any sauce that's come in contact with raw chicken meat to avoid potential contamination.

Grilled Cheddar Chicken Sandwiches

 Serves:
4

1 TB. margarine or butter
8 slices whole-wheat bread
½ tsp. dried oregano

8 slices cheddar cheese
1½ cups thinly (¼ in.) sliced cooked chicken

1. Spread margarine on 4 slices of bread, and dust each with pinch oregano.

2. In a large skillet over medium heat, place bread, margarine side down. (Depending on the size of your skillet, you may need to do this in batches.)

3. Place 1 slice cheddar cheese on each piece of bread in the skillet, followed by several pieces of chicken.

4. Spread remaining pieces of bread with margarine, dust with oregano, and place bread on sandwiches in the skillet, margarine side up. Cook for 4 minutes or until cheese begins to melt and bread is browned. Flip sandwich carefully, and cook for 4 more minutes.

Chicken Quesadillas

 Serves:
6 (½ *quesadilla* each)

1 (10-oz.) can chunk white chicken meat, drained
6 (8-in.) soft low-carb tortillas
1 (8-oz.) pkg. shredded cheddar or Monterey Jack cheese

1 tsp. chili powder
1 cup salsa
1 cup light sour cream

1. Preheat the broiler.

2. Using a spoon or fork, break up any large chunks of chicken in the can.

3. Place 3 tortillas on a baking tray, and top each with shredded cheddar cheese and chicken. Sprinkle pinch chili powder over each, and top with remaining 3 tortillas.

4. Broil for 3 minutes, watching carefully to prevent burning. Turn over quesadillas, and broil for 2 more minutes or until cheese is melted and tortillas are crisp. Remove quesadillas to a cutting board, cut into wedges, and serve with salsa and sour cream.

Variation: Substitute whole-wheat tortillas for low-carb tortillas. Quesadillas can also be cooked in an oiled skillet over medium heat for about 2 minutes per side.

DEFINITION

A **quesadilla** is, at its most basic, two tortillas with something in between, sort of like a grilled cheese sandwich. The "in between" is what makes all the difference. Cheese is a natural—start with Monterey Jack or cheddar. Swiss is also delicious. Also include meats, vegetables, and, of course, Southwest-style seasonings.

Quick Tacos

Spice from the seasoned ground beef and guacamole balances deliciously with the coolness of the tomato and sour cream.

20	**Serves:** 4 to 6

1 lb. ground beef

¼ cup water

1 tsp. chopped garlic

2 tsp. chili powder

½ tsp. salt

10 taco shells

1 large tomato, diced

1 cup guacamole

1 cup shredded Monterey Jack cheese

1 cup sour cream (optional)

1. In a large skillet over medium heat, brown ground beef for 7 minutes or until cooked. Drain fat from the skillet.

2. Add water, garlic, chili powder, and salt. Stir and cook for 5 minutes.

3. Distribute seasoned meat among taco shells. Spoon tomato over ground beef, add guacamole, and top with shredded Monterey Jack cheese. Top with sour cream (if using) before serving.

Kid-Friendly Enchiladas

Hearty and quick, this version is vegetarian, although meat can be added for even more heft.

	Serves: 4

1 (16-oz.) can fat-free refried beans	1 tsp. chili powder
4 large flour tortillas	2 cups shredded cheddar cheese
1 large tomato, finely chopped	

1. Preheat the broiler.

2. In a microwave-safe bowl, heat refried beans on high for 3 minutes or until hot. Stir beans to loosen.

3. Place 1 tortilla on a plate, scoop ¼ of beans onto tortilla in a roughly straight line across center. Top with ¼ chopped tomato and 1 pinch chili powder. Repeat with remaining tortillas and filling ingredients.

4. Roll tortilla around filling, and place in a baking dish, leaving room for the other 3. Repeat with remaining tortillas, placing them next to each other in the baking dish.

5. Sprinkle cheddar cheese over top of *enchiladas*, and sprinkle remaining chili powder over cheese. Broil for 3 minutes or until cheese is melted, and serve.

DEFINITION

An **enchilada** is a dish made by wrapping a tortilla around a savory filling, often served with a sauce or topping. They're delicious with guacamole, sour cream, and salsa.

Tortilla "Pizza"

10	**Serves:** 4

4 (8-in.) soft low-carb tortillas

1 (8-oz.) pkg. shredded Mexican-style cheese

½ cup sliced pepperoni

½ cup light sour cream

1. Preheat the broiler.

2. Arrange tortillas on a baking tray in a single layer and broil for 1 minute, watching carefully to prevent burning. Remove tray from broiler.

3. Distribute Mexican-style cheese among tortillas, spread to an even layer, and top with pepperoni slices. Broil for 2 or 3 minutes or until cheese melts.

4. Remove your pizzas to a cutting board, cut into wedges, and serve. Top each slice with dollop of sour cream.

Variation: Use other shredded cheeses in place of the Mexican-style cheese. You can also substitute whole-wheat tortillas for low-carb tortillas.

Pepperoni Pizza Dip

10	**Serves:** 6 to 8

1 cup cream cheese or light cream cheese, softened

1 cup sour cream

1 tsp. dried oregano

¼ tsp. garlic powder

⅛ tsp. crushed red pepper flakes

½ cup pizza sauce

½ cup chopped pepperoni

¼ cup chopped green bell pepper

½ cup shredded mozzarella cheese

1. In a medium bowl, combine cream cheese, sour cream, oregano, garlic powder, and crushed red pepper flakes. Scrape into a 9- or 10-inch microwave-safe quiche dish or pie plate, and spread evenly.

2. Spread pizza sauce over top, sprinkle with pepperoni and green bell pepper, and microwave on high for 3 minutes, turning the dish after the first and second minutes.

3. Top with mozzarella cheese, and microwave for 2 more minutes or until cheese is melted and mixture is heated through. Serve with breadsticks or anything else your kids feel like dipping.

Variation: For a little extra kick, add 2 tablespoons sliced scallions with pepperoni and green bell pepper.

Onion Rings

A classic that's always popular, I've called for whole-wheat flour for added flavor and a bit of nutrition.

 20

Serves:
4

¾ cup canola oil

1 egg

¼ cup milk

1 cup whole-wheat flour

1 large Vidalia or other sweet onion, sliced crosswise and rings separated

Salt

1. In a small skillet over medium-high heat, heat canola oil. (Oil should be at least ⅓ inch deep.)

2. In a small bowl, whisk egg and milk.

3. In a separate small bowl, spread whole-wheat flour.

4. Dip Vidalia onion rings in flour, followed by a dip in egg-milk mixture, and dredge one more time through flour to thoroughly coat. Add to the skillet, and cook several rings at once in oil for 4 minutes per piece or until browned and crispy, turning once. Drain on paper towels, sprinkle with salt, and serve.

Garlic Toast with Tomato Dipping Sauce

Crisp toast with warm, savory tomato sauce—all is right with the world.

 Serves:
6 to 8

1 loaf store-bought garlic bread	2 TB. shredded Parmesan cheese
1 (14- to 15-oz.) can pizza sauce	

1. Preheat the broiler.

2. Cut garlic bread into rounds about $1\frac{1}{2}$ inches wide, and place garlic side up on a baking sheet. Broil for about 2 minutes or until bread begins to brown and crisp.

3. Meanwhile, pour pizza sauce into a serving bowl, and microwave for 1 minute or until warm.

4. Serve toasted garlic bread in a basket lined with a cloth napkin. Sprinkle Parmesan cheese on top of warm pizza sauce, and place that bowl next to bread. Invite your kids to "dip in," and watch the whole thing vanish.

Fruit and Cream Platter

This is a dipping dessert made in fruit-and-cream heaven.

 Serves:
6 to 8

1 cup light sour cream	$\frac{1}{2}$ lb. seedless grapes
$\frac{1}{4}$ cup sugar	1 fresh, crisp apple, cored, seeded, and sliced lengthwise into about $\frac{1}{2}$-in.-wide slices
1 pt. fresh strawberries	

1. In a serving bowl, combine sour cream and sugar.

2. Place the bowl on a platter, and surround the bowl with strawberries, grapes, and apple slices.

3. Serve, inviting your children to dip fruit into cream. If apple slices will be out for a while, rub with a cut lemon half to delay browning.

Variation: Serve with just one type of fruit (grapes or strawberries are terrific), or pick another fruit to try.

Grapes Rockefeller

 Serves:
2

$\frac{1}{2}$ lb. seedless grapes, cut in half	$\frac{1}{8}$ cup brown sugar
$\frac{1}{2}$ cup low-fat sour cream	

1. In a serving bowl, combine grapes, sour cream, and brown sugar.

2. Serve, or chill and serve cold.

Variation: For **Grapes and Cream,** use sweetener instead of the brown sugar.

Stars on the Side

Now for the side dishes. These quick and delicious vegetable, rice, and bread recipes round out the perfect meal.

Vegetable side dishes are a natural for the dinner table. They're quick to cook and pack a real nutritional punch. Rice and grains are also fitting side dishes. With the right seasonings and spices, they shine on the side.

Baked goods form a comforting, essential part of many of our meals. You might be wondering how you can have something fresh from the oven and on the table in 30 minutes or less. With a few tricks, it's easy.

Quick
Vegetable Sides

In This Chapter

- Taking advantage of fresh flavors
- Quick-cooking vegetable recipes
- Vegetable comfort foods
- Baked, broiled, steamed, and sautéed veggies

Almost more than any other ingredient, vegetables are perfect for getting on the table in 30 minutes or less. They often require either no cooking or a bare minimum. Most of the flavor is already there, bursting from the fresh peppers, onions, tomatoes, greens, and herbs you'll be using; to subject them to extensive heating and preparation is to risk losing the taste and nutrition that's already there.

This chapter focuses on fresh and offers several ways to prepare, serve, and enjoy many of your favorite vegetables, including beans, artichokes, peppers, broccoli, cauliflower, and potatoes.

Vichy Soy Carrots

Serves:
6

1 (16-oz.) pkg. baby carrots

½ cup water

3 TB. soy sauce

3 TB. sugar

¼ cup butter, cut into ½-TB. pieces

6 sprigs fresh parsley

1. In a flat-bottomed, microwave-safe container, arrange carrots in a single layer.

2. Pour water and soy sauce over carrots, sprinkle with sugar, and scatter butter around the dish. Microwave on high for 2 minutes, stir, and microwave for 1 more minute or until carrots begin to soften.

3. Distribute carrots among small serving plates, garnish with parsley, and serve.

DEFINITION

Vichy carrots are a classic French vegetable dish of carrots cooked in water, butter, and sugar.

Pinzimonio

10	**Serves:** 6

4 scallions, roots and dark green parts removed, sliced into quarters lengthwise, leaves reserved

1 red bell pepper, ribs and seeds removed and cut into ¼×4-in. strips

1 green bell pepper, ribs and seeds removed and cut into ¼×4-in. strips

2 carrots, peeled and cut into ¼×4-in. strips

2 celery stalks, cut into ¼×4-in. strips

6 long arugula or cress leaves, rinsed and stemmed

1 cup olive oil

⅓ cup balsamic vinegar

Salt

Black pepper

1. Lay 1 long green scallion leaf (at least 7 inches, if possible) on a cutting board. Lay 1 red bell pepper strip across middle of leaf, followed by 1 green bell pepper strip, 1 carrot strip, 1 celery strip, and 1 arugula leaf. Gently tie scallion leaf around vegetable bunch, and repeat with remaining leaves.

2. Distribute olive oil equally among 6 small serving bowls, and top each bowl with balsamic vinegar.

3. To eat, dip vegetable bunches in oil-vinegar mix, season with salt and pepper, and crunch away while visualizing the Italian vegetable gardens in the distance.

Variation: Choose your own favorite vegetables that can be prepared long and skinny for bunching.

DEFINITION

Pinzimonio is an Italian vegetable dish in which combinations of sliced vegetables are served with olive oil, vinegar, salt, and pepper.

Sautéed Peppers

10	Serves: 4

3 TB. olive oil

1 small onion, chopped into ½-in. pieces

1 tsp. Italian seasoning

2 tsp. crushed garlic

1 large yellow bell pepper, ribs and seeds removed, and sliced crosswise into rings

1 large red bell pepper, ribs and seeds removed, and sliced crosswise into rings

1 large green bell pepper, ribs and seeds removed, and sliced crosswise into rings

Salt

Black pepper

1. In a large skillet over medium heat, heat olive oil. Add onion, Italian seasoning, and garlic, and sauté for 5 minutes.

2. Add yellow bell pepper, red bell pepper, and green bell pepper, and cook, stirring, for 5 minutes or until tender-crisp.

3. Season with salt and pepper, and serve.

ON THE CLOCK

In the freezer section of some grocery stores, you'll find 1-pound bags of sliced red, yellow, and green bell peppers. Keep a bag in your freezer, and you'll have instant appeal for a side dish.

Corn and Red Pepper Mélange

 20

Serves:
4 to 6

2 TB. olive oil

1 large onion, chopped

2 tsp. chopped garlic

1 (1-lb.) pkg. frozen corn, or
    2 (15.5-oz.) cans corn kernels,
    drained

2 large sweet red peppers,
    chopped

1 tsp. crushed red pepper flakes

1 tsp. paprika

2 cups crumbled feta cheese

Salt

Black pepper

1. In a large skillet over medium heat, heat olive oil. Add onion and garlic, and cook for 5 minutes.

2. Add corn, red pepper, crushed red pepper flakes, and paprika, and cook for 4 minutes. (If using frozen corn, add it to the skillet first, cook for 2 minutes, and add red pepper, crushed red pepper flakes, and paprika and cook for 4 minutes.)

3. Add feta cheese, cover, and cook for 1 minute.

4. Serve with salt and pepper.

Variation: Serve mixed with 1 pound cooked lamb pieces to make a tempting one-dish meal.

Green Beans with Almonds

10	**Serves:** 4

2 TB. butter

1 lb. fresh green beans, rinsed, stems removed, and sliced into 2-in. pieces

¼ cup slivered almonds

1 TB. fresh dill or ½ tsp. dried

Salt

1. In a large skillet over medium heat, melt butter. Add green beans, almonds, and dill, and cook, stirring, for 4 minutes or until tender-crisp.

2. Season with salt, and distribute to serving plates.

Balsamic Green Beans

20	**Serves:** 4

3 TB. butter or olive oil

4 scallions, roots and dark green leaves removed, cut into ¼-in. sections

1 lb. green beans

Balsamic vinegar

Salt

Black pepper

1. In a large skillet over medium heat, melt butter. Add scallions, and cook, stirring, for 5 minutes.

2. Add green beans, and cook, stirring, for 6 minutes or until beans are tender-crisp.

3. Distribute beans to serving plates, and serve, seasoning with balsamic vinegar, salt, and pepper.

Variation: If you'd rather use olive oil, it will work, but the butter flavor is just terrific.

White Beans and Dark Greens

20	Serves: 10

3 TB. olive oil

1 large onion, cut into $\frac{1}{2}$-in. pieces

2 tsp. chopped garlic

4 large kale leaves, rinsed, stemmed, and chopped into 1×2-in. pieces

1 (10-oz.) pkg. frozen leaf spinach, thawed

7 cups chicken broth

1 (15-oz.) can white beans, drained and rinsed

2 tsp. Italian seasoning

$\frac{1}{2}$ tsp. salt

$\frac{1}{4}$ tsp. black pepper

Dash hot pepper sauce

1. In a stockpot over medium heat, heat olive oil. Add onion, and cook, stirring, for 4 minutes.

2. Add garlic, and cook for 1 more minute.

3. Add kale, spinach, chicken broth, white beans, Italian seasoning, salt, pepper, and hot pepper sauce, and cook, stirring, for 10 minutes or until kale is tender.

Variation: Season with Parmesan cheese for even more flavor.

Sesame Broccoli

10	Serves: 4

$1\frac{1}{2}$ lb. broccoli florets

1 TB. lemon juice

2 TB. sesame or olive oil

2 tsp. grated fresh ginger, or $\frac{1}{2}$ tsp. powdered

Dash hot pepper sauce (optional)

2 TB. sesame seeds

Salt

1. In a stovetop steamer or a saucepan with a lid over medium-high heat, bring $\frac{1}{2}$ inch water to a boil. Add broccoli florets, and steam for 4 minutes or until tender-crisp. Scoop broccoli into a bowl.

2. In a cup, combine lemon juice, sesame oil, ginger, and hot pepper sauce (if using) in a cup. Pour oil mixture over broccoli and toss to coat.

3. Serve, sprinkling each serving with sesame seeds and seasoning with salt.

Variation: For **Sesame Asparagus,** replace the broccoli florets with fresh asparagus spears cut into 2-inch sections.

 ON THE CLOCK

To save even more time, use prepackaged fresh broccoli florets, available in the vegetable section of your grocery store.

Broccoli with Cheese Sauce

 20   **Serves:**
4

1 (16-oz.) head broccoli, broken
 into serving-size florets
$\frac{1}{2}$ cup light sour cream

$\frac{1}{2}$ cup shredded cheddar cheese
2 TB. olive oil
Salt

1. In a stovetop steamer or a saucepan with a lid, bring $\frac{1}{2}$ inch water to a boil. Add broccoli florets, and steam for 7 minutes or until broccoli is tender-crisp.

2. Meanwhile, in a microwave-safe cup, combine sour cream, cheddar cheese, and olive oil. Microwave on high for 1 minute or until beginning to bubble and cheese is melted.

3. Distribute broccoli to serving plates, and pour cheese sauce over broccoli. Serve, seasoning with salt.

Baked Cauliflower

10	**Serves:** 6

1 (1½-lb.) head cauliflower	Butter or margarine (optional)
3 TB. olive oil	Salt
1 tsp. ground cumin	Black pepper

1. In a microwave-safe baking dish, pour ½ inch water.

2. Thoroughly rinse cauliflower in cold water, pat dry with paper towels, and cut head in half lengthwise from stem to top. Place two halves flat side down in the baking dish.

3. Drizzle cauliflower with olive oil, covering as much of the top as you can, and sprinkle with cumin. Microwave on high for 5 to 8 minutes or until cauliflower softens to tender-crisp. Remove the dish from the oven.

4. Slice each piece into 3 pieces, and distribute to serving plates. Season with butter (if using), salt, and pepper.

Asparagus with Tarragon-Dill Dip

20	**Serves:** 4

¾ cup low-fat sour cream	1 tsp. lemon juice
½ cup low-fat mayonnaise	¼ tsp. black pepper
3 scallions, roots and dark green leaves removed, minced	1 lb. fresh baby asparagus, tough ends removed, blanched for 1 minute in boiling water
1 TB. fresh dill or 1 tsp. dried	
1½ tsp. chopped fresh tarragon or ½ tsp. dried	

1. In a serving bowl, combine sour cream, mayonnaise, scallions, dill, tarragon, lemon juice, and pepper. If you've got time, allow dip to sit for an hour or so for flavors to mix.

2. Use tender-crisp asparagus to scoop dip.

Variation: Baby carrots, snow peas, French green beans, or a combination of these veggies are also delicious with this dip.

 TIME WASTER

When a recipe relies on fresh vegetable texture, be sure the "star" veggie is in good shape. Pick only in-season, crisp, fresh vegetables. Your best bet for flavor, color, and nutrition (not to mention the most fun) are veggies from a local farmstand.

Steamed Asparagus

 Serves:
4

1 bunch (about 1 lb.) fresh asparagus, washed, stem ends removed, each stalk cut in half and separated into heads and stems	Butter or margarine
	1 tsp. dried tarragon
	1 tsp. chives
	Salt

1. In a stovetop steamer, bring 1 inch water to a boil. Add stem pieces of asparagus, and cook for 3 minutes.

2. Add head end pieces, and steam for 4 minutes. Test with a fork for softness. If necessary, steam for 1 or 2 minutes longer.

3. Remove to serving plates, top with butter, and sprinkle with tarragon, chives, and salt. Delicious!

Variation: For **Roasted Asparagus,** cut asparagus into 3-inch sections, coat with 2 tablespoons olive oil, sprinkle with 1 tablespoon chopped fresh tarragon (or 1 teaspoon dried) and salt, and broil for 3 minutes. Roll over spars, and broil for 2 more minutes. Serve, seasoning with salt if desired.

Sautéed Herbed Summer Squash

 Serves:
4

2 TB. olive oil	1½ tsp. fresh thyme or ½ tsp. dried
1 TB. chopped garlic	½ tsp. fresh dill or 1 pinch dried
2 (9-in.) zucchini squash, ends removed, cut into ½-in. crosswise sections	Salt
	Black pepper
2 (9-in.) yellow squash, ends removed, cut into ½-in. crosswise sections	

1. In a large skillet over medium heat, heat olive oil. Add garlic, and cook, stirring, for 2 minutes.

2. Add zucchini squash, yellow squash, thyme, and dill to the skillet, and cook, stirring, for 5 minutes or until squash is tender.

3. Serve, seasoning with salt and pepper.

Variation: A splash of balsamic vinegar is a delicious addition.

Baked Acorn Squash

 Serves:
4

2 small acorn squashes (4 or 5 in. long), halved lengthwise, seeds scooped out

¼ cup molasses (4 TB.)

2 TB. butter or margarine

Salt

Black pepper

1. In a microwave-safe baking dish, pour ¼ inch water. Place acorn squash halves, cut side down, side by side in the dish, and microwave on high for 7 minutes. Remove dish from the microwave, and turn squash over. (Careful, it's hot!)

2. Place 1 tablespoon molasses and 1½ teaspoons butter in each squash cavity. Microwave on high for 7 minutes or until squash is soft and you can scoop it out with a fork, rotating dish to ensure even cooking.

3. Serve with salt and pepper, using a fork to mash flesh of squash with any remaining molasses and margarine.

Skillet Parmesan Artichokes

 Serves:
4

2 TB. olive oil

1 TB. chopped garlic

½ tsp. dried oregano

2 (9-oz.) pkg. frozen artichoke hearts, thawed

2 TB. shredded Parmesan cheese

Salt

Black pepper

1. In a 12-inch skillet over medium heat, heat olive oil. Add garlic and oregano. Add artichoke hearts, and sauté, stirring, for 4 minutes.

2. Distribute artichokes to serving plates, sprinkle with Parmesan cheese, and season with salt and pepper. Serve with a lot of napkins.

Sautéed Spinach

10	Serves: 4

3 TB. olive oil

1 tsp. chopped garlic

1 lb. fresh spinach, rinsed, stemmed, and dried

Salt

Black pepper

1. In a large skillet with a lid over medium heat, heat olive oil. Add garlic, and cook, stirring, for 1 minute.

2. Add spinach, cover, and cook for 3 minutes. Lift the lid (note how much spinach has shrunk), and stir to mix spinach with olive oil and garlic.

3. Distribute to serving plates, and season with salt and pepper.

Variation: Balsamic vinegar is delicious on sautéed spinach. Shredded Parmesan cheese is also very tasty.

Fried Tomatoes

I came across this method when looking for a way to use up extra ripe and unripe tomatoes at the end of the season. Whether you like 'em fried green (like the movie), or fried red, this is another unusual vegetable dish that will have people asking for seconds.

20	Serves: 4

$\frac{1}{3}$ cup plus 2 TB. olive oil

2 large red or green tomatoes, sliced in $\frac{1}{2}$-in. pieces

1 tsp. salt

Pinch ground red pepper

1 cup dried breadcrumbs

$\frac{1}{4}$ cup Parmesan cheese

1. In a large skillet over medium heat, heat ⅓ cup olive oil.

2. In a large bowl, place tomato slices. Drizzle with remaining 2 tablespoons olive oil, turning to coat.

3. In a small bowl, combine salt, red pepper, and breadcrumbs, and pour crumbs onto a plate.

4. One at a time, coat tomato slices in breadcrumb mixture, and place in the skillet. Fry for 3 minutes for red tomato slices, 5 minutes for green, or until coating begins to crisp, turning once.

5. Distribute pieces to serving plates, sprinkling each piece with Parmesan cheese.

TIME WASTER

When frying tomatoes, be sure to both use firm fruit (if red—green tomatoes will be firm) and watch them closely to avoid overcooking. Otherwise, you'll find yourself picking up pieces.

Tuna-Stuffed Tomatoes

20

Serves:
4

1 (6-oz.) can chunk white tuna in water, drained

½ cup celery, chopped into ¼-in. chunks (about ½ stalk)

½ cup water-packed artichoke hearts, drained and chopped into ¼-in. pieces

¼ cup real mayonnaise

¼ cup toasted pine nuts

1 TB. freshly squeezed lemon juice

1 tsp. Italian seasoning

Dash hot pepper sauce

½ tsp. salt

Black pepper

4 medium tomatoes, top ½ in. removed, insides scooped out and discarded

½ cup shredded mozzarella cheese

1. In a medium bowl, mix tuna, celery, artichoke pieces, mayonnaise, pine nuts, lemon juice, Italian seasoning, hot pepper sauce, salt, and pepper.

2. Stuff each tomato with an equal amount of tuna salad, and arrange tomatoes in a microwave- and oven-safe dish.

3. Preheat the broiler.

4. Microwave on high for 4 minutes or until filling is hot, turning once or twice if your microwave doesn't have a turntable. Remove tomatoes from the microwave.

5. Top each tomato with mozzarella cheese, and broil for 3 minutes or until cheese is melted and bubbling.

Garden Broil

 Serves:
4 to 6

2 large, ripe tomatoes, sliced thickly	¼ cup extra-virgin olive oil
1 large eggplant, peeled and sliced thickly	Basil (fresh leaves are perfect, 1 tsp. dried will do)
2 zucchini squash, striped and sliced thickly	¼ cup kalamata olives
	Kosher salt

1. Preheat the broiler to high. Lightly coat a cookie sheet with cooking oil spray.

2. Arrange sliced tomatoes, eggplant, and zucchini squash in a single layer on the cookie sheet, and drizzle with extra-virgin olive oil.

3. Broil for 3 minutes or until surface of vegetables begins to bubble and crisp. Flip over each piece, and broil for 2 or 3 more minutes.

4. Serve over rice, drizzle with more olive oil, and top with basil, kalamata olives, and kosher salt.

Vegetables au Gratin

20 **Serves:** 4

5 TB. olive oil

2 TB. chopped garlic

2 TB. fresh chopped basil or 2 tsp. dried

1 tsp. dried rosemary

$\frac{1}{2}$ tsp. dried marjoram

2 large celery stalks, chopped into $\frac{1}{2}$-in. pieces

2 (10-in.) zucchini squash, ends removed, cut in half lengthwise, and cut into $\frac{1}{2}$-in. crosswise sections

2 large tomatoes, cored, seeded, and chopped into $\frac{1}{2}$-in. pieces, or 1 (15-oz.) can diced tomatoes, with juice

$\frac{1}{3}$ cup unprocessed bran

$\frac{1}{3}$ cup shredded Parmesan cheese

Salt

Black pepper

1. Preheat the broiler.

2. In a large skillet over medium heat, heat 3 tablespoons olive oil. Add garlic, basil, rosemary, and marjoram, and cook, stirring, for 1 minute.

3. Add celery and zucchini squash, and cook, stirring, for 5 minutes.

4. Add tomatoes, and cook, stirring, for 3 more minutes or until celery and zucchini squash are tender-crisp.

5. Scrape herbed vegetables into a baking dish, sprinkle with unprocessed bran and Parmesan cheese, and drizzle with remaining 2 tablespoons olive oil.

6. Broil for 2 minutes or until topping begins to crisp. Serve, seasoning with salt and pepper.

DEFINITION

Au gratin is the quick broiling of a dish before serving to brown the top ingredients.

Jen's Potato Salad

 Serves:
8

1½ lb. new potatoes, skin on and scrubbed

1 tsp. salt, plus more as needed

3 TB. white vinegar

⅓ cup mayonnaise

3 TB. prepared mustard

½ tsp. dried dill

Black pepper

1. Place potatoes in a large saucepan, cover with cold water, sprinkle with 1 teaspoon salt, and bring to a boil over high heat. Boil for about 15 minutes or until tender enough for a fork to easily penetrate.

2. Place potatoes in a large bowl, splash with white vinegar, and slice them into ⅓-inch-thick medallions.

3. In a small bowl, combine mayonnaise, mustard, and dill. Pour over potatoes, and toss to coat. Season with additional salt and pepper.

Variation: You could also add 3 tablespoons sweet relish or 1 small sweet onion, finely chopped.

 MINUTE MORSEL

New potatoes are generally small, thin-skinned potatoes that are sweeter (less starchy) than older potatoes and great for boiling and salads. Baking potatoes (you can also use "all-purpose" potatoes) are usually larger, thick-skinned, starchier potatoes great for baking, frying, mashing, and other uses. If you're using organic potatoes, scrub 'em but keep the peels on for nutrition and flavor.

Skillet Potatoes

These potatoes, crisp outside and tender inside, are given a head start in the microwave and finished in the frying pan. They're great with ketchup.

20

Serves:
4 to 6

4 large baking potatoes, skin on and scrubbed	2 TB. plus ½ cup canola oil
	1 tsp. salt

1. Slice potatoes lengthwise into sections that resemble dill pickle spears. Place in a large microwave-safe bowl, drizzle with 2 tablespoons canola oil, and microwave on high for 5 minutes.

2. Meanwhile, in a large skillet over medium heat, heat remaining ½ cup canola oil.

3. Using a fork, transfer potato spears to the skillet, and arrange in a single layer. Sprinkle with salt, and cook for 10 minutes, turning to ensure that all sides are cooked. When done, drain on a paper towel–lined plate.

Fast and Easy Scalloped Potatoes

20

Serves:
4 to 6

1½ lb. baking potatoes	3 TB. butter
1 cup milk	1 large onion, sliced thin
½ tsp. salt	

1. Peel and slice potatoes crosswise into sections about ½ inch thick. Arrange slices in a microwave-safe baking dish with a lid, pour milk over, and sprinkle with salt. Microwave, covered, on high for 8 minutes or until soft, turning dish 180 degrees once.

2. Meanwhile, in a large skillet over medium heat, heat butter. Add onion, and cook while potatoes are cooking until they're soft, translucent, and sweet.

3. When potatoes are done, add them to the skillet with milk and onion, increase heat to high, and cook for 8 minutes.

4. Serve with salt and pepper.

Variation: If you like, add a sprinkling of Parmesan cheese when serving. Or add chopped ham when adding potatoes to the skillet for a quick, hearty main course.

ON THE CLOCK

Milk adds richness to these potatoes, and butter adds flavor. Olive oil will work fine if you prefer.

Garlic Mashed Potatoes

20   **Serves:**
4

5 cloves garlic
4 large potatoes, peeled and cut
  into 1-in. cubes

Salt
$\frac{1}{2}$ cup milk
4 TB. butter

1. In a small saucepan with a little water, add garlic. Bring to a boil, and boil for about 15 minutes or until cloves are soft.

2. Meanwhile, arrange potato cubes in a microwave-safe baking dish, and sprinkle with salt. Cover and microwave on high for 12 minutes or until soft.

3. In another microwave-safe bowl, heat milk on high for 1 minute, adding butter during the last 30 seconds. (Butter won't totally melt, but it will soften.)

4. In a food processor fitted with a chopping blade, or in a blender, thoroughly mix garlic with butter-milk mixture.

5. Pour garlic mixture over potatoes, and mash with a fork or a potato masher to get rid of the big lumps. Blend with a whisk or hand beater to make potatoes lighter and creamier. Don't mash too much; some lumps are okay.

Quick Chinese Cabbage Stir-Fry

Serves:
4 to 6

2 TB. canola oil, or 1 TB. canola oil
   and 1 TB. sesame oil

1 small onion, sliced thin

½ head *bok choy* or *Chinese
   cabbage,* sliced into bite-size
   pieces, stalk ends separate from
   leaves

1 TB. soy sauce

Salt

Black pepper

1. In a wok or a large skillet over medium heat, heat canola oil. Add onion, and cook for 5 minutes.

2. Add bok choy stalks, and cook for 4 minutes.

3. Add leaves and soy sauce, and cook for 2 or 3 minutes or until leaves have wilted.

4. Serve with salt and pepper.

DEFINITION

Bok choy and **Chinese cabbage** are both members of the cabbage family, with thick stems, crisp texture, and fresh flavor. They're perfect for stir-frying.

Sautéed Cabbage with Bacon

20   **Serves:**
                        4

½ head cabbage, sliced into
   ½×3-in. pieces

5 strips bacon

1 tsp. caraway seed

½ tsp. dried sage

Salt

Black pepper

1. In a vegetable steamer over medium-high heat, steam cabbage for 10 minutes or until soft.

2. Meanwhile, in a large skillet over medium heat, cook bacon for 6 minutes or until crispy. Remove bacon to a paper towel–lined plate.

3. Add caraway seed and sage to bacon fat in the skillet, and heat for 1 minute.

4. Add cabbage, and cook, stirring, for 1 more minute.

5. Crumble bacon into cabbage, stir to mix, and season with salt and pepper.

Variation: Stir in 1½ cups cooked brown rice.

MINUTE MORSEL

Caraway is a popular seasoning in many German and central European dishes. One possible reason is that caraway is traditionally believed to relieve indigestion and gas—side effects associated with vegetables in the cabbage family.

Chard with Balsamic Vinegar

 Serves:
4

2 TB. olive oil

8 to 10 large chard leaves, washed and chopped, stems separated

1 TB. balsamic vinegar

Salt

Black pepper

1. In a large skillet over medium heat, heat olive oil. Add chard stem pieces, and sauté for 3 minutes.

2. Add leaves, cover, and cook for 3 minutes, uncovering to stir every minute, or until leaves are wilted.

3. Drizzle with balsamic vinegar, and serve, seasoning with salt and pepper.

Rice and Pasta Sides

In This Chapter

- Hearty rice-based sides
- Spicy rice dishes from around the world
- Perfect pasta to pair with main dishes
- Filling pasta salads

A main dish tastes better with a good side or two. And this chapter contains some delicious and nutritious rice and grain side dishes to accompany your favorite main dishes.

Rice and grain are grown throughout the world, from the United States to the Far East, and are staples for many people. As if wearing a new suit of clothes, rice and grains take on a new character with each seasoning variation—here, Italian, Mexican, Asian, and Middle Eastern. Let's look at some of my favorites.

Rice with Mozzarella, Bacon, and Scallions

This rich, hearty dish is quick to make but will disappear even more quickly.

 Serves:
4

6 strips bacon

4 scallions, dark green parts removed, white and light green parts sliced into 1/4-in. pieces

4 cups cooked rice

1/3 cup shredded mozzarella cheese

Salt

Black pepper

1. In a large skillet over medium heat, cook bacon for 6 minutes, turning once, or until crisp. Remove bacon to a paper towel–lined plate.

2. Discard all but about 3 tablespoons bacon fat from the skillet. Add scallions, and cook for 2 minutes.

3. Add rice, and cook, stirring, for 4 minutes.

4. Add mozzarella cheese, and stir to mix. Turn off heat, and serve, seasoning with salt and pepper.

Chicken and Tomato Rice

 Serves:
4

1 TB. olive oil

1/2 onion, chopped

3/4 lb. cooked chicken, chopped into 1-in. pieces

1 cup 20-Minute Tomato Sauce (recipe in Chapter 24)

3 cups cooked rice

Salt

Black pepper

Parmesan cheese

1. In a large skillet over medium heat, heat olive oil. Add onion, and sauté for 5 minutes.

2. Add chicken, and cook for 2 minutes.

3. Add 20-Minute Tomato Sauce, and cook for 3 minutes.

4. Stir in rice, and heat through, about 2 minutes. Season with salt, pepper, and Parmesan cheese, and serve.

Bacon, Eggs, and Rice

20	**Serves:** 4

½ lb. bacon	4 cups cooked rice
1 large onion, chopped	Salt
½ tsp. crushed red pepper flakes	Black pepper
4 eggs	

1. In a large skillet over medium-high heat, cook bacon for 6 minutes, turning once, or until crispy. Remove bacon to a paper towel–lined plate.

2. Add onion and crushed red pepper flakes to the skillet, and cook for 3 minutes.

3. Meanwhile, in a small bowl, whisk eggs. Add eggs to the skillet, and cook, stirring, for about 4 minutes or until done.

4. Crumble bacon. Add bacon and rice to the skillet, and heat thoroughly. Serve with salt and pepper.

Variation: You can make this dish as simple or complex, bland or spicy as you want. This basic recipe will start you on your culinary way.

Salsa Rice

 Serves:
4

1 TB. olive oil

2 scallions, dark green parts removed, white and light green parts sliced into $\frac{1}{4}$-in. pieces

$\frac{3}{4}$ lb. cooked chicken, chopped into 1-in. pieces

1 cup salsa

3 cups cooked rice

Salt

Black pepper

$\frac{1}{2}$ cup sour cream

1. In a large skillet over medium heat, heat olive oil. Add scallions, and sauté for 2 minutes.

2. Add chicken, and cook for 2 minutes.

3. Add salsa and rice, and cook for 4 more minutes.

4. Distribute to serving plates, season with salt and pepper, and spoon dollop of sour cream on each serving.

Za's Peanut Sauce and Rice

 Serves:
4

3 tsp. crushed garlic

3 TB. creamy peanut butter

$\frac{1}{4}$ cup white wine vinegar

$\frac{1}{4}$ cup soy sauce

$\frac{1}{4}$ cup warm water

2 TB. sesame oil

Pinch cayenne

$\frac{1}{2}$ tsp. fennel seeds

1 tsp. dried basil

4 cups cooked rice

1. In a saucepan over medium heat, whisk together garlic, peanut butter, white wine vinegar, soy sauce, warm water, sesame oil, cayenne, fennel seeds, and basil, and cook until just boiling.

2. Remove from heat, and let sit for 1 minute.

3. Serve over rice for a flavor explosion.

Korean-Style Fried Rice

 Serves:
4

4 TB. canola oil

1 cup green beans, cut into 1-in. pieces

$\frac{1}{2}$ cup carrots, peeled and cut into $\frac{1}{2}$-in. pieces

2 cups cooked rice

2 tsp. peanut sauce

1 TB. soy sauce

$\frac{1}{2}$ TB. sesame oil

3 TB. sesame seeds

$\frac{1}{4}$ cup cashews

$\frac{1}{4}$ cup pickled hot vegetables, with liquid

4 eggs

Hot pepper sauce

1. In a large skillet over medium heat, heat 2 tablespoons canola oil. Add green beans and carrots, and sauté for about 5 minutes or until just done.

2. Add rice, peanut sauce, soy sauce, sesame oil, sesame seeds, cashews, and pickled hot vegetables with juice. Mix thoroughly, heating. Distribute to 4 plates.

3. In a small skillet over medium heat, heat remaining 2 tablespoons oil. Add eggs, one at a time, and fry for 4 minutes, turning once.

4. When done, put 1 egg on top of each plate of fried-rice mixture. Season with hot pepper sauce, and serve.

Stir-Fried Teriyaki Beef, Pea Pods, and Rice

 20

Serves:
4

1 cup cooked steak, cut into ½-in. pieces

3 TB. teriyaki sauce

4 cups cooked rice

1 TB. olive oil

1 onion, chopped

1 (9-oz.) box frozen snow peas or sugar snap peas (or fresh)

1. In a medium bowl, combine steak pieces and teriyaki sauce, turning steak to coat each piece. Set aside.

2. In a microwave-safe bowl, heat rice for 3 minutes or until hot.

3. Meanwhile, in a large skillet over medium heat, heat olive oil. Add onion, and sauté for 5 minutes.

4. Add snow peas, and cook for 4 minutes.

5. Add steak pieces with teriyaki sauce, and cook for 3 minutes or until heated through.

6. Distribute rice to serving plates, and top with steak and snow pea mixture.

Curried Rice

The flavorful, somewhat unusual treatment of these ingredients is a delicious wake-up for the taste buds.

20   **Serves:**
4

4 cups cooked rice

2 TB. olive oil

1 onion, chopped

2 tsp. curry powder

$\frac{1}{2}$ lb. cooked chicken, cut into $\frac{1}{2}$-in. pieces

$\frac{1}{2}$ cup raisins

1 crisp apple, cored and cut into small ($\frac{1}{4}$-in.) pieces

1 tsp. salt

$\frac{1}{4}$ tsp. black pepper

1. In a microwave-safe bowl, heat rice for 3 minutes or until hot.

2. Meanwhile, in a large skillet over medium heat, heat olive oil. Add onion and curry powder, and sauté for 5 minutes.

3. Add chicken and raisins, and cook for 3 minutes.

4. Add apple, salt, and pepper, and heat, stirring, for 1 more minute.

5. Distribute rice to serving plates or bowls, top with curried chicken mixture, and serve.

Thai Couscous Salad

 Serves:
4

1 cup *couscous*

1 (16-oz.) can sweet corn, drained

1 large red bell pepper, ribs and seeds removed, and chopped

2 medium tomatoes, chopped

$\frac{1}{2}$ cup diced cucumber

$\frac{1}{2}$ cup scallions, finely chopped

$\frac{1}{2}$ cup dried raisins, currants, figs, or cranberries

1 tsp. Thai peanut sauce (optional)

1. Cook couscous according to package instructions.

2. When couscous is ready, add sweet corn, red bell pepper, tomatoes, cucumber, scallions, dried fruit, and Thai peanut sauce (if using), and mix thoroughly. Vegetables will be warmed by couscous but will still be crisp.

 DEFINITION

Couscous is a wheat-based staple similar in usage and nutritional value to pasta, bread, or rice.

Lamb and Feta Orzo

 Serves:
4

1 lb. ground lamb

1 TB. garlic

1 tsp. oregano

$\frac{1}{2}$ tsp. rosemary

$\frac{1}{2}$ tsp. crushed red pepper flakes

5 cups cooked *orzo* pasta

6 oz. crumbled feta cheese

1. In a large skillet over medium-high heat, cook lamb, garlic, oregano, rosemary, and crushed red pepper flakes, stirring, for 7 minutes or until done.

2. Meanwhile, in a microwave-safe bowl, heat orzo for 3 minutes or until warm.

3. Distribute orzo to serving plates, top with seasoned lamb and feta cheese, and serve.

> **DEFINITION**
>
> **Orzo** pasta, with its tiny oblong shape, might be mistaken for rice. It provides an interesting variation on the pasta theme and mixes well with other small ingredients.

Whole-Wheat Penne with Summer Squash, Tomatoes, and Mushrooms

 20   **Serves:**
6

1 lb. whole-wheat penne pasta	1 small yellow (summer) squash, sliced lengthwise and cross cut in ½-in.-thick pieces
½ tsp. salt	
2 tsp. plus 2 TB. olive oil	
1 TB. chopped garlic	2 large fresh tomatoes, chopped into 1-in. pieces, or 1 (16-oz.) can chopped tomatoes with juice
1 tsp. crushed red pepper flakes	
1 tsp. dried basil	Parmesan cheese
½ tsp. dried tarragon	Salt
8 oz. sliced fresh mushrooms	Black pepper

1. Cook penne according to the package directions, adding salt and 2 teaspoons olive oil to the water.

2. Meanwhile, in a large skillet over medium-low heat, heat remaining 2 tablespoons olive oil. Add garlic, crushed red pepper flakes, basil, and tarragon, and sauté for 2 minutes.

3. Add mushrooms, yellow squash, and tomatoes, and cook, covered, for 6 minutes, stirring a couple times while cooking.

4. Distribute pasta to serving plates, top with tomato and pepper mixtures, and season with Parmesan cheese, salt, and pepper.

MINUTE MORSEL

Whole wheat in breads and pasta brings much higher nutritional value than white flour. Whole-wheat flour also brings a characteristic rich, nutty taste that many people prefer.

Anya's Smoked Salmon Penne Pasta

Sweet red (or yellow) peppers work beautifully with the rich taste of smoked salmon.

 20 **Serves:**
4 to 6

1 lb. penne pasta	2 TB. cream cheese, plus more as needed
3 TB. olive oil	
2 large sweet red bell peppers, ribs and seeds removed, and sliced thin	2 TB. capers
	Black pepper
	6 to 8 oz. smoked salmon, chopped into bite-size chunks
1 small red onion, sliced very thin	
¾ cup whipping cream	⅓ cup chopped fresh parsley
1½ TB. cloves garlic, minced	¼ cup grated Parmesan cheese

1. Cook penne according to package directions.

2. Meanwhile, in a large skillet over medium heat, heat olive oil. Add sweet red bell peppers and red onion, and sauté, covered, for 5 minutes to wilt and soften vegetables. Set vegetables aside.

3. Add whipping cream and garlic to the skillet, and boil for 1 or 2 minutes to soften garlic and reduce cream 25 percent.

4. Add cream cheese, and stir gently to ensure cream cheese melts into sauce and thickens it. Sauce should coat back of spoon. Add another tablespoon cream cheese, if necessary, to thicken.

5. Drain pasta, and toss with cream sauce, capers, pepper, salmon, parsley, and Parmesan cheese. Serve immediately.

ON THE CLOCK

Shorten this recipe even more by using a 16- to 20-ounce jar of roasted red peppers, sliced. If you're using a jar of roasted red peppers in this smoked salmon dish, be sure they're not pickled or preserved in vinegar. They won't taste good.

Penne with Sweet Sausage and Tomato Sauce

 20

Serves:
4

1 lb. sweet Italian sausage, sliced into ¼-in. sections

1 onion, chopped

1 tsp. chopped garlic

3 cups 20-Minute Tomato Sauce (recipe in Chapter 24)

5 cups penne pasta

Parmesan cheese

1. In a large skillet over medium heat, cook Italian sausage with onion for 8 minutes, stirring.

2. Add garlic, and cook for 2 or 3 more minutes or until sausage is done. Drain excess fat from the skillet.

3. Add 20-Minute Tomato Sauce, and cook for 5 minutes.

4. Meanwhile, in a microwave-safe bowl, heat penne for 3 minutes or until hot. Distribute to serving plates, pour sauce over each serving, and top with Parmesan cheese.

TIME WASTER

Fatty meats, such as sausage, bacon, and ground lamb and beef, release fat when they cook. This fat can be used as a flavorful cooking medium for other ingredients, such as onion and garlic. Just keep in mind that, although delicious, this is saturated fat we're talking about, to be enjoyed in moderation. Discard extra fat to minimize your saturated fat intake.

Sautéed Mushrooms, Olives, and Sun-Dried Tomato Penne

20 **Serves:**
4 to 6

1 lb. penne pasta

$\frac{1}{3}$ cup olive oil

2 tsp. chopped garlic

1 tsp. dried oregano

1 tsp. dried basil

$\frac{1}{2}$ tsp. salt

1 bay leaf

$\frac{1}{3}$ cup chicken broth

1 lb. button mushrooms, cut in half

1 cup kalamata olives

$\frac{1}{2}$ cup oil-packed sun-dried tomatoes, drained and chopped

1 TB. lime juice

1. Cook penne according to package directions. Drain.

2. Meanwhile, in a large saucepan over medium heat, combine olive oil, garlic, oregano, basil, salt, and bay leaf. Cook, stirring, for 3 minutes.

3. Add chicken broth, increase heat to medium-high, and cook for 5 minutes.

4. Add mushrooms, reduce heat to low, and cook, covered, for 5 minutes.

5. Add kalamata olives and sun-dried tomatoes, cook for 1 more minute, remove from heat, and drizzle with lime juice.

6. Distribute pasta to serving plates, top with mushroom mixture, and serve.

Bowties with Sherry Pepper Cream

Luxuriant cream with distinctive sherry richness make this a special dish.

 20

Serves:
6

1 lb. bowtie pasta	½ tsp. crushed red pepper flakes
2 TB. butter	1½ tsp. dried basil
1 TB. crushed garlic	¼ tsp. black pepper
3 large tomatoes, chopped, or	⅔ cup heavy cream
1 (28-oz.) can whole Italian	½ cup cooking sherry
tomatoes, chopped	Parmesan cheese

1. Cook bowtie pasta according to package directions, but only for 5 minutes.

2. In a large skillet over medium-low heat, heat butter. Add garlic, and sauté for 2 minutes.

3. Cut tomatoes in the can. Add tomatoes, crushed red pepper flakes, basil, pepper, heavy cream, and sherry to the skillet, and cook for 5 minutes.

4. Add partially cooked pasta, and cook for 5 more minutes.

5. Serve with Parmesan cheese, Italian bread, and steamed asparagus.

Black Tie and Red Dress Pasta

The "black" in this recipe comes from sliced olives, the "tie" is the bowtie pasta, and the "red" represents the sweet grape tomatoes.

 Serves:
4

2 TB. olive oil	5 cups bowtie pasta
2 TB. chopped garlic	Salt
²/₃ cup sliced black olives	Black pepper
½ tsp. crushed red pepper flakes	Parmesan cheese
2 cups grape tomatoes, each sliced in half	

1. In a large skillet over medium heat, heat olive oil. Add garlic, and sauté for 2 minutes.

2. Add black olives and crushed red pepper flakes, and sauté for 2 more minutes.

3. Add tomatoes and pasta, and cook for about 4 minutes or until heated through.

4. Season with salt, pepper, and Parmesan cheese.

Skillet-Broiled Double Cheese and Macaroni Casserole

 Serves:
4

1 lb. ground beef

1 onion, chopped

1 tsp. salt

$\frac{1}{4}$ tsp. black pepper

1 tsp. crushed red pepper flakes

1 cup 20-Minute Tomato Sauce (recipe in Chapter 24)

5 cups cooked macaroni

1 cup shredded mozzarella cheese

3 slices provolone cheese

1. Preheat the broiler.

2. In a large oven-safe skillet over medium heat, cook ground beef, onion, salt, pepper, and crushed red pepper flakes for about 7 minutes or until beef loses its pink color. Pour off excess fat.

3. Add 20-Minute Tomato Sauce and macaroni, and cook, stirring, for 5 more minutes.

4. Turn off heat, stir in mozzarella cheese, and top with slices of provolone cheese.

5. Slide the skillet under the broiler, and cook for 3 minutes or until cheese melts and bubbles.

Romano Pasta

 Serves:
4

4 TB. olive oil

2 TB. chopped garlic

5 cups cooked spaghetti

1 tsp. salt

¼ tsp. black pepper

½ cup shredded or grated Romano cheese

1. In a large skillet over medium heat, heat olive oil. Add garlic, and sauté for 2 minutes.

2. Add spaghetti, and sprinkle with salt and pepper. Heat, stirring, for 3 or 4 minutes or until pasta is heated.

3. Serve, topping generously with Romano cheese.

Pasta with Broiled Tomatoes and Garlic

Broiled tomatoes gain a richness that stands up to hearty whole wheat in this filling pasta dish.

 Serves:
6 to 8

1 lb. whole-wheat spaghetti

3 large tomatoes, chopped into ½-in. pieces

1 TB. chopped garlic

1 tsp. dried basil

1 tsp. dried oregano

½ tsp. dried thyme

½ tsp. salt

Pinch black pepper

1. Cook spaghetti according to package directions. Drain.

2. Preheat the broiler.

3. Meanwhile, in a large bowl, combine tomatoes, garlic, basil, oregano, thyme, salt, and pepper.

4. Spread mixture in a glass baking tray, and broil for 10 to 12 minutes, stirring every few minutes.

5. Toss sauce with spaghetti, and serve.

Spaghetti Carbonara

20	**Serves:** 4 to 6

1 lb. spaghetti	2 eggs, well beaten
8 to 12 slices bacon	Salt
¾ cup Parmesan cheese, shredded	Black pepper
¼ cup sour cream	

1. Cook spaghetti according to the package directions.

2. Meanwhile, in a large skillet over medium heat, cook bacon for 6 minutes, turning once, or until crispy. Drain on a paper towel–lined plate, and crumble.

3. When spaghetti is done, drain, return to the pan, and quickly toss with crumbled bacon, Parmesan cheese, sour cream, and beaten eggs. (Hot pasta will cook eggs.)

4. Season with salt and pepper, and serve to rave reviews.

Penne Pasta Salad

 Serves:
6 to 8

1 (1-lb. pkg.) penne pasta, cooked

1 bag (10- to 16-oz.) spinach, washed and coarsely chopped

1 large Vidalia or other sweet onion, minced

1 (6.5-oz.) can sliced olives, drained

2 or 3 cups feta cheese, crumbled

1 (8-oz.) bottle Caesar dressing

1. In a serving bowl, combine penne, spinach, Vidalia onion, olives, and feta cheese.

2. Pour $\frac{1}{2}$ or more of Caesar dressing over, and toss to coat. Serve, sit back, and watch it disappear. Served warm or cold, it's delicious.

Carol Ann's Tortellini Salad

 Serves:
6 to 8

1 lb. tortellini

1 lb. frozen Italian vegetables

$\frac{1}{2}$ cup Italian dressing

$\frac{1}{4}$ cup shredded Parmesan cheese

$\frac{1}{4}$ tsp. garlic powder

$\frac{1}{2}$ tsp. dried basil

Salt

Black pepper

1. Cook tortellini according to package directions.

2. Put frozen Italian vegetables in a colander in the sink. Drain cooked tortellini over the colander to rapidly heat vegetables. Rinse with cold water.

3. In a large bowl, combine tortellini-vegetable mixture, Italian dressing, Parmesan cheese, garlic powder, and basil.

4. Season with salt and pepper, and serve.

The 30-Minute Bakery

In This Chapter

- Bakery-worthy biscuits and scones
- Quick breads
- Recipes where bread is the star

No discussion of any meal, whether it takes 30 minutes or a week, is complete without some discussion of bread. From the simplest slice to the heartiest loaf, bread brings with it connotations of warmth, richness, and comfort.

Quick breads rely on a chemical agent such as baking powder or baking soda to create the little bubbles of carbon dioxide that raise bread and make it light. And they're called "quick" for a reason: they don't have to sit and rise like yeast breads, so they're perfect for meals in 30 minutes or less. In this chapter, I share a few of my favorites.

I've also included a few of my favorite bruschettas and other recipes where bread is the star. If you're craving bread, this chapter is for you.

Buttermilk Biscuits

These biscuits—nicely browned on the outside and moist and chewy on the inside—won't last long in the bread basket.

20 **Serves:**
4 to 6

1¾ cups flour
¼ cup buttermilk powder
2 tsp. sugar
1 TB. baking powder

½ tsp. salt
5 TB. butter, cut into pieces
⅔ cup water

1. Preheat the oven to 450°F. Lightly coat a baking pan or cookie sheet with cooking spray.

2. In a large bowl, mix flour, buttermilk powder, sugar, baking powder, and salt. Add mixture to a food processor fitted with a cutting blade, and blend in butter until mixture is fine and crumbly.

3. Remove mixture to a large bowl, and stir in water until it's absorbed and dough becomes uniform.

4. Turn out dough onto a floured counter, knead for 1 minute, and using your hands, flatten dough to about ¾ inch thick. Cut into wedges (or shapes if you have a cookie cutter), and place in the prepared baking pan. Bake for 15 minutes or until browned and crusty.

Variation: If you like to use salted butter, omit the ½ teaspoon salt called for. And if you have fresh buttermilk, use ⅔ cup buttermilk instead of the water and 2 cups flour. Finally, substitute whole-wheat flour for some of the white flour for added nutrition and flavor.

Scones

Less sweet than scones you might find at the bakery, these are hearty and rich and just perfect with butter and jelly.

20	**Serves:** 4 to 6

1¾ cups flour	4 TB. butter
¼ cup wheat germ	¾ cup sour cream
2 tsp. baking powder	2 eggs, beaten
1 tsp. sugar	½ cup currants (optional)
½ tsp. salt	

1. Preheat the oven to 425°F. Lightly coat a baking pan or cookie sheet with cooking spray.

2. In a large bowl, mix flour, wheat germ, baking powder, sugar, and salt. Add mixture to a food processor fitted with a cutting blade, and blend in butter until mixture is fine and crumbly.

3. Mix in sour cream and eggs, and add currants (if using).

4. Turn out dough onto a floured counter, knead for 1 minute, and using your hands, flatten dough to about ¾ inch thick. Cut into wedges, place in the prepared baking pan, and bake for 15 minutes or until done.

Variation: Substitute ½ cup whole-wheat flour for ½ cup white flour for added nutrition and flavor.

ON THE CLOCK

If you'd like sweeter scones, add 1 tablespoon sugar to the dough, and, before putting scones in the oven, brush them with melted butter and sprinkle them with more sugar. That brushed butter also gives scones a great glazed look.

Skillet-Baked Cornbread

 Serves:
4 to 6

1 cup flour	1 egg
1 tsp. salt	1 TB. honey
2 tsp. baking powder	¾ cup milk
1 cup cornmeal	¼ cup sour cream
¼ cup sugar	¼ cup canola oil

1. Preheat the oven to 425°F.

2. In a large bowl, mix flour, salt, baking powder, cornmeal, and sugar.

3. In a small bowl, whisk egg, honey, milk, and sour cream, and mix into dry ingredients.

4. In a medium (12-inch) cast-iron or oven-safe skillet, heat canola oil. Pour hot canola oil onto dough, and stir to mix. Scrape dough into the hot skillet, and bake for 17 minutes or until top browns.

 Garden Bruschetta

 Serves:
4

2 tsp. chopped garlic	¼ tsp. black pepper
¼ cup olive oil	1 large fresh tomato, chopped into ¼-in. pieces
4 slices low-carb bread, each cut into 4 triangles	⅓ cup shredded Parmesan cheese
3 TB. fresh basil, minced	
1 tsp. salt	

1. Preheat the broiler.

2. In a small bowl, mix garlic and olive oil.

3. Arrange bread triangles in a single layer on a baking tray, brush each piece with garlic–olive oil mixture, and broil for 1 minute per side or until browned.

4. While bread is toasting, mix basil, salt, pepper, and tomato. Spread some tomato mixture onto each piece of toasted bread, and sprinkle with Parmesan cheese. Serve *bruschetta* to sighs of appreciation.

Variation: If you prefer, use 100 percent whole-wheat bread in place of the low-carb bread.

 DEFINITION

Bruschetta is an Italian favorite. In the classic version, slices of good bread are toasted or grilled, rubbed with garlic, and drizzled with olive oil.

Roasted Red Pepper Bruschetta

These glistening red peppers topped with rich Romano cheese make this bruschetta irresistible.

 10 | **Serves:**
6 to 8

1 baguette or slender loaf of crusty bread, sliced into $\frac{1}{2}$-in. rounds	2 cups roasted red peppers, chopped into $\frac{1}{2}$-in. pieces
1 TB. chopped garlic	$\frac{1}{3}$ cup shredded Romano or Parmesan cheese
2 TB. olive oil	1 tsp. kosher salt

1. Preheat the broiler.

2. Arrange bread in a single layer on a baking sheet.

3. In a small cup, mix garlic and olive oil, and brush each slice of bread with garlic–olive oil mixture. Broil for 1 minute or until lightly browned. Turn over slices, brush other side with garlic–olive oil mixture, and broil for 1 more minute.

4. Remove the baking sheet from the broiler, leaving broiler on. Spoon some red peppers onto each slice of bread, and sprinkle with Romano cheese.

5. Broil for 1 more minute or until cheese begins to melt. Sprinkle with kosher salt, transfer to a large platter, and serve.

Olive and Feta Bruschetta

This recipe provides a delicious flavor combination evocative of the Mediterranean. The cream cheese anchors the feta.

10	Serves: 6 to 8

8 slices white or wheat bread, crusts removed, each cut into 4 triangles	1 (4.25-oz.) can chopped black olives
1 cup crumbled feta cheese	$\frac{1}{2}$ tsp. dried chopped rosemary
$\frac{1}{2}$ cup cream cheese or light cream cheese, softened	$\frac{1}{8}$ tsp. garlic powder
	2 TB. finely chopped fresh chives

1. Preheat the broiler.

2. Arrange bread in a single layer on a baking sheet, and broil for about 1 minute on each side or until lightly browned.

3. Meanwhile, in a medium bowl, combine feta cheese, cream cheese, black olives, rosemary, and garlic powder.

4. Remove the baking sheet from the oven, and arrange toast points on a work surface. Spread about 2 teaspoons feta mixture on each, and arrange on a serving tray.

5. Sprinkle each with pinch of chives, and serve.

Quick-Broiled Garlic and Herb Bread

 Serves:
8

⅓ cup olive oil
1½ TB. chopped garlic
1½ TB. prepared *pesto*

1 baguette or slender loaf of crusty
bread, cut into ½-in. slices
Warm pizza sauce (optional)

1. Preheat the broiler.

2. In a small bowl, whisk together olive oil, garlic, and pesto.

3. Arrange bread in a single layer on a baking sheet, and brush each piece with garlic-oil mixture. Broil for 1 or 2 minutes or until bread begins to brown. Flip over bread, brush other side, and broil for 1 more minute.

4. Serve with a bowl of warm pizza sauce for dipping (if using) or as is.

 DEFINITION

Pesto is a thick spread or sauce traditionally made with basil, garlic, olive oil, and pine nuts. (New versions sometimes call for different herbs or sun-dried tomatoes.) Rich and flavorful, pesto can be used on anything from appetizers to pasta and other main dishes.

Jamie's Welsh Rarebit

This version of rarebit, from friends in Scotland, is quicker than stateside rarebit and perfect for thick slices of whole-grain bread.

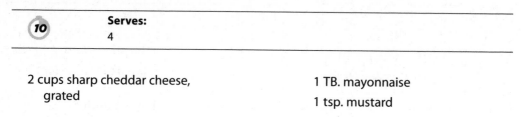

Serves:
4

2 cups sharp cheddar cheese, grated

1 TB. mayonnaise

1 tsp. mustard

1. Preheat the broiler.

2. In a small bowl, combine cheddar cheese, mayonnaise, and mustard. Spread mixture over toast, and place under the broiler for 3 minutes or until hot and bubbling. Serve immediately.

And for Dessert ...

Life is short—eat dessert first! Okay, maybe not *first*, but certainly save room for it.

Fruit is a natural when it comes to dessert. Packed with sweetness and flavor, they're perfect for quick desserts. Pair fresh fruit with a sweet and creamy dip, and you've got a slice of heaven on your plate. When you want a little something more, like cookies and pie, I've also included some rich and decadent desserts I think you'll love.

And you weight-conscious cooks, I haven't forgotten about you! I've included a whole chapter of reduced-carb desserts so you can satisfy your sweet tooth without wrecking your diet.

Fantastic Fruit Desserts

In This Chapter

- Sweet fruit treats
- Dream cream themes
- Quick-cooked fruit treats

Fruits were probably one of the first desserts. Naturally sweet and needing little or no preparation, fresh fruit offers a self-contained quick dessert. Fruits are delicious by themselves, but add cream, and you've got something irresistible. And there's just something about cooked fruit desserts. From apple crisp to blueberry pies, they evoke the dinner table of yesteryear. I share my favorite recipes for these and other delicious fruit desserts in this chapter.

I've found that my dessert tastes have changed as I've learned more about fruits. I have less of a sweet tooth for sugar, but nothing beats a dessert of dried apricots or a bowl of blueberries and cream. Knowing that what you eat is not only good but also good for you—and doesn't take all day to cook—makes it all the more appealing. In my book, you can't get much better than that!

Orchard Fruit Bowl

20

Serves:
8

3 cups green grapes, rinsed and halved

2 crisp apples, cored, and chopped into $\frac{1}{4}$-in. pieces

2 cups fresh blueberries, rinsed

3 TB. lemon juice

1. In a large bowl, combine grapes, apples, and blueberries.

2. Drizzle with lemon juice, toss to coat, and distribute to serving bowls.

Variation: For **Tropical Fruit Bowl,** instead use 3 kiwi fruit, peeled and sliced into $\frac{1}{4}$-inch rounds; 1 grapefruit, sectioned, sections cut in half, and juice reserved; 1 seedless orange, peeled and sectioned, and sections cut in half; and $\frac{1}{4}$ medium ($1\frac{1}{2}$ cups) ripe cantaloupe, carved into balls with a melon baler. Drizzle with lemon juice as directed.

Peach Yogurt Parfait

10

Serves:
4

1 cup low-fat plain yogurt

3 TB. sweetener

3 medium ripe peaches, peeled, pitted, and chopped into $\frac{1}{4}$-in. pieces

1. In a small bowl, combine yogurt and sweetener.

2. In 4 tall glasses, layer 1 inch chopped peaches, about $\frac{1}{2}$ inch yogurt, and repeat to fill each glass equally.

ON THE CLOCK

Many grocery stores carry Greek-style yogurt these days, which even in the low-fat and nonfat forms offers a rich, creamy base for desserts. It also has more protein than the "regular" versions. If you find it, try it in place of regular low-fat plain yogurt.

Apricots and Almond Cream

 Serves:
4

¼ cup plus 1 TB. light cream cheese, softened

Pinch ground cinnamon

¼ tsp. pure almond extract

20 dried apricots

1 TB. sliced almonds

1. In a small bowl, combine cream cheese, cinnamon, and almond extract.

2. Scoop about ⅔ teaspoon cream cheese on top of each dried apricot, distribute 5 apricots to each of 4 serving plates, and top each with 1 slivered almond.

Variation: Mix 1 or 2 tablespoons sweetener with the cream cheese. As a fruity alternative in place of almond extract, crush a handful of ripe raspberries into the cream cheese before topping apricots.

Blueberries and Cream

(10)	**Serves:**
	4

1 cup light sour cream   3 TB. sweetener (optional)
1 tsp. pure vanilla extract   2 cups fresh blueberries, rinsed

1. In a medium bowl, combine sour cream, vanilla extract, and sweetener (if using).

2. Gently stir in blueberries, taking care not to break them too much.

3. Distribute to serving bowls, and enjoy on your patio as you look out over Blueberry Hill.

Variation: Frozen blueberries, thawed, will work in place of fresh blueberries. And raspberries will work. And blackberries. And strawberries ....

Almond Piecrust

This quick and easy crust can serve as the base for any number of fruity desserts.

(20)	**Serves:**
	8 (as part of a pie)

$1\frac{1}{2}$ cups chopped unsalted $\frac{1}{4}$ tsp. salt
   almonds   4 TB. butter or Smart Balance–type
2 TB. sweetener   spread
$\frac{1}{2}$ tsp. ground cinnamon   1 egg, beaten

1. Preheat the oven to 375°F. Lightly coat a pie plate with cooking spray.

2. In a food processor fitted with a steel blade, process almonds, sweetener, cinnamon, and salt to a coarse powder.

3. In a microwave-safe bowl, heat butter for 30 seconds or until melted. Add melted spread and beaten egg to almonds, and pulse to mix.

4. Spread crust mixture across the bottom and the sides of the prepared pie plate, spreading to approximately even thickness throughout. Bake for 10 to 12 minutes or until piecrust is crisp.

Variation: If you can find almond flour at your grocery store, use that (1½ cups) in place of the almonds to save processing time.

ON THE CLOCK

Make two of these crusts at a time. Keep one, in its pie plate, in the freezer, ready to accelerate your next dessert masterpiece.

Strawberry Cheesecake Cupcakes

30	**Serves:** 6

1 (8-oz.) pkg. light cream cheese, at room temperature

1 cup part-skim ricotta cheese

1 tsp. pure vanilla extract

¼ cup sweetener

2 cups fresh strawberries, caps removed and cut into ¼-in. slices

1. Line 6 muffin cups with paper liners.

2. In a large bowl, combine cream cheese, ricotta cheese, vanilla extract, and sweetener.

3. Distribute cheese mixture among muffin cups, and chill in the freezer for 20 minutes or until cheesecakes are firm.

4. When ready to serve, carefully remove the muffin liners and place cheesecake "muffins" on serving plates. Top with a big spoonful of sliced strawberries, and serve.

Variation: Chill this cheesecake in an Almond Piecrust (recipe earlier in this chapter) for a delicious, pie-style cheesecake. If you have small serving-size bowls, chill your cheesecake in those and serve topped with strawberries.

Raspberry Cheesecake Mousse

 10   **Serves:**
                  6

1½ cups skim milk

1 (1.4-oz.) pkg. sugar-free, fat-free instant vanilla pudding mix

1 cup part-skim ricotta cheese

1 cup fresh raspberries

1. In a large bowl, combine skim milk and vanilla pudding mix. Thoroughly whisk in ricotta cheese.

2. Distribute cheese mixture among 6 ramekins or small bowls, and chill for 5 minutes.

3. Top with raspberries, and serve in their individual serving bowls.

Variation: Chill this cheesecake in an Almond Piecrust (recipe earlier in this chapter) for a delicious, pie-style cheesecake.

Baked Cherry Miel

Miel is French for "honey." This will provide two nights' dessert … if you can restrain yourself that long.

20   **Serves:**
              8

1 lb. fresh ripe cherries, sliced in half and pitted

1 TB. flour

¼ cup plus 1 TB. honey

4 TB. butter, melted

1 cup uncooked oatmeal

¼ tsp. ground cinnamon

Pinch nutmeg

1. Preheat the oven to 425°F. Lightly coat an 8×8 baking dish with cooking spray.

2. In a bowl, gently combine cherries with flour and stir to coat.

3. Pour ¼ cup honey over cherries, stir again, and pour cherries into the prepared baking dish.

4. In a small bowl, combine butter, remaining 1 tablespoon honey, oatmeal, and cinnamon, and spoon over cherries. Sprinkle with nutmeg.

5. Bake for 18 to 20 minutes or until mixture is bubbling and top is crispy.

6. Distribute to serving plates and eat as is, or if you want to be decadent, add a scoop of vanilla ice cream.

 ON THE CLOCK

On vacation in France years ago, our rental house had two huge cherry trees. While we were there, we discovered the branches dripping with white cherries. The kids spent an hour eating them, with plenty to spare. Without a fully stocked pantry, we took a crack at whipping up a dessert. Baked Cherry Miel is a slightly improved version.

Mixed Fruit Betty

 20   **Serves:**
8

1 (1-lb.) pkg. frozen mixed berries, about 1 cup each blueberries, blackberries, and raspberries

3 TB. lemon juice

1¼ cups sweetener

4 TB. butter or Smart Balance–type spread, at room temperature and sliced into tablespoon-size chunks

¼ cup old-fashioned oatmeal (not instant)

¼ cup unprocessed bran

½ tsp. apple pie spice, or ½ tsp. ground cinnamon

1. Preheat the broiler.

2. In a large bowl, gently toss berries with lemon juice and then 1 cup sweetener. Pour mixture into a microwave- and oven-safe pie plate or 8×8 baking dish. Microwave for 5 minutes, stirring occasionally, to thaw berries, and then cook on high for 4 minutes or until fruit is beginning to bubble. Remove from the microwave, and stir fruit.

3. Meanwhile, in a separate bowl, combine butter, remaining ¼ cup sweetener, oatmeal, unprocessed bran, and apple pie spice to a crumbly texture by pinching together with your fingers.

4. When fruit is done, sprinkle oatmeal mixture over top in an even layer. Broil on the next-to-highest rack for 5 minutes or until top begins to crisp.

Variation: If you've got extra time, you can bake this *Betty* in a preheated 375°F oven for 30 to 40 minutes.

> **DEFINITION**
>
> A **Betty** is a dessert dish of sweet baked fruit topped with a crisp topping, usually breadcrumbs.

(How 'Bout Them) Warm Apples

 20 | **Serves:** 4

4 TB. butter or Smart Balance–type spread	2 crisp Granny Smith apples, peeled, cored, and thinly sliced
8 dried apricots, chopped into ¼-in. pieces (about ¼ cup)	2 TB. heavy cream (optional)
½ tsp. apple pie spice, or ½ tsp. ground cinnamon	Ground cinnamon

1. In a large skillet over medium-low heat, melt butter. Add apricots and apple pie spice, and cook, stirring, for 3 minutes.

2. Add apples, and cook for 5 more minutes.

3. Serve, drizzling each serving with heavy cream (if using) and sprinkling each serving with 1 pinch cinnamon.

Variation: If you've got a sweet tooth, sprinkle ¼ cup spoon-for-spoon sweetener over apples as you're stirring. For a **Warm Apple Betty,** top apples with oatmeal mixture used for the Mixed Fruit Betty (recipe earlier in this chapter), and broil for 5 minutes.

MINUTE MORSEL

Each variety of apple has a distinct texture and tartness that will show through when you use it to make a dessert. For some dishes, the type of apple is very important. For warm apples, you can use your favorite. I use Granny Smith, because I like the firm texture and tart flavor, even as a dessert. Another variety, such as a golden delicious, will translate as a sweeter, softer dish.

 Sherried Pears

20	Serves: 4

1½ cups cooking sherry or red wine

½ cup water

½ cup sweetener

1 tsp. apple pie spice, or 1 tsp. ground cinnamon

1 tsp. lemon juice

4 pears, peeled, sliced in half lengthwise, and *cored*

Confectioners' sugar

1. In a saucepan over medium heat, combine sherry, water, sweetener, apple pie spice, and lemon juice, and bring to a simmer.

2. Reduce heat to medium-low, add pear halves, and cook for 10 minutes or until pears are tender.

3. Turn off the heat, and allow fruit to cool in its juices. Place 2 halves on each plate, spoon some sauce over, and garnish with a sprinkle of confectioners' sugar.

DEFINITION

To **core** a piece of fruit is to remove the unappetizing middle membranes and seeds. To core pear halves, use a paring knife or other small, sharp knife to cut out the center part of the fruit.

Dad's Baked Fruit

This recipe can use many different fruits, depending on your mood and the season. This is one delicious example, but feel free to modify it as you like.

 Serves:
4 to 6

1 (1-lb.) pkg. frozen mixed berries (approximately 1 cup each blueberries, blackberries, and raspberries)

3 TB. sugar

2 TB. plus ¼ cup flour

Juice of ½ lemon

¼ cup brown sugar, firmly packed

¾ cup oatmeal

½ tsp. baking spice or ½ tsp. cinnamon

4 TB. butter, chilled and cut into small pieces

1. Place berries in an 8×8 microwave-safe pie pan or baking pan. Add sugar, 2 tablespoons flour, and lemon juice, and toss together.

2. In a separate bowl, combine brown sugar, oatmeal, remaining ¼ cup flour, and baking spice.

3. Add butter by pinching together with your fingers until it's incorporated and a crumble texture. Sprinkle evenly over top of fruit, and cover dish with plastic wrap.

4. Microwave on high for 7 minutes. Turn once or twice if your microwave doesn't have a carousel tray.

5. Meanwhile, preheat the broiler.

6. Remove plastic wrap, and place dish under the broiler (not too close), and broil for 2 minutes or until top begins to crisp.

Variation: Fresh fruit is even better in this recipe. I've listed frozen for the convenience.

Strawberries and Sour-Sweet Cream Dip

 10

Serves:
4

1 qt. fresh strawberries, caps removed	$\frac{1}{2}$ tsp. pure vanilla extract
1 cup sour cream or light sour cream	$\frac{1}{4}$ cup sweetener

1. Place strawberries in a large serving bowl.

2. In a smaller serving bowl, combine sour cream, vanilla extract, and sweetener.

3. Dip strawberries in cream, and enjoy.

Variation: Distribute strawberries and cream to individual serving plates and use a dipping bowl. Other large berries, such as blackberries, are delicious with this cream, too.

ON THE CLOCK

With fruit-based desserts, you'll get the best flavor from fresh, in-season produce. And whether it's time for strawberries, peaches, blueberries, apples, or something else, they'll always taste better when they're local. Check out your local farmers' market for fresh goods.

Lemon-Cranberry Fruit Dip

 Serves:
4

1 cup plain low-fat yogurt

¼ cup unsweetened cranberries, minced

2 TB. sweetener

1 TB. lemon zest

¼ tsp. ground cinnamon

Pinch ground cloves

3 apples or 3 crisp pears, sliced

1. In a serving bowl, combine yogurt, cranberries, sweetener, lemon zest, cinnamon, and cloves.

2. Serve yogurt dip surrounded by apple and pear slices.

Variation: If possible, mix yogurt ahead of time and chill to allow the flavors to spread.

Fluff Fruit Dip

For the certifiable sweet tooth, even when it comes to appetizers, may I present Fluff Fruit Dip.

 Serves:
6 to 8

1 cup cream cheese or light cream cheese, softened

1 cup marshmallow topping

Assorted fruit

1. In a serving bowl, combine cream cheese and marshmallow topping.

2. Serve with an assortment of fruit such as strawberries, raspberries, and pear slices as dippers.

 MINUTE MORSEL

Remember that sweet marshmallow topping from your school days? Check the ingredients—no fat or cholesterol to be found. Of course, there's plenty of sugar ....

Raspberry Fruit Dip

Here's another creamy, fruity dip for those warm summer evenings.

	Serves:
	6 to 8

2 cups whipped topping

1 cup seedless raspberry yogurt

Assorted fruit

1. In a serving bowl, combine whipped topping and yogurt.

2. Serve with an assortment of fruit such as strawberries, raspberries, and pear slices as dippers.

Madeira Cream Fruit Dip

This is a creamy, irresistible fruit dip. The optional addition of heavy cream loosens up the dip just a bit. Try it with a sweet wine.

	Serves:
	4 to 6

1 (8-oz.) pkg. *mascarpone*

2 TB. Madeira

1 TB. honey

1 TB. heavy or whipping cream (optional)

1 ripe pear, seeds removed, and sliced

2 cups ripe red pitted cherries

2 cups ripe strawberries

1. In a small bowl, combine mascarpone, Madeira, honey, and heavy cream (if using).

2. Serve surround by pear slices, cherries, and strawberries for dipping. If pear slices will be out for long, rub them with a cut lemon half to delay browning.

Variation: Try other fruits with this delicious dip such as apple slices or pineapple pieces.

DEFINITION

Mascarpone is a thick, rich, buttery cheese that resembles cream. It's traditionally from Italy, although versions using the same name are made in the United States. It is perhaps one of the most delicious and decadent cheeses to use as a base for desserts or for a fruit dip.

Rhubarb Sauce

Many gardeners have a patch of rhubarb, quietly growing those elephantine leaves and thick red stalks. This sauce is simple, tart, and sweet, and delicious warm or cold.

20	**Serves:** 4 to 6

½ cup water

3 stalks (about 1 lb.) rhubarb, scrubbed and cut into 1-in. segments

1 cup sugar or equivalent sweetener

1. In a large saucepan over medium heat, heat water.

2. Place rhubarb in a large bowl, pour sugar over, and mix.

3. Scrape into the saucepan, cover, and cook for 14 minutes or until rhubarb pieces are completely soft and mixture is more like a thick liquid.

4. Serve in bowls with a little bit of cream stirred in.

Variation: Stevia extract works perfectly as a sweetener if you'd rather not use the sugar.

ON THE CLOCK

For a little something extra, serve warm Rhubarb Sauce over vanilla ice cream. Yum.

Sweet-Tooth Teasers

In This Chapter

- Rich chocolate desserts
- Light and creamy delights
- Quick cookies
- Sweet, nutty noshes

Need to satisfy your sweet tooth but still need to watch your waistline? This is the chapter for you!

In this chapter, we explore solutions to this delicious challenge. We bite into textures and flavors such as chocolate and cream that enable delicious desserts with ingredient choices other than sugar.

Velvet Fudge

 20

Serves:
24

2 cups heavy cream

1 (8-oz.) box bittersweet chocolate

$\frac{1}{3}$ cup sugar or equivalent sweetener

$\frac{1}{2}$ tsp. pure vanilla extract

2 egg yolks

1. Line a small baking pan with waxed paper.

2. In a medium saucepan over medium-low heat, heat heavy cream to a simmer. Stir in chocolate until melted and creamy.

3. Meanwhile, in a small bowl, combine sugar and vanilla extract into egg yolks.

4. When chocolate is completely melted, turn off heat and slowly stir in egg yolk mixture until thoroughly blended.

5. Scrape mixture onto the waxed paper using a rubber spatula, and smooth to a flat layer. Chill until firm and cut into 1-inch squares.

Variation: Mix in $\frac{1}{3}$ cup toasted walnuts or almonds.

 MINUTE MORSEL

If chocolate is good for you, one bite of this and you'll live forever. This one's adapted from Dr. Atkins' *New Diet Revolution*.

Mocha Mousse

 Serves:
4

1 TB. cocoa powder	2 cups whipping cream
2 tsp. instant espresso powder	1 tsp. pure vanilla extract
½ cup sugar or equivalent sweetener	

1. In a small bowl, combine cocoa powder, espresso powder, and sugar.

2. In a large bowl, whip cream, slowly adding cocoa-sweetener mixture and vanilla extract as you whip. When cream doubles and forms soft peaks, you're done.

3. Serve in small bowls.

Variation: For pure chocolate flavor, use 1 extra tablespoon cocoa powder in place of the espresso powder.

ON THE CLOCK

To add visual appeal, scoop the Mocha Mousse into a zipper-type freezer bag. Cut off about ½ inch from one corner of the bag and, squeezing gently, swirl servings into each bowl. Irresistible.

Blueberry Chocolate Pudding

10 | **Serves:** 4

1 (1.4-oz.) pkg. sugar-free instant chocolate pudding

Skim milk (as much as pudding instructions call for)

¼ cup light sour cream

½ cup fresh or frozen blueberries

¼ tsp. vanilla extract

1. In a large bowl, prepare chocolate pudding with skim milk according to package instructions.

2. Quickly stir in sour cream, blueberries, and vanilla extract.

3. Distribute to small serving bowls, and refrigerate for 5 minutes or until set.

Variation: Substitute small pieces of other fruits for blueberries. Sliced almonds and chopped walnuts are also tasty in place of fruits.

Almond Chocolate Parfaits

 | **Serves:** 4

1 (1.4-oz.) pkg. sugar-free instant chocolate pudding

Skim milk (as much as pudding instructions call for)

1 cup light sour cream

2 TB. sweetener

½ tsp. pure almond extract

1. In a medium bowl, prepare chocolate pudding with skim milk according to package instructions.

2. In a separate bowl, combine sour cream, sweetener, and almond extract.

3. Spoon a 1-inch layer of chocolate pudding into 4 tall, slender glasses. Add ½ inch sour cream, and repeat with pudding until glasses are filled equally. Refrigerate for 5 minutes or until set.

MINUTE MORSEL

More and more alternatives to sugar are available all the time. Increasingly, grocery stores are carrying "natural" low-calorie or low-carb sweeteners, such as stevia extract. Stevia extract is derived from the stevia plant and is promoted as a safer alternative to "artificial" sweeteners.

Chocolate-Chip Cookies

 20

Serves:
about 24 cookies

$^2/_3$ cup butter or Smart Balance–
type spread (suitable for
baking), softened

2 large eggs

1 tsp. pure vanilla extract

$1^1/_2$ cups sugar or equivalent
sweetener

2 cups all-purpose flour

$^1/_2$ tsp. baking powder

$^1/_2$ tsp. salt

1 cup bittersweet chocolate chips

1. Preheat the oven to 375°F.

2. In a large bowl, combine butter, eggs, vanilla extract, and sugar.

3. In a medium bowl, combine all-purpose flour, baking powder, and salt. Beat dry ingredients into egg-butter mixture, and stir in chocolate chips.

4. Using rounded tablespoonfuls, spoon dough onto an ungreased baking tray, and cook for 10 minutes. The longer cookies cook, the crispier they get.

Variation: Substitute up to half of the flour with whole-wheat flour.

ON THE CLOCK

Whole-wheat baked goods, like cookies, are still a healthier bet than traditional white-flour cookies.

Almond Oatmeal Cookies

20	**Serves:** about 24 cookies

²⁄₃ cup butter or Smart Balance–type spread (suitable for baking), softened

2 large eggs

½ tsp. pure almond extract

1 cup sugar or equivalent sweetener

1 cup old-fashioned oatmeal (not instant)

1 cup all-purpose flour

½ cup unprocessed bran

1 tsp. ground cinnamon

½ tsp. baking soda

½ tsp. salt

½ cup slivered almonds

1. Preheat the oven to 375°F.

2. In a large bowl, combine butter, eggs, almond extract, and sugar.

3. In a medium bowl, combine oatmeal, all-purpose flour, bran, cinnamon, baking soda, and salt. Beat dry ingredients into egg-butter mixture, add almonds, and mix again.

4. Using a tablespoon, spoon dough onto an ungreased baking tray. Cook for 9 minutes or until cookies are just done. (Don't let them overcook.)

Variation: Use whole-wheat flour instead of all-purpose flour if you want.

 ON THE CLOCK

If you're using more than one baking tray in the oven at a time, rotate the trays halfway through the cooking time for even cooking. And when using butterlike spreads such as Smart Balance for baking, be sure to read the label. Some are appropriate for use in baking; others are not.

Chocolate Macadamia Nut Clusters

 Serves:
24

2 cups heavy cream

1 (8-oz.) box bittersweet chocolate

⅓ cup sugar or equivalent
   sweetener

2 egg yolks, lightly beaten

½ tsp. pure vanilla extract

1 cup roasted and salted
   macadamia nuts

1. Line a baking tray with waxed paper.

2. In a saucepan over medium-low heat, heat heavy cream to a simmer. Stir in chocolate until melted and creamy.

3. Meanwhile, in a small bowl, combine sugar and egg yolks.

4. When chocolate is melted, turn off heat and slowly stir in egg yolk mixture and vanilla extract until thoroughly blended. Stir in macadamia nuts.

5. Scoop tablespoonfuls of chocolate-nut mixture onto the waxed paper using a rubber spatula, taking care to be sure they don't touch each other. Chill clusters for about 20 minutes or until firm, and cut into 1-inch squares.

"Honeyed" Almonds

20 **Serves:**
8

½ lb. roasted, lightly salted
   almonds

1 egg white

½ cup sugar or equivalent
   sweetener

1 TB. grated lemon zest

½ tsp. apple pie spice or ground
   cinnamon

1. Preheat the broiler.

2. In a mixing bowl, toss almonds with egg white. Add sugar, lemon zest, and apple pie spice.

3. Spread almonds in a single layer on a baking sheet, and broil for 6 minutes, stirring a couple times, or until nuts are beginning to tan. (Watch carefully to prevent burning.)

4. Remove from the broiler, cool, and serve.

Variation: Other nuts such as pecans, peanuts, and walnuts—or a mixture—also work well in this recipe.

ON THE CLOCK

I find that salted nuts work well for "honeyed" nuts. It might be counterintuitive to include salt in a sweet recipe, but that savory backbone balances the dessert and makes it even more irresistible.

Rich and Delectable Desserts

In This Chapter

- Perfect pies
- Quick and easy pudding and mousse
- Fruity shortcake
- Delicious cookies

For some people, dessert is the most important meal of the day. My editor is one of those people! "Life is short," she says. "Eat dessert first!"

You might think you don't have time to make a pie in 30 minutes or less. I'm happy to tell you, you'd be wrong. You might not be able to make an old-fashioned fruit pie in less than 30 minutes, but you can still have some fun pies on the table within 30 minutes. In this chapter, I share some fun pies my family love. I've also included some rich and delicious pudding and mousse, strawberry shortcake, and tasty chocolate-chip oatmeal cookies.

Grammalane's Lemon Pie

Not too sweet. Definitely too delicious.

30 **Serves:**
6

1 cup plus 4 TB. sugar	1 TB. butter
1⅓ cups water	1 prebaked pie shell
Juice of 2 lemons	3 egg whites, at room temperature
4 TB. plus 2 tsp. cornstarch	½ tsp. salt
3 egg yolks	⅛ tsp. cream of tartar

1. In the top part of a double boiler, heat 1 cup sugar and 1 cup water. Add lemon juice.

2. Pour remaining ⅓ cup water in a small bowl, and whisk in cornstarch until blended and smooth. Slowly add to the double boiler, stirring. It will thicken.

3. In a small bowl, beat egg yolks. Add 1 spoonful lemon mixture to egg yolks, stirring. Add 2 more spoonfuls, stirring. Repeat one more time. Pour egg mixture into double boiler, stirring, along with butter.

4. Pour mixture into prebaked pie shell, and chill to set.

5. Preheat the broiler.

6. While pie chills, in a small bowl, combine egg whites, salt, and cream of tartar, and beat rapidly until mixture expands and forms stiff peaks.

7. Add remaining 4 tablespoons sugar slowly, gently folding it into stiff egg whites so as not to deflate them. Meringue will firm up.

8. Spread over chilled pie, and place under the broiler for 4 minutes or until meringue begins to brown.

MINUTE MORSEL

Rather than simply dumping eggs into a hot mixture, we add spoonfuls of that mixture to the eggs first to start warming them so they don't cook and cause lumps.

Charles River Mud Pie

This quick pie is decadent and rich. I've included my favorite flavors, but feel free to experiment.

 Serves:
4

2 cups coffee ice cream	1 cup fudge sauce, heated
2 cups chocolate ice cream	1 store-bought graham-cracker or
$\frac{1}{2}$ cup chopped walnuts	chocolate-cookie-crumb crust
$\frac{1}{2}$ cup semisweet chocolate chips	$1\frac{1}{2}$ cups whipped cream

1. In a large bowl, combine coffee ice cream and chocolate ice cream. Stir in walnuts, chocolate chips, and fudge sauce.

2. Scrape into graham-cracker crust, and press to smooth. Top with whipped cream, and serve.

 ON THE CLOCK

If you've got a few extra minutes, put the pie in the freezer to firm up before spreading on the whipped cream.

Sara's Instant Chocolate Mousse

 Serves:
4

1 pt. whipping cream	$\frac{1}{2}$ cup sugar
4 TB. instant hot chocolate powder	2 tsp. vanilla extract

1. Pour whipping cream into a medium bowl, and whip.

2. Slowly add hot chocolate powder, sugar, and vanilla extract, and continue to whip until mousse has doubled in size and has soft waves standing.

Grampa Phil's Pudding

Serves:
8

2½ cups milk	2 TB. flour
¾ cup sugar	3 TB. cornstarch
2 oz. unsweetened solid baking chocolate	2 eggs
½ tsp. salt	1½ tsp. vanilla extract
	1 tsp. butter

1. In the top part of a *double boiler*, heat 2 cups milk, sugar, baking chocolate, and salt. Heat until just simmering.

2. Pour remaining ½ cup milk in a small bowl, and with a fork, mix in flour and cornstarch until thoroughly combined. Slowly pour milk-flour mixture into milk-chocolate mixture in the double boiler, stirring constantly.

3. Crack eggs into a small bowl, and beat. Add 1 spoonful chocolate mixture, stirring. Add 2 more spoonfuls, stirring. Pour egg mixture into pudding, stirring. Cook for 1 minute.

4. Add vanilla extract and butter, cook for 1 more minute, and serve.

Variation: To make a chocolate pie, simply pour prepared pudding into a store-bought graham-cracker or chocolate-cookie-crumb crust. To dress it up even more, sprinkle whipped cream with chocolate shavings or dust with powdered chocolate (like from instant cocoa).

DEFINITION

A **double boiler** is a set of two pots designed to nest together, one inside the other. The bottom one holds water (not quite touching the bottom of the top pot), the top one holds the ingredient you are trying to heat. A double boiler provides consistent heat for things that need delicate treatment.

Lightning Strawberry Shortcake

 20

Serves:
6

1 pt. strawberries, cut into quarters

3 TB. sugar

2¼ cups baking mix (the kind that
    only requires addition of milk)

¾ cup milk

Whipped cream

1. Preheat oven to 450°F.

2. Place strawberries in a medium bowl, sprinkle with sugar, cover, and set aside to *macerate*.

3. Pour baking mix into a large bowl, and stir in milk to create dough. Turn out dough onto a floured counter, and knead for 30 seconds. Using your hands, flatten dough to about ½ inch thick. Cut into your favorite shape (circles if you have a cookie cutter, squares, triangles ... have some fun!), and place on an ungreased baking pan or cookie sheet. Bake for 8 minutes or until browned and crusty.

4. When shortcakes are done, cool to handling temperature and slice horizontally so you have 2 flat pieces. Distribute bottom pieces to serving plates, top each with a large spoonful of strawberries and juice. Place top of each biscuit on strawberries, and top each with the remaining strawberry and juice mixture. Top with whipped cream before serving.

 DEFINITION

Mixing sugar or another sweetener with fruit initiates a process called **maceration.** The fruit softens and releases delicious juice.

Oatmeal Chocolate-Chip Cookies

I can't resist the whole wheat in cookies. I pretend that eating one extra cookie is good for me.

20	**Serves:** 8

½ cup shortening	½ tsp. baking powder
1 cup brown sugar, firmly packed	½ tsp. salt
½ cup white flour	2 eggs
½ cup whole-wheat flour	1 tsp. vanilla extract
1 cup oatmeal	1 cup semisweet chocolate chips

1. Preheat the oven to 375°F. Lightly coat a baking pan or cookie sheet with cooking spray.

2. In a large bowl, thoroughly mix shortening and brown sugar.

3. In a separate bowl, whisk together white flour, whole-wheat flour, oatmeal, baking powder, and salt, and stir into shortening-sugar mixture.

4. Add eggs and vanilla extract, and mix well. Add chocolate chips, and mix again.

5. Scoop spoonfuls of cookie dough onto the prepared baking pan, and bake for 10 minutes or until done.

Variation: For moist, chewy cookies, cook for slightly less time than 10 minutes. For crisp, crunchy cookies, cook for a little longer.

ON THE CLOCK

If we're using more than one cookie sheet when making these cookies, my wife insists on rotating trays from bottom to top oven shelves after 5 minutes to ensure uniform cooking.

Glossary

al dente   Italian for "against the teeth." Refers to pasta or rice that's neither soft nor hard, but just slightly firm against the teeth.

all-purpose flour   Flour that contains only the inner part of the wheat grain. Usable for all purposes from cakes to gravies.

allspice   Named for its flavor echoes of several spices (cinnamon, cloves, nutmeg), allspice is used in many desserts and in rich marinades and stews.

almonds   Mild, sweet, and crunchy nuts that combine nicely with creamy and sweet food items.

anchovies (also **sardines**)   Tiny, flavorful preserved fish that typically come in cans. Anchovies are a traditional garnish for Caesar salad, the dressing of which contains anchovy paste.

andouille sausage   A sausage made with highly seasoned pork chitterlings and tripe, and a standard component of many Cajun dishes.

arborio rice   A plump Italian rice used, among other purposes, for risotto.

artichoke hearts   The center part of the artichoke flower, often found canned in grocery stores.

arugula   A spicy-peppery garden plant with leaves that resemble a dandelion and have a distinctive—and very sharp—flavor.

baba ghanouj   A Middle Eastern–style spread composed of eggplant, lemon juice, garlic, olive oil, and tahini.

bake   To cook in a dry oven. Dry-heat cooking often results in a crisping of the exterior of the food being cooked. Moist-heat cooking, through methods such as steaming, poaching, etc., brings a much different, moist quality to the food.

balsamic vinegar   Vinegar produced primarily in Italy from a specific type of grape and aged in wood barrels. It is heavier, darker, and sweeter than most vinegars.

bamboo shoots Crunchy, tasty white parts of the growing bamboo plant, often purchased canned.

barbecue To quick-cook over high heat, or to cook something long and slow in a rich liquid (barbecue sauce).

basil A flavorful, almost sweet, resinous herb delicious with tomatoes and used in all kinds of Italian or Mediterranean-style dishes.

baste To keep foods moist during cooking by spooning, brushing, or drizzling with a liquid.

beat To quickly mix substances.

Belgian endive A plant that resembles a small, elongated, tightly packed head of romaine lettuce. The thick, crunchy leaves can be broken off and used with dips and spreads.

bisque A creamy, thick soup made with puréed vegetables, meats, and especially seafood.

black pepper A biting and pungent seasoning, freshly ground pepper is a must for many dishes and adds an extra level of flavor and taste.

blackening To cook something quickly in a very hot skillet over high heat, usually with a seasoning mixture. Cajun cooking makes frequent use of blackening.

blanch To place a food in boiling water for about 1 minute (or less) to partially cook the exterior and then submerge in or rinse with cool water to halt the cooking.

blend To completely mix something, usually with a blender or food processor, more slowly than beating.

blue cheese A blue-veined cheese that crumbles easily and has a somewhat soft texture, usually sold in a block. The color is from a flavorful, edible mold that is often added or injected into the cheese.

boil To heat a liquid to a point where water is forced to turn into steam, causing the liquid to bubble. To boil something is to insert it into boiling water. A rapid boil is when a lot of bubbles form on the surface of the liquid.

bok choy (also **Chinese cabbage**) A member of the cabbage family with thick stems, crisp texture, and fresh flavor. It's perfect for stir-frying.

bouillon Dried essence of stock from chicken, beef, vegetable, or other ingredients. This is a popular starting ingredient for soups as it adds flavor (and often a lot of salt).

braise To cook with the introduction of some liquid, usually over an extended period of time.

bread flour   Wheat flour used for bread and other recipes.

breadcrumbs   Tiny pieces of crumbled dry bread, often used for topping or coating.

Brie   A creamy cow's milk cheese from France with a soft, edible rind and a mild flavor.

brine   A highly salted, often seasoned, liquid used to flavor and preserve foods. To brine a food is to soak, or preserve, it by submerging it in brine. The salt in the brine penetrates the fibers of the meat and makes it moist and tender.

broil   To cook in a dry oven under the overhead high-heat element.

broth   *See* stock.

brown   To cook in a skillet, turning, until the food's surface is seared and brown in color, to lock in the juices.

brown rice   Whole-grain rice including the germ with a characteristic pale brown or tan color; more nutritious and flavorful than white rice.

bruschetta (or **crostini**)   Slices of toasted or grilled bread with garlic and olive oil, often with other toppings.

brush   To coat food with a liquid.

bulgur   A wheat kernel that's been steamed, dried, and crushed and is sold in fine and coarse textures.

Cajun cooking   A style of cooking that combines French and Southern characteristics and includes many highly seasoned stews and meats.

cake flour   A high-starch, soft, and fine flour used primarily for cakes.

canapés   Bite-size hors d'oeuvres usually served on a small piece of bread or toast.

capers   Flavorful buds of a Mediterranean plant, ranging in size from *nonpareil* (about the size of a small pea) to larger, grape-size caper berries produced in Spain.

capicolla   Seasoned, aged pork shoulder; a traditional component of antipasto dishes.

caramelize   To cook sugar over low heat until it develops a sweet caramel flavor. The term is increasingly gaining use to describe cooking vegetables (especially onions) or meat in butter or oil over low heat until they soften, sweeten, and develop a caramel color.

caraway   A distinctive spicy seed used for bread, pork, cheese, and cabbage dishes. It is known to reduce stomach upset, which is why it is often paired with, for example, sauerkraut.

cardamom An intense, sweet-smelling spice, common to Indian cooking, used in baking and coffee.

carob A tropical tree that produces long pods. The dried, baked, and powdered flesh (carob powder) is used in baking, and the fresh and dried pods are used for a variety of recipes. The flavor is sweet and reminiscent of chocolate.

cayenne A fiery spice made from (hot) chili peppers, especially the cayenne chili, a slender, red, and very hot pepper.

ceviche A seafood dish in which fresh fish or seafood is marinated for several hours in highly acidic lemon or lime juice, tomato, onion, and cilantro. The acid "cooks" the seafood.

cheddar The ubiquitous hard cow's milk cheese with a rich, buttery flavor that ranges from mellow to sharp. Originally produced in England, cheddar is now produced worldwide.

chevre French for "goat's milk cheese," chevre is a typically creamy-salty soft cheese delicious by itself or paired with fruits or chutney. Chevres vary in style from mild and creamy to aged, firm, and flavorful.

chiles (or **chilis**) Any one of many different "hot" peppers, ranging in intensity from the relatively mild ancho pepper to the blisteringly hot habañero.

chili powder A seasoning blend that includes chili pepper, cumin, garlic, and oregano. Proportions vary among different versions, but they all offer a warm, rich flavor.

Chinese five-spice powder A seasoning blend of cinnamon, anise, ginger, fennel, and pepper.

chives A member of the onion family, chives grow in bunches of long leaves that resemble tall grass or the green tops of onions and offer a light onion flavor.

chop To cut into pieces, usually qualified by an adverb such as "*coarsely* chopped," or by a size measurement such as "chopped into $1/2$-inch pieces." "Finely chopped" is much closer to mince.

chorizo A spiced pork sausage eaten alone and as a component in many recipes.

chutney A thick condiment often served with Indian curries made with fruits and/ or vegetables with vinegar, sugar, and spices.

cider vinegar Vinegar produced from apple cider, popular in North America.

cilantro   A member of the parsley family and used in Mexican cooking (especially salsa) and some Asian dishes. Use in moderation, as the flavor can overwhelm. The seed of the cilantro plant is the spice coriander.

cinnamon   A rich, aromatic spice commonly used in baking or desserts. Cinnamon can also be used for delicious and interesting entrées.

clove   A sweet, strong, almost wintergreen-flavor spice used in baking and with meats such as ham.

coat   To cover all sides of a food with a liquid, sauce, or solid.

core   To core a piece of fruit or a vegetable is to remove the unappetizing middle membranes and seeds.

coriander   A rich, warm, spicy seed used in all types of recipes, from African to South American, from entrées to desserts.

coulis   A thick paste, often made with vegetables or fruits, used as a sauce for many recipes.

count   In terms of seafood or other foods that come in small sizes, the number of that item that compose 1 pound. For example, 31 to 40 count shrimp are large appetizer shrimp often served with cocktail sauce; 51 to 60 are much smaller.

couscous   Granular semolina (durum wheat) that is cooked and used in many Mediterranean and North African dishes.

cream   To blend an ingredient to get a soft, creamy liquid or substance.

crimini mushrooms   A relative of the white button mushroom but brown in color and with a richer flavor. The larger, fully grown version is the portobello. *See also* portobello mushrooms.

croutons   Chunks of bread, usually between $\frac{1}{4}$ and $\frac{1}{2}$ inch in size, sometimes seasoned and baked, broiled, or fried to a crisp texture and used in soups and salads.

crudités   Fresh vegetables served as an appetizer, often all together on one tray.

cumin   A fiery, smoky-tasting spice popular in Middle-Eastern and Indian dishes. Cumin is a seed; ground cumin seed is the most common form used in cooking.

curing   A method of preserving uncooked foods, usually meats or fish, by either salting and smoking or pickling.

curry   Rich, spicy, Indian-style sauces and the dishes prepared with them. A curry uses curry powder as its base seasoning.

curry powder   A ground blend of rich and flavorful spices used as a basis for curry and many other Indian-influenced dishes. Common ingredients include hot pepper, nutmeg, cumin, cinnamon, pepper, and turmeric. Some curry can also be found in paste form.

custard   A cooked mixture of eggs and milk popular as base for desserts.

dash   A few drops, usually of a liquid, released by a quick shake of, for example, a bottle of hot sauce.

deglaze   To scrape up the bits of meat and seasoning left in a pan or skillet after cooking. Usually this is done by adding a liquid such as wine or broth and creating a flavorful stock that can be used to create sauces.

devein   The removal of the dark vein from the back of a large shrimp with a sharp knife.

dice   To cut into small cubes about ¼-inch square.

Dijon mustard   Hearty, spicy mustard made in the style of the Dijon region of France.

dill   A herb perfect for eggs, salmon, cheese dishes, and, of course, vegetables (pickles!).

dolce   Italian for "sweet." Refers to desserts as well as styles of a food (*Gorgonzola dolce* is a style of Gorgonzola cheese).

dollop   A spoonful of something creamy and thick, like sour cream or whipped cream.

double boiler   A set of two pots designed to nest together, one inside the other, and provide consistent, moist heat for foods that need delicate treatment. The bottom pot holds water (not quite touching the bottom of the top pot); the top pot holds the ingredient you want to heat.

dredge   To cover a piece of food with a dry substance such as flour or corn meal.

drizzle   To lightly sprinkle drops of a liquid over food, often as the finishing touch to a dish.

dry   In the context of wine, a wine that contains little or no residual sugar, so it's not very sweet.

dust   To sprinkle a dry substance, often a seasoning, over a food or dish.

emulsion A combination of liquid ingredients that do not normally mix well beaten together to create a thick liquid, such as a fat or oil with water. Creation of an emulsion must be done carefully and rapidly to ensure that particles of one ingredient are suspended in the other.

espresso Strong coffee made by forcing steam through finely ground coffee beans.

ètouffèe Cajun for "smothered." This savory, rich sauce (often made with crayfish) is served over rice.

extra-virgin olive oil *See* olive oil.

falafel Middle Eastern hand food composed of seasoned, ground chickpeas formed into balls, cooked, and often used as a filling for pita bread.

fennel In seed form, a fragrant, licorice-tasting herb. The bulbs have a much milder flavor and a celery-like crunch and are used as a vegetable in salads or cooked recipes.

feta A white, crumbly, sharp, and salty cheese popular in Greek cooking and on salads. Traditional feta is usually made with sheep's milk, but feta-style cheese can be made from sheep's, cow's, or goat's milk.

fish basket A grill-top metal frame that holds a whole fish intact, making it easier to turn.

flake To break into thin sections, as with fish.

floret The flower or bud end of broccoli or cauliflower.

flour Grains ground into a meal. Wheat is perhaps the most common flour. Flour is also made from oats, rye, buckwheat, soybeans, etc. *See also* all-purpose flour; cake flour; whole-wheat flour.

fold To combine a dense and light mixture with a circular action from the middle of the bowl.

fricassee A dish, usually chicken, cut into pieces and cooked in a liquid or sauce.

frittata A skillet-cooked mixture of eggs and other ingredients that's not stirred but is cooked slowly and then either flipped or finished under the broiler.

fritter A food such as apples or corn coated or mixed with batter and deep-fried for a crispy, crunchy exterior.

fry *See* sauté.

fusion To blend two or more styles of cooking, such as Chinese and French.

garam masala A famous Indian seasoning mix, rich with cinnamon, pepper, nutmeg, cardamom, and other spices.

garlic   A member of the onion family, a pungent and flavorful element in many savory dishes. A garlic bulb contains multiple cloves. Each clove, when chopped, provides about 1 teaspoon garlic. Most recipes call for cloves or chopped garlic by the teaspoon.

ginger   Available in fresh root or dried, ground form, ginger adds a pungent, sweet, and spicy quality to a dish.

Gorgonzola   A creamy and rich Italian blue cheese. "Dolce" is sweet, and that's the kind you want.

goulash   A rich, Hungarian-style meat-and-vegetable stew seasoned with paprika, among other spices.

grits   Coarsely ground grains, usually corn.

Gruyère   A rich, sharp cow's milk cheese made in Switzerland that has a nutty flavor.

gyoza (also **pot stickers**)   Small, usually $1\frac{1}{2}$- to 2-inch-long, Chinese dumplings filled with chicken, seafood, or vegetables. They are traditionally served with soy sauce for dipping.

handful   An unscientific measurement; the amount of an ingredient you can hold in your hand.

Havarti   A creamy, Danish, mild cow's milk cheese perhaps most enjoyed in its herbed versions such as Havarti with dill.

hazelnuts (also **filberts**)   A sweet nut popular in desserts and, to a lesser degree, in savory dishes.

hearts of palm   Firm, elongated, off-white cylinders from the inside of a palm tree stem tip.

herbes de Provence   A seasoning mix including basil, fennel, marjoram, rosemary, sage, and thyme, common in the south of France.

hoisin sauce   A sweet Asian condiment similar to ketchup made with soybeans, sesame, chili peppers, and sugar.

hors d'oeuvre   French for "outside of work" (the "work" being the main meal), an hors d'oeuvre can be any dish served as a starter before the meal.

hummus   A thick, Middle Eastern spread made of puréed garbanzo beans, lemon juice, olive oil, garlic, and often tahini (sesame seed paste).

infusion   A liquid in which flavorful ingredients such as herbs have been soaked or steeped to extract that flavor into the liquid.

Italian seasoning   A blend of dried herbs, including basil, oregano, rosemary, and thyme.

jicama   A juicy, crunchy, sweet, large, round Central American vegetable. If you can't find jicama, try substituting sliced water chestnuts.

julienne   A French word meaning "to slice into very thin pieces."

kalamata olives   Traditionally from Greece, these medium-small long black olives have a smoky rich flavor.

Key limes   Very small limes grown primarily in Florida known for their tart taste.

knead   To work dough to make it pliable so it holds gas bubbles as it bakes. Kneading is fundamental in the process of making yeast breads.

kosher salt   A coarse-grained salt made without any additives or iodine.

lentils   Tiny lens-shape pulses used in European, Middle Eastern, and Indian cuisines.

macerate   To mix sugar or another sweetener with fruit. The fruit softens, and its juice is released to mix with the sweetener.

marinate   To soak meat, seafood, or other food in a seasoned sauce, called a marinade, which is high in acid content. The acids break down the muscle of the meat, making it tender and adding flavor.

marjoram   A sweet herb, a cousin of and similar to oregano, popular in Greek, Spanish, and Italian dishes.

mascarpone   A thick, creamy, spreadable cheese, traditionally from Italy.

medallion   A small round cut, usually of meat or vegetables such as carrots or cucumbers.

meld   To allow flavors to blend and spread over time. Melding is often why recipes call for overnight refrigeration and is also why some dishes taste better as leftovers.

meringue   A baked mixture of sugar and beaten egg whites, often used as a dessert topping.

mesclun   Mixed salad greens, usually containing lettuce and assorted greens such as arugula, cress, endive, and others.

mince   To cut into very small pieces smaller than diced pieces, about $\frac{1}{8}$ inch or smaller.

mirin   A thick, sweet wine or liqueur made from rice. Mirin is an important component in many Japanese-style dishes such as teriyaki.

miso   A fermented, flavorful soybean paste, key in many Japanese dishes.

muhammara   A classic Turkish dip or spread that contains walnuts, onion, garlic, breadcrumbs, and hot peppers.

mull (or **mulled**)   To heat a liquid with the addition of spices and sometimes sweeteners.

mushrooms   Any one of a huge variety of *edible* fungi (note emphasis on "edible"; there are also poisonous mushrooms). *See also* crimini mushrooms; porcini mushrooms; portobello mushrooms; shiitake mushrooms; white mushrooms.

nutmeg   A sweet, fragrant, musky spice used primarily in baking.

olivada   A simple spread composed of olives, olive oil, and pepper that carries a wealth of flavor.

olive oil   A fragrant liquid produced by crushing or pressing olives. Extra-virgin olive oil—the most flavorful and highest quality—is produced from the first pressing of a batch of olives; oil is also produced from later pressings.

olives   The fruit of the olive tree commonly grown on all sides of the Mediterranean. Black olives are also called ripe olives. Green olives are immature, although they are also widely eaten. *See also* kalamata olives.

oregano   A fragrant, slightly astringent herb used in Greek, Spanish, and Italian dishes.

orzo   A rice-shape pasta used in Greek cooking.

oxidation   The browning of fruit flesh that happens over time and with exposure to air. Minimize oxidation by rubbing the cut surfaces with a lemon half.

paella   A grand Spanish dish of rice, shellfish, onion, meats, rich broth, and herbs.

pan-broil   Quick-cooking over high heat in a skillet with a minimum of butter or oil. (Frying, on the other hand, uses more butter or oil.)

pancetta   Salted, seasoned bacon; an important element in many Italian-style dishes.

paprika   A rich, red, warm, earthy spice that also lends a rich red color to many dishes.

parboil   To partially cook in boiling water or broth, similar to blanching (although blanched foods are quickly cooled with cold water).

pare   To scrape away the skin of a food, usually a vegetable or fruit, as part of preparation for serving or cooking.

Parmesan   A hard, dry, flavorful cheese primarily used grated or shredded as a seasoning for Italian-style dishes.

parsley   A fresh-tasting green leafy herb, often used as a garnish.

pâté   A savory loaf that contains meats, poultry, or seafood; spices; and often a lot of fat, served cold spread or sliced on crusty bread or crackers.

pecans   Rich, buttery nuts, native to North America, that have a high unsaturated fat content.

pesto   A thick spread or sauce made with fresh basil leaves, garlic, olive oil, pine nuts, and Parmesan cheese. Some newer versions are made with other herbs.

pickle   A food, usually a vegetable such as a cucumber, that's been pickled in brine.

pilaf   A rice dish in which the rice is browned in butter or oil and then cooked in a flavorful liquid such as a broth, often with the addition of meats or vegetables. The rice absorbs the broth, resulting in a savory dish.

pinch   An unscientific measurement term, the amount of an ingredient—typically a dry, granular substance such as an herb or seasoning—you can hold between your finger and thumb.

pinzimonio   An Italian vegetable dish in which combinations of sliced vegetables are served with olive oil, vinegar, salt, and pepper.

pita bread   A flat, hollow wheat bread often used for sandwiches or sliced, pizza style, into slices. Terrific soft with dips or baked or broiled as a vehicle for other ingredients.

pizza stone   Preheated with the oven, a pizza stone cooks a crust to a delicious, crispy, pizza-parlor texture. It also holds heat well, so a pizza or other food removed from the oven on the stone stay hot for as long as a half hour at the table.

plantain   A relative of the banana, a plantain is larger, milder in flavor, and used as a staple in many Latin American dishes.

poach   To cook a food in simmering liquid, such as water, wine, or broth.

porcini mushrooms   Rich and flavorful mushrooms used in rice and Italian-style dishes.

portobello mushrooms   A mature and larger form of the smaller crimini mushroom, portobellos are brownish, chewy, and flavorful. Often served as whole caps, grilled, and as thin sautéed slices. *See also* crimini mushrooms.

pot stickers   *See* gyoza.

preheat   To turn on an oven, broiler, or other cooking appliance in advance of cooking so the temperature will be at the desired level when the assembled dish is ready for cooking.

prosciutto   Dry, salt-cured ham, that originated in Italy.

purée   To reduce a food to a thick, creamy texture, usually using a blender or food processor.

ragout (pronounced *rag-OO*)   A thick, spicy stew.

red pepper flakes   Hot yet rich, crushed red pepper, used in moderation, brings flavor and interest to many savory dishes.

reduce   To boil or simmer a broth or sauce to remove some of the water content, resulting in more concentrated flavor and color.

render   To cook a meat to the point where its fat melts and can be removed.

reserve   To hold a specified ingredient for another use later in the recipe.

rice vinegar   Vinegar produced from fermented rice or rice wine, popular in Asian-style dishes. Different from rice wine vinegar.

ricotta   A fresh Italian cheese smoother than cottage cheese with a slightly sweet flavor.

risotto   A popular Italian rice dish made by browning arborio rice in butter or oil and then slowly adding liquid to cook the rice, resulting in a creamy texture.

roast   To cook something uncovered in an oven, usually without additional liquid.

Roquefort   A world-famous (French) creamy but sharp sheep's milk cheese containing blue lines of mold.

rosemary   A pungent, sweet herb used with chicken, pork, fish, and especially lamb. A little of it goes a long way.

roux   A mixture of butter or another fat and flour, used to thicken sauces and soups.

saffron   A spice made from the stamens of crocus flowers, saffron lends a dramatic yellow color and distinctive flavor to a dish. Use only tiny amounts of this expensive herb.

sage   An herb with a musty yet fruity, lemon-rind scent and "sunny" flavor.

satay (also **sate**)   A popular Southeast Asian dish of broiled skewers of fish or meat, often served with peanut sauce.

sauté   To pan-cook over lower heat than used for frying.

savory   A popular herb with a fresh, woody taste.

scant   A measurement modification that specifies "include no extra," as in 1 scant teaspoon.

scrapple   A sausagelike mixture of seasoned pork and cornmeal that is formed into loaves and sliced for cooking.

sear   To quickly brown the exterior of a food, especially meat, over high heat to preserve interior moisture.

sesame oil   An oil, made from pressing sesame seeds, that's tasteless if clear and aromatic and flavorful if brown.

shallot   A member of the onion family that grows in a bulb somewhat like garlic and has a milder onion flavor. When a recipe calls for shallot, use the entire bulb.

shellfish   A broad range of seafood, including clams, mussels, oysters, crabs, shrimp, and lobster. Some people are allergic to shellfish, so take care with its inclusion in recipes.

shiitake mushrooms   Large, dark brown mushrooms with a hearty, meaty flavor. Can be used either fresh or dried, grilled or as a component in other recipes and as a flavoring source for broth.

short-grain rice   A starchy rice popular for Asian-style dishes because it readily clumps (perfect for eating with chopsticks).

shred   To cut into many long, thin slices.

simmer   To boil gently so the liquid barely bubbles.

skillet (also **frying pan**)   A generally heavy, flat-bottomed metal pan with a handle designed to cook food over heat on a stovetop or campfire.

skim   To remove fat or other material from the top of liquid.

slice   To cut into thin pieces.

steam   To suspend a food over boiling water and allow the heat of the steam (water vapor) to cook the food. A quick-cooking method, steaming preserves the flavor and texture of a food.

steep   To let sit in hot water, as in steeping tea in hot water for 10 minutes.

stew   To slowly cook pieces of food submerged in a liquid. Also, a dish that has been prepared by this method.

sticky rice (or **glutinous rice**)   *See* short-grain rice.

Stilton   The famous English blue-veined cheese, delicious with toasted nuts and renowned for its pairing with port wine.

stir-fry   To cook small pieces of food in a wok or skillet over high heat, moving and turning the food quickly to cook all sides.

strata   A savory bread pudding made with eggs and cheese.

succotash   A cooked vegetable dish usually made of corn and peppers.

tahini   A paste made from sesame seeds used to flavor many Middle Eastern recipes.

tamarind   A sweet, pungent, flavorful fruit used in Indian-style sauces and curries, made into a sweet sauce popular in Indian dishes.

tapenade   A thick, chunky spread made from savory ingredients such as olives, lemon juice, and anchovies.

taro   A popular root vegetable that is similar to the potato and is used in African and Caribbean cuisines.

tarragon   A sweet, rich-smelling herb perfect with seafood, vegetables (especially asparagus), chicken, and pork.

tender-crisp   To cook something, usually a vegetable, just to the point of holding some appetizing crisp texture.

teriyaki   A Japanese-style sauce composed of soy sauce, rice wine, ginger, and sugar that works well with seafood as well as most meats.

thyme   A minty, zesty herb.

toast   To heat something, usually bread, so it's browned and crisp.

toast points (also **toast triangles**)   Pieces of toast with the crusts removed that are then cut on the diagonal from each corner, resulting in four triangle-shape pieces.

tofu   A cheeselike substance made from soybeans and soy milk.

turmeric   A spicy, pungent yellow root used in many dishes, especially Indian cuisine, for color and flavor. Turmeric is the source of the yellow color in many prepared mustards.

veal   Meat from a calf, generally characterized by mild flavor and tenderness.

vegetable broth   Vegetable broth is a liquid that adds body and flavor to many dishes, and serves as an alternative to chicken or beef broth in many recipes.

venison   Deer meat.

vichy   A classic French vegetable dish of carrots cooked in water, butter, and sugar.

vindaloo   A famous spicy Indian curry dish.

vinegar   An acidic liquid widely used as dressing and seasoning, often made from fermented grapes, apples, or rice. *See also* balsamic vinegar; cider vinegar; rice vinegar; white vinegar; wine vinegar.

walnuts   A rich, slightly woody flavored nut.

wasabi   Japanese horseradish, a fiery, pungent condiment used with many Japanese-style dishes. Most often sold as a powder; add water to create a paste.

water chestnuts   A tuber, popular in many types of Asian-style cooking. The flesh is white, crunchy, and juicy, and the vegetable holds its texture whether cool or hot.

whisk   To rapidly mix, introducing air to the mixture.

white mushrooms   Button mushrooms. When fresh, they have an earthy smell and an appealing "soft crunch."

white vinegar   The most common type of vinegar, produced from grain.

whole-wheat flour   Wheat flour that contains the entire grain.

wild rice   Actually a grass with a rich, nutty flavor, popular as an unusual and nutritious side dish.

wine vinegar   Vinegar produced from red or white wine.

yeast   Tiny fungi that, when mixed with water, sugar, flour, and heat, release carbon dioxide bubbles, which, in turn, cause the bread to rise.

zest   Small slivers of peel, usually from a citrus fruit such as lemon, lime, or orange.

zester   A kitchen tool used to scrape zest off a fruit. A small grater also works well.

Index

W-X

Y-Z